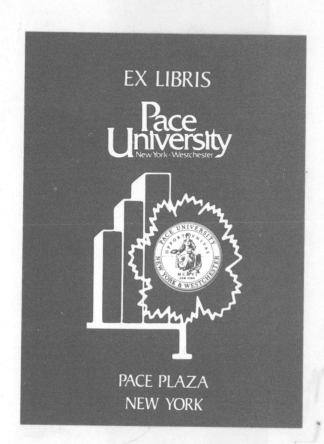

THE POLITICS OF
URBAN DEVELOPMENT
IN SINGAPORE

ROBERT E. GAMER

The Politics of Urban Development in Singapore

CORNELL UNIVERSITY PRESS | Ithaca and London

First published 1972 by Cornell University Press.
Published in the United Kingdom by Cornell University Press Ltd., 2–4 Brook Street, London W1Y 1AA.

International Standard Book Number 0-8014-0708-7
Library of Congress Catalog Card Number 78-37778
PRINTED IN THE UNITED STATES OF AMERICA
BY VAIL-BALLOU PRESS, INC.

Librarians: Library of Congress cataloging information appears on the last page of the book.

To my father,

Carl Wesley Gamer,

who grieved over the human condition, but never wavered in his conviction that the good earth will support us all when we learn to treat one another with compassion.

Acknowledgments

I did the research for this book from 1964 to 1968 while teaching courses on the politics of developing nations as a Lecturer in the Political Science Department of the University of Singapore. From the time of my arrival in Singapore, I was fascinated by the dynamism of Singapore's housing and industrialization programs. I took long walks through the housing estates, eating in the outdoor stalls and talking to people. How was public housing affecting their lives and political orientations? Soon I formalized the questions into a social survey. After obtaining permission from Minister of Social Affairs S. Rajaratnam, I conducted this survey—with the aid of students—both in a public housing estate and in an area of run-down housing in the central city. The survey raised more questions than it answered. Because it seemed important to find out how the planning mechanisms were geared to dealing with such questions, I asked the Permanent Secretary of National Development, Howe Yoon Chong, whether I might study the administration of some public project. He received the idea favorably, and provided me with authorization to examine all file data on the Kallang Basin Reclamation Project.

Literature on bureaucracy has always appeared dull and lifeless to me. In contrast, the people I met in the Singapore agencies, and the files of their correspondence, were human and vital. I have never been more warmly received anywhere than by these many individuals. The things they told me about their concerns and interests gave me new eyes, to notice phenomena that I had hitherto thought trivial. I found politically relevant meanings in writings other than those on public administration and political science. On many trips to other countries I spied details I would previously have overlooked and was able to learn about political processes through them. What evolved, as the reader will discover, is a book about far more than the socialization of people in public housing or the planning mechanisms of the Kallang Basin Reclamation Project.

On May 28, 1971, after several more subtle attempts at suppression, the Singapore Government closed the doors of an English-language newspaper whose editorial policy allowed for mild but continual criticism of Government policy, and also in May 1971 four senior officials of a leading Chinese-language daily were imprisoned on the grounds that their paper was furthering the cause of communism and communalism. These actions can be seen as an extension of the Government's continuing program (discussed in Chapter II) to maintain political capabilities. Yet they have raised doubts in some circles as to whether Prime Minister Lee Kuan Yew is prepared to harbor any criticism.

The Government's cooperation with my research stands in marked contrast to these incidents. The day before leaving Singapore I called on Howe Yoon Chong to ask him if he would like to see a copy of my manuscript prior to publication. "No," he said, "but I would be pleased to get a free copy of the book, with your autograph." (I shall be sending him one.) He then remarked that his ministry's cooperation with me constitutes some proof that Singapore is an open society. I agree, and am grateful for the remarkable cooperation at all levels during my research. I have attempted to make objective comparisons of Singapore's development with that of other nations and to assess trends. As Chapter VI suggests, there seems to be no time when such comparisons and assessments have been more urgently needed in Singapore than at present. I hope that readers in Singapore, as elsewhere, will approach my evaluations with minds that are both open and critical, so that they may make comparisons and assessments of their own.

As is usual (probably more than is usual) this study has involved considerable intellectual interaction with others. A great many people —in Singapore, the United States, and elsewhere—have furnished data, read chapters, and discussed ideas with me (sometimes heatedly). I shall simply and sincerely say that they are remembered and appreciated. While I take full responsibility for what I say in this book, many of the ideas in it came from these friends and associates or resulted from my consideration of their differing ideas.

The Political Science Departments of the University of Singapore and the University of Missouri at Kansas City, and the Office of Graduate Studies at the latter institution, aided in typing various drafts. I especially wish to thank Lilian Wong, Betty Stevenson, and Carolyn Zeis for this typing, which was done expertly and with an added element of loving care. The maps were originally designed with the assistance of Wong Poh Poh and Rudolphe De Koninck; Michael Scammon made the final drafts. Michael also drew Chart 4—based on an illustration in the Housing and Development Board pamphlet "Home Ownership for the People." Tay Kheng Soon and I took the aerial photographs. Bruce L. Ottley and Jennifer Tebbe are thanked for their assistance with the bibliography; Jennifer helped me, in addition, with the index. I also owe a debt to Professors Samuel Thompson at Monmouth College, Illinois, and Whitney Perkins at Brown University. Their areas of specialization (philosophy of religion and international relations) are fairly far afield from these pages. It may surprise (and I hope not alarm) them that I doubt whether I could have written this book had they both not been my teachers.

ROBERT E. GAMER

Kansas City, Missouri

Contents

Index   **257**

Maps

Aerial Photographs, 1968

Charts

Table

Introduction: Meeting the Challenges of Change

A Singapore delegate to an international housing conference was surprised to hear another delegate brag that his nation had no housing problem. The Singaporean, knowing the country in question to be very poor and quickly urbanizing, could not believe his ears and asked for clarification. "Yes," came the reply, "we have plenty of tents and huts for everyone."

When Singapore secured independence from the British in 1959, under the leadership of the People's Action Party, it boldly confronted two common contemporary problems—political instability and urban deterioration—and found solutions for them. Singapore's 1,500,000 inhabitants faced an acute housing shortage; virtually the whole built-up portion of the island's 225 square miles was rapidly decaying into a wretched slum. Racial tension was mounting between the majority group and minority groups. Unemployment was on the rise and was especially serious among minority groups. The students were expressing their restlessness by street demonstrations, sit-ins, camp-ins, and other forms of civil disobedience. The Communists, who had recently accepted a truce that largely ended their guerilla warfare in the countryside of Malaya, were marshaling their forces to take over Singapore. Feelings ran high, and several times the city had been torn by bloody rioting.

In 1959, Singapore's new government began a frontal attack on these problems. Within a decade it had changed the face of them all. It successfully implemented techniques and institutions with which American cities and federal agencies are currently experimenting: urban renewal; public housing (every twenty-five minutes, a new flat is completed); community centers; neighborhood committees; the adaptation of communications media to promote social and political ends; grassroots political party restructuring; coordination of bureaucratic and political agencies; improvement of police training; reorganization of elementary, secondary, and vocational education; a Job Corps; fair employment legislation; a heavy conscription into peacetime military service; construction of industrial estates; loans, tax incentives, and other assistance for new businesses; construction of new water, sewerage, electrical, and road facilities; and more.

Cumulatively, these programs have helped Singapore move within a decade into political peace and economic prosperity. The massive inflow of foreign capital attests to this success.[1] This book discusses these programs and analyzes the role they played in bringing stability out of turmoil. Singapore has faced the challenges of change with remarkable vigor.

Despite these accomplishments, however, I remain pessimistic about urban development—in Singapore and elsewhere. Many cities fall far behind Singapore in the dynamism of their urban development programs; in an era of rapid change such as the present, this is a cause for special concern. Yet even when a city like Singapore has developed vigorous programs that are politically astute, administratively convenient, and fiscally sound, there is still no assurance that they benefit the poor (who, in the case of Singapore, constitute the majority of the populace). What distresses me most is that my careful perusal of the inner workings of the Kallang Basin Reclamation Project, and of literature on urban development programs elsewhere, produces little evidence that the problems of the poor have been basically assuaged by these programs. In fact, there is some evidence that these programs may be disrupting life patterns in a manner that could ultimately hold back the economic progress of the most disadvantaged portions of the populace.

Furthermore, the answer to this problem does not seem to lie in the direction of bigger and better urban planning. In Part Three of this book, I think about possibilities for modifying Singapore's planning procedures, and find little latitude for changing them. I also explore planning in some other cities with differing economic bases and bureaucratic setups, and find similar inadequacies in meeting the needs of the poor. Whether simple or sophisticated, fledgling or grandiose, planning decisions remain ensconced in the hands of middle and up-

---

[1] At the end of 1969, US$335 million in foreign capital was invested in Singapore. By the end of 1970 that figure had grown to US$570 million. During 1970 US$350 million in foreign capital was committed for investment in the Republic. Cf. James Morgan, "Singapore's Future," *Far Eastern Economic Review,* Vol. LXXIII, No. 35, August 28, 1971, 33.

per class groups; this, I conclude, is the major problem. In the closing chapters of the book I explore means for grappling with this problem by infusing poorer elements with greater political efficacy. I argue that poorer people once had such efficacy in a rural setting, and that those who have moved to the city must attempt to regain this efficacy by recreating some of the cohesion that characterized preindustrial social life. The last chapter ends on a mildly positive note by suggesting some guidelines that might be followed in achieving this objective.

The book is divided into three parts. The following subsections explain the theoretical concerns of each part.

PRECONDITIONS FOR PLANNING

The land of tents and huts cited in the epigraph at the beginning of this Introduction had no housing program. This lack of response to a probable need must partly be blamed on the attitude of the delegate and his government. Yet the delegate may have been disguising a sheer inability to act. There are a number of objective conditions that need to be established before a government can actually institute reform programs. It took Singapore many years to develop these preconditions for planning. In comprehending how a government plans, it is as important to analyze how it developed these preconditions as it is to look into the planning itself:

Resources Some nations have extensive resources; others, few. The extensiveness of natural, financial, and human resources is of less consequence than their accessibility to one another. A basic transportation system must link populated areas and natural resources. The government needs means to lure a percentage of extant financial resources into development projects. Agricultural development requires reliable supplies of water; urban development, a steady source of inexpensive electrical power.

Skills Human resources are the most essential components of development. Planning requires engineers, economists, architects, and statisticians. Skilled bureaucrats and entrepreneurs, and various types of skilled and semiskilled laborers, must also emerge from the culture and the schools. Of secondary, but vital, importance are agronomists, urban planners, geographers, sociologists, lawyers, survey researchers, mathematicians, and economists with advanced specialized skills. Personnel can sometimes be temporarily recruited from abroad. Yet because of the fast turnover, general shortage, and high cost of expatriate staff (not to mention the need for maintenance of national independence) at least some nationals trained in these skills are necessary. Since the educational process is complex and requires many years for each individual, it needs long and careful cultivation.

Administrative capabilities People with necessary skills may have become available. Still, they must be brought together into organizations with the ability to conceive and carry out socially useful projects. Key administrators must achieve enough command over resources to create such organizations out of existing bureaucracy.

Political capabilities Resources, skills, and administrative capabilities can become accessible during times of chaos. To follow through on development programs, however, the Government needs enough stability to concentrate on development rather than simply on its own continuance in office. Its development goals must be acceptable to its principal political supporters. It must be in a position to mobilize available resources, skills, and administrative capabilities.

To develop efficient programs, a city or nation will need a modicum of each of the above preconditions. Even many wealthy nations (the United States included) and wealthy cities (New York and Los Angeles included) lack several of the above attributes. These partially endowed places can do something about their problems, but run a risk that what they do will be inappropriate. Singapore has developed a modicum of all these preconditions. Part One discusses how it has done so.

THE DYNAMICS OF PLANNING

As the preconditions take root, a government needs to organize planning in a manner that will provide socially beneficial programs and neutralize the influence of rivals who would use their power to adapt these programs to serve their own purposes. Older and younger civil servants, economic and political groups, private developers and landowners, planners and financiers, and various government agencies all compete for scarce resources in Singapore, as elsewhere. In the second part of the book we shall follow the interaction of the government with all of these groups in its efforts to make its programs socially beneficial. As we shall see, it has not been entirely successful in this regard.

This inadequacy partly stems from the programs themselves—their initial objectives do not always jibe with the needs of the people. To make its priorities conform with societal values, a government needs specific information about the needs and aspirations of a wide variety of societal groups. Both an atmosphere of freedom in which grievances will be expressed, and trained personnel capable of doing surveys and studies to evaluate such grievances, are necessary in this process. These are lacking in Singapore.

Another reason these programs fall short is the fact that the Singapore Government has not always found it possible to neutralize the power of those who would divert programs to more limited objectives. An individual's ability to divert the objectives of programs may derive from his possession of needed skills or resources, or from the fact that his political support is desired. If the government must rely upon wealthier people for its resources, it may find them demanding the use of the resources in a manner that tends to favor their interests at the expense of some of the objectives of the original program. If it must rely on bureaucrats for skills, they may slant the programs to the needs of their own agencies. If it must rely on partisans for information, they may supply a distorted picture of societal aspirations. In Singapore, as in many other places, these problems are endemic. Not uncommonly, Singapore finds them hard to eradicate.

It is sometimes suggested that such problems can be erased by manipulating the structural organization of planning. Louis J. Walinsky, for instance, suggests the creation of a Planning Group and a Planning Authority—both very different from anything that exists in Singapore.[2] The Planning Group would be separate from all functional agencies of the bureaucracy, and would carry out all aspects of planning. It would be in a position to consult with all kinds of citizen groups, and to coor-

---

[2] Louis J. Walinsky, *The Planning and Execution of Economic Development* (New York: McGraw-Hill, 1963), 13–20. He suggests that the Planning Group be headed by a man who is "intelligent, capable, interested, alert, dynamic, politically sophisticated, and possessed of considerable initiative." This group, staffed by experts from a variety of disciplines, will do economic and social planning, statistics-gathering, research, budgeting, and will create the administrative means to carry out projects. It would draw up a broad framework for economic and physical planning. The Planning Authority would preferably be chaired by the Prime Minister and, in addition to some other ministers, would contain chief civil servants. It would be furnished with a staff of economic and technical advisers, and the Head of the Planning Group would serve as its secretary. It would approve new projects, make major modifications in policy or in the overall plan, approve financial measures, settle major disputes among agencies, and sometimes reorganize agencies.

dinate the activities of the bureaucratic agencies. The Planning Authority would be a Cabinet level group that would give final authorization to the Planning Group's programs, back them when they could not settle conflicts among other groups, and periodically check to see that projects are being implemented as planned. Walinsky reminds one that planning is more than a succession of five-year plans, maps, econometric analyses, statistics, budgets, and projects. Planning is a flexible process involving continuing interactions among people and their values. He suggests that good planning involves care in assigning responsibility and routinizing methods of coordination.

From time to time, outside experts and academics have suggested changes in Singapore's planning structure that would move it in the direction of Walinsky's approach to planning. Before these suggestions can be placed in proper perspective, it is important to examine the degree to which her present procedures provide for flexibility in coordinating the interactions among people and their values.

Part Two of the book, then, explores the organizational processes that produced the Kallang Basin Reclamation Project. It also examines some of the above shortcomings in those processes, and raises the question of whether these shortcomings might be overcome by structural reorganization of planning.

THE SOCIAL ENVIRONMENT OF PLANNING

Were Singapore to top off its exceptional resources, skills, and administrative and political capabilities with exceptional planning procedure on the order of that suggested by Walinsky, trouble might still ensue. In fact, it might be argued that Singapore has done *too* well in establishing these capabilities, and that a streamlining of planning structure might actually make the situation worse unless it were accompanied by an improvement in the social environment within which planning operates. Enhancing the power of those with planning capabilities may simply allow those whose interests run counter to the needs of people to wield broader power.

There was an age when man could do little to manipulate his environment. Today he is capable of effecting enormous changes in short periods of time. As the economy develops, it affects many aspects of life. And, whether this development is by government or private citizens, it may cause more upset than uplift to human lives.

In many places, sectoral planning is poorly coordinated. An agricultural board clears land, a zoning board approves private clearance of land, an engineering section produces irrigation, a housing authority produces housing, and so on. Meanwhile, private businesses are also active, causing unrelated changes in the individual's living pattern. An individual needs housing that satisfies him and that he can afford. He needs neighbors and cultural facilities with which he feels comfortable. His job must offer him both security and an above-subsistence income. The educational system has to promise his children the same advantages. If any of these aspects are lacking for an individual, his environment becomes unstable. At the same time, his political efficacy can be weakened, as he must devote increasing time to straightening out his personal affairs.

As urbanization progresses, it becomes increasingly difficult to get all these parts working together. Planning means more than undertaking desired activities; it also involves creating stable environments for individual citizens. Ironically, as one comes to depend on ever-larger economic and bureaucratic organizations to achieve these results, their power to divert programs from the objective of creating stable individual environments increases. A sophisticated planning procedure—even one with Walinsky's central control facilities—could be controlled as easily by people with a stake in unstable environments (or in growth at whatever human costs) as by those who place broad human needs first. Furthermore, the very attributes that contribute to government's power to intervene—preconditions of planning and organizing techniques—tend to speed economic growth rather than to hold it in check. They help produce newer, more powerful moguls who can even more effectively divert planning—and the political processes—to their own ends.

Job centers that train people for menial jobs which provide no mobility might increase discontent rather than diminish it. Urban renewal that moves people away from their jobs, or raises the cost of living, or destroys small businesses, might increase economic misery rather than end it. Rural development programs that create dissatisfaction with a rural way of life faster than they make rural living viable are likely to cause more instability than they remove. A growing gross national product can itself be an imbalancing factor if it increases the gap between the rich and the poor, the city and the countryside, the ethnic majority and ethnic minorities, or the capital city and the rest of the country. All of these can result from an accretion in the power of the upper and middle classes through augmented planning potentials. By enhancing the power of these classes, massive urban development and industrialization programs may be weakening government's ability to serve human needs, rather than strengthening it as is commonly assumed.

Perhaps there is a basic incompatibility between the planning mechanisms of urban industrialization and the needs of the poor. This is the central concern of Part Three of the book. Can the social and economic systems of the postindustrial world support urban planning that is compatible with the needs of human beings?

PART ONE

SINGAPORE'S PRECONDITIONS FOR PLANNING

CHAPTER I

Resources, Skills, and Administrative Capabilities

> There are a number of objective conditions that need to be established before a government can actually institute reform programs. In comprehending how a government plans, it is as important to analyze how it developed these preconditions as it is to look into the planning itself.[1]

Few new nations have yet developed resources, skills, and administrative capabilities to as advanced a stage as Singapore already enjoyed in 1959—the year she began internal self-government. When Prime Minister Lee Kuan Yew and the People's Action Party came to power that year, they inherited—from the British and from Singapore's own peculiar history—talents, facilities, and institutions that allowed them to immediately initiate vast development programs. These capabilities and their historic evolution are described below; Prime Minister Lee's ascent to power and the achievements of his Government will be discussed in the two chapters immediately following.

RESOURCES

> accessible natural resources . . . a basic transportation system . . . means to lure financial resources into development projects . . . water . . . inexpensive electrical power.[2]

The island of Singapore is not large; the entire nation comprises a land area of 224 square miles (see Map 1). Her 1968 population was two million.

The visitor flying in from abroad often expects to find an island covered with buildings and people. To his surprise, as he looks from the aircraft after crossing the narrow Straits of Johore from Malaya he sees below him a stretch of land that is largely green, with dense urbanization confined principally to the southeast corner of the island. Since Sin-

---

[1] See Introduction, p. xix.   [2] *Ibid.*

3

gapore is near the equator, a greenish hue might bring to mind a vision of virgin jungle. The vision is not entirely askew; the center of Singapore island contains a patch of virgin jungle. But much of Singapore's flora and fauna are used for productive purposes. Each year the island produces approximately 850,000 pigs, 20 million chickens, 750,000 ducks, and 290 million eggs. She markets 44,000 tons of vegetables and 18,000 tons of fish (fresh and salt water). She raises S$383,000 worth of orchids; [3] some fruits and sugar cane; S$1,193,000 worth of coconut; S$2,200,000 worth of tobacco; S$3,000,000 of rubber; and reaps S$15,500,000 from fish and prawns. [4] These marketed goods contribute a substantial proportion of the island's total consumption of pork, poultry, eggs, and vegetables. There is surplus pork for export. The additional portion of the diet supplied from fruits, vegetables, and livestock grown in the back yard and never reaching the market is difficult to determine, but probably also substantial. Singapore's agricultural sector, according to one source, had an annual per capita output of S$113 and S$108 in 1960 and 1966 respectively. [5] Per capita income from industrial output was S$369 and S$654 in those years. [6] Hence the agricultural sector by no means contributes the major portion of the island's income. It is, at the same time, not an insignificant economic factor. Singaporeans have learned to reap a high return from scarce nat-

[3] These figures come from Mrs. A. N. F. Hill, "The Physical Characteristics, Climate, and Their Effect on Trade, Agriculture, and Fishing," in Republic of Singapore, State and City Planning, *Notes for Consultant Briefing at Node One in the Plan of Operations* (Singapore: GPO, 1967). Three Singapore dollars equal approximately one U.S. dollar.

[4] Lan Kwok Weng, "Production, Trade, and Tourism," in State and City Planning, *ibid.*

[5] Lan, *op. cit.* Annual output of S$172 million in 1960 and S$226 million in 1966. The 1966 figure is estimated. For a developing nation, this is an unusually high per capita income from agriculture. Tobacco, rubber, coconut, fish, and prawn production are not included in these figures. Goh Chok Tong, "Industrial Growth, 1959–66," in Ooi Jin-Bee and Chiang Hai Ding, eds., *Modern Singapore* (Singapore: University of Singapore, 1969), 131, gives the respective figures for gross domestic product in the agricultural sector in 1960 and 1966 as S$124 million and S$164 million. He cites the Department of Statistics, Singapore, as his source. This would make the figures in the text slightly high.

[6] Lan, *op. cit.* Annual output of S$563,600,000 in 1960 and S$1,250,000,000 in 1966. The 1966 figure is estimated. This includes only private firms with ten or more employees. Goh, *op. cit.*, gives 1960 and 1966 figures for gross domestic product in manufacturing (10 or more employees) of S$126 million and S$345 million respectively. The total for all sectors in the two years is given as S$2,122 million and S$3,218 million. Hence the per capita income figures quoted in the text may be far too high.

ural resources. As in many cities, however, this well-developed resource base is gradually being displaced as urban development expands.

The Republic's chief resources are financial. From the founding of the city in 1819 by Sir Stamford Raffles, it was the policy of the British governors to attract to the island from China large numbers of commercially inclined entrepreneurs. Most of these immigrants followed a similar pattern: Arriving virtually penniless, they set to work at commercial pursuits and saved most of their earnings. Part of these savings were sent back to families in China, and part were invested. Finally, the individual either returned to China with his savings or sent for a wife and settled down. In this manner a stable and highly enterprising class of entrepôt [7] traders gradually began to form the principal demographic group on the island.[8] A number of millionaires emerged from among this populace. Late in the nineteenth century these Singaporeans began to invest in the development of tin, rubber, transport, and real estate in the surrounding Federation of Malaya and the Dutch East Indies. In addition, British importation of laborers from South India added another savings-conscious element to Singapore's populace. Arab traders and some Sephardic Jewish immigrants also established businesses and investments on the island and in surrounding territories.

[7] Warehousing and middlemanning. Ships sell cargoes to Singaporeans, who warehouse them, and sell them to tourists, Singaporeans, Malayans, or other middlemen via other ships. Singaporeans refer to warehouses as godowns.

[8] Goh, *op. cit.*, indicates a 1966 gross domestic product from domestic and entrepôt trade of S$928 million. One of Singapore's millionaires was Aw Boon Haw, who made his fortune on Tiger Balm, a patent medicine to rub on sore muscles. He was highly philanthropic—endowing several Chinese-language schools, and co-sponsoring the China Relief drive discussed in Chapter II, footnote 21. He left behind in Singapore (and in Hong Kong) a monument—Tiger Balm Gardens—which tells something about the mentality of the enterprising businessman of his era. Here, in a somewhat garish and gargantuan fashion, are displayed painted plaster dioramas depicting folk and religious tales from China. Along one promenade, up a stairway leading from the Taoist purgatory torture scenes and behind the artificial mountain containing the bloody war between the rats and rabbits, is a set of dioramas setting forth moral maxims for modern Singaporeans. Their messages are primarily directed at the evils of gambling, debauchery, and loose spending. "After all is lost and reduced to mendicancy," warns one scene, "it will be too late to make amends for one's recklessness with money and immoral deeds." There is also a warning that money itself can be a great obstacle to ambition and success when it leads to "pleasant dissipation." A "good lesson for youngsters who do not study hard" depicts a boy who did not study hard in school and later was unable to handle the books of his father's small business when the duty fell to him. He was then remorseful over his malfeasance.

As a result of its small territory and its business-inclined demographic base, nearly the entire populace of the nation is involved in a monetary economy, saves, invests, and is susceptible to taxation. This is an extremely rare situation in developing nations. In addition, there are many relatively large enterprises that can serve as sources for both private and public investment capital.[9] The budget-balancing propensities of the British governors also contributed to the island's fiscal solvency; for many years the island's governments have taken in more revenue than they have spent. As a result, the present-day Singapore government is blessed with unusually high per-capita capital reserves.[10] Singapore possesses the enviable capacity to finance many of her development projects without foreign aid assistance.

Furthermore, Singapore made unusually early strides in development planning. It was from its inception a planned city. When Sir Stamford Raffles arrived on Singapore Island during 1819 he found at the mouth of the Singapore River a nearly uninhabited swamp ringed by hills; here he laid out a town. For the next 130 years, the built-up area of the city remained essentially within Raffles' original outline (see Map 2); [11] his original city simply became increasingly crowded. There are several reasons for this situation. The edge of the southern portion of his city touched the base of hillsides, and to the north of his city lay mangrove swamps. The hills immediately inland were soon occupied by the expansive homes and gardens of Europeans. Wealthy Chinese preferred to

[9] Singapore is the largest banking center in Southeast Asia, and provides the Southeast Asian headquarters for many major industrial and commercial firms. There are several large multicommodity export and import firms based on the island, and some moderately large factories and shipping lines. Esso, Mobil, and Shell have refineries in Singapore, and all major oil companies exploring the offshore oil discoveries are operating out of Singapore.

[10] The government's reserves at year's end 1954 were S$290 million. Colony of Singapore, *Singapore Annual Report, 1954.* In December 1967 the Minister of Finance announced that Singapore's reserves then stood at S$1,251,600,000. The March 1971 budget speech placed overseas reserves at S$3,556 million at the end of 1970. A review of the *Singapore Annual Reports* (1947–1963) and *Year Books* (1964–1966) shows that only in 1954 and 1963 did governmental expenditures surpass revenues.

[11] Raffles located the commercial section on the south bank of the Singapore River. Since this area consisted entirely of mangrove swamp, laborers carried earth in baskets from nearby hills to produce dry land. Roads and rows of shophouses were laid out. The land immediately to the north of the Singapore River was used for the government sector (see Photo 1). North of this, a tract of land was set aside for the main mosque and for general habitation by Europeans and other non-Chinese elements of the population.

live close to their place of business, while most of the remaining populace was forced to stay in town to be close to their employment. The rest of the island became inhabited only by small vegetable farmers and fishermen, and by the operators of the nutmeg, coconut, gambier, pepper, and tapioca estates which began to replace the rain forest and mangrove. The city itself had only one direction to grow—toward the sea. A succession of reclamation projects extended the city's boundaries westward into the sea and removed some of the hills immediately to the south.[12] Only after 1945 did the urban spread, discussed later, begin to develop.

Meanwhile, the growth of agriculture had necessitated the establishment of a road network for the island. Soon small trails that previously served outlying villages were being expanded into roads to serve the estates. Already in 1863 the Surveyor General's Office reported basic roads serving all but the westernmost portions of the island. By the beginning of World War II, 275 miles of paved roads criss-crossed the island;[13] by 1959 this figure had not been greatly increased, but there were several new roads, and the surfaces of others had been improved. As of the end of 1947 there were 17,703 motor vehicles on the island, including 210 buses and 5,406 lorries;[14] by the end of 1958 there were 82,584 motor vehicles, including 950 buses and 12,253 goods carriers.[15] For a small developing nation, this was an exceptional number of vehicles.

From the beginning, Singapore's economic activities were principally dependent upon the sea. At first its natural harbor served the small trading ships. Construction of wharves began in 1852. In 1864 the Tanjong Pagar Dock Company started construction of more substantial facilities, which continued to expand along the south and southeast shore line of the city.[16] With the opening of the Suez Canal in 1869, more substantial vessels began to call at the port; the Singapore Straits serve

[12] Cf. Wong Poh Poh, "The Changing Landscapes of Singapore Island," in Ooi, *ibid.*, 27–35. This reclaimed area is indicated on Photo 1.

[13] *Singapore Annual Report, 1947,* 112.   [14] *Ibid.*

[15] *Singapore Annual Report, 1958,* 256.

[16] See George Boggars, *The Tanjong Pagar Dock Company 1864–1905* (Singapore: GPO, 1956). In 1899 the Tanjong Pagar Dock Company amalgamated with a number of smaller dock companies which had built along the southern shore line. The government soon entered into protracted arbitration regarding price, and six years later expropriated the company to form the Tanjong Pagar Dock Board. See also Wong, *op. cit.,* 33–35.

as the most convenient route for any ship traveling from there to the Far East. In 1913 the Singapore Harbour Board took over these facilities. By 1959, Singapore had two and a half miles of modern wharfage, a one-mile breakwater, six major drydocks for ships 400–885 feet in length, a fleet of water and service boats, mechanized cargo handling, heavy repair services, and considerable dockside warehouse and bulk storage facilities. It had become one of the world's largest and most active ports.

Civil and military aviation began operating off the island before World War II. In 1955, Singapore opened the Paya Lebar International Airport, sufficient to handle the largest jet commercial airliners.

Public water services began in 1857 and have constantly expanded since then at a rate fast enough to meet demand.[17]

Electrical services also started relatively early. During 1953 the supply of electrical power surpassed demand, with increases in power facilities progressing at a steady pace.[18] The city was, in addition, supplied with piped gas.[19]

[17] Singapore's first water installation was made in 1857, with the construction of a culvert from MacRitchie Reservoir (in the center of the island) into town. The Municipal Council took responsibility for the water supply in 1878. By 1950 the island was using an average of 32 million gallons of water a day; in 1955 this had increased to 50 million gallons per day. *Singapore Annual Report, 1955.* However, there was still a water shortage. Hence Singapore had to turn to Johore to begin construction on its next major waterworks, with water from these facilities piped across the Causeway. By 1959, with pumping capacity of 191 million gallons a day established or under construction, consumption had risen to 63 million gallons a day. In addition to indoor installations, there were 2,046 outdoor standpipes (507 of which were constructed in 1959) *Singapore Annual Report, 1959.*

Modern sewage began in 1912. By 1955 there were 210.43 miles of sewers and 10 pumping stations, with 238 small purification plants located outside the city area. By the end of 1958, 262.5 miles of sewers and 13 pumping stations served 35,218 premises and 615,000 people.

[18] Electrical service was inaugurated in 1906 by the Tramway Company. In 1926, the St. James Power Station was constructed; by 1948 it had reached a capacity of 37,000 kilowatts. This equipment was modernized in 1958. In 1950 work began on the Pasir Panjang Power Station, which attained a capacity of 150,000 kilowatts in 1959. The maximum demand for electricity was 87,500 kilowatts in 1956 and 105,700 kilowatts in 1958. By the end of 1958 there were 86,-621 consumers with 148,778 meters, and 269.93 miles of street lighting. During 1958, 571,256,225 units of electricity were generated. *Singapore Annual Report, 1955, 1958, 1959.*

[19] In 1861 the Singapore Gas Company started delivery, primarily to light the streets; in 1901 it was taken over by a local authority. Coal carbonization was used as fuel source. In 1928, 1932, and 1951 the gas manufacturing plant was ex-

C. Northcott Parkinson taught for a time at the University of Singapore. It is perhaps a corollary of his Law that demand expands to absorb the available supply of basic services. At least that corollary was to apply in Singapore. As with work spreading out to fill available time, the blessing may be a mixed one.

SKILLS

> engineers, economists, architects, statisticians, skilled bureaucrats and entrepreneurs, and various types of skilled and semiskilled laborers . . . agronomists, urban planners, educationists, geographers, sociologists, lawyers, survey researchers, mathematicians, and economists with advanced specialized skills.[20]

Singapore had acquired a pool of trained personnel by the time it achieved independence.

Its chief human resource, the skilled entrepreneur, has already been mentioned. Because it had not had to create large numbers of achievement-oriented entrepreneurs from scratch—or from among minority groups—Singapore was far ahead of most countries in the developing world.

Before World War II, Singapore's educational system was primarily privately endowed.[21] Instruction was in one of several Chinese or Indian dialects, in Malay, or in English, depending on the school. Advanced textbooks were unavailable in the non-English languages. The syllabus of most schools centered around classical subjects, and standards were not high. For many older Singaporeans, education had meant three or four years of schooling in China or India. The education of many younger people was interrupted by the war. Practically no women were educated, and high percentages of males remained illiterate.[22]

---

tended. By 1955 the gas works had developed the capacity to produce and store 2 million cubic feet per day. In 1958 a new gas plant, which burns oil, was commissioned. During that year 14,723 consumers used 630 million cubic feet of gas. There were 305 miles of gas mains. *Singapore Annual Report, 1955, 1959.*

[20] See Introduction, p. xix.

[21] Nearly all Chinese education was supported by wealthy businessmen. Christian Missions started some primary and a few secondary schools, both for boys and girls. See footnote 22.

[22] In 1941 there were 72,100 students enrolled in school, including 17,500 (one-third girls) in 31 government and government-aided English-stream schools (i.e., with instruction conducted in the English language), 9,500 (under one-third girls) in 50 private English-stream schools, and 38,000 in 370 private Chinese-

A small number of schools—with instruction conducted in the English language—did offer a high quality secondary school education,[23] and Raffles College [24] gave university level courses and a diploma in arts and sciences. Many of the graduates of these institutions went to England to study—primarily in law and medicine, but also in architecture, engineering, and other fields.[25] Prime Minister Lee Kuan Yew, with his First Honours in law from Cambridge, Minister of Finance Dr. Goh Keng Swee (Ph.D. in economics), Minister of Law Edwin Barker, Deputy Prime Minister Dr. Toh Chin Chye (a physiologist), Foreign Minister S. Rajaratnam, and many top administrators in the present bureaucracy followed an educational path through one or more of these secondary institutions and thence to England. Special scholarships to England were instituted after World War II for senior civil servants and

---

stream schools. About 700 pupils in the English-stream schools passed their Cambridge School Certificate Examinations that year. Colony of Singapore, Department of Education, *Annual Report of the Department of Education, 1947* (Singapore: GPO), 16–17.

The 1947 census showed a total island population of 940,824; probably a third of these were of school age. Hence many school-age youth were not in school.

[23] Among the principal secondary schools in Singapore were Raffles Institution, founded under the patronage of Sir Stamford Raffles himself in 1823, the Anglo-Chinese School (1885), St. Joseph's Institution (1852), St. Andrew's School (1862), Raffles Girls' School (1844) and Convent of the Holy Infant Jesus Girls' School (1854).

[24] Raffles College was founded in 1929 from public funds. During the 1934–1935 school year it had 80 students. By 1941 it had 300 students, the majority of whom were fee-paying. It had departments of English, history, geography, mathematics, economics, chemistry, physics, law, and education. In 1946 Raffles College had 211 students, and the College of Medicine 200 (see footnote 35).

[25] In 1886 the colonial government instituted Queen's Scholarships to allow two individuals per year from Singapore and Malaya to be sent to England for university studies. These scholarships were abandoned in 1910, but they were revived again in 1924—after agitation from the Straits Chinese British Association (an organization of priminent English-speaking Chinese that had advocated the introduction of the scholarships in the first place). In 1939 new regulations were introduced that limited these scholarships to graduates of Raffles College and the College of Medicine. *Annual Report of the Department of Education, 1947, op. cit.,* 7. Among the first three Queen's Scholars to go to England after the war in 1946 was E. W. Barker, Minister of Law in the PAP Government. After World War II, the number studying abroad both on scholarships and with assistance from their own families increased considerably. By 1956 there were 152 Singaporeans abroad on scholarships at foreign universities. *Singapore Annual Report, 1956.*

for teacher training.[26] Between 1955 and 1957 fifty-six students from English- and Chinese-stream backgrounds were sent abroad under such scholarships.[27]

Immediately after World War II the government began a program to increase primary and secondary school facilities and to upgrade school curricula—primarily within the English-language schools. Teacher training began in 1939, with a two-year course for teachers in private English schools.[28] In 1950 the Teachers' Training College was established with 760 students in training to teach in English schools;[29] by 1958 enrollment had grown to 2,513.[30] Between the end of World War II and 1958, the government constructed 113 primary and 17 secondary school buildings.[31] In 1949 there was an estimated school enrollment of 145,000—principally in primary schools; by 1958 this figure had increased to 313,792.[32] The 1957 secondary school enrollment was 37,385 (including 15,210 in Chinese middle schools); by 1958 there were 10,292 teachers.[33] Furthermore, reforms begun in 1957 [34] were bringing a common modernized syllabus and the teaching of science to most secondary schools. Some of the secondary schools were technical schools.

There were still many individuals without primary education, and few had secondary education. The roots of a modern school system were firmly set, however.

Higher education was also well established by 1959. The year 1905 marked the founding of King Edward VII College of Medicine; in 1949

[26] In 1947 seven senior civil servants went to England on scholarships. *Singapore Annual Report, 1948.* By 1953, 21 civil servants were on training courses in Malaya, and 130 were studying overseas. *Singapore Annual Report, 1953.*

[27] Colony of Singapore, *First Education Triennial Survey, 1955–57* (Singapore: GPO, 1959), 48.

[28] The program was interrupted by the war. By 1946 the program had resumed and had 101 enrolled.

[29] *Singapore Annual Report, 1950.* These were all training to teach in English-language schools. Normal classes began in Kuala Lumpur, Malaya, in 1905.

[30] *Singapore Annual Report, 1958.* Of these, 892 were training to teach in Chinese-language schools.

[31] *Singapore Annual Report, 1954–58.* By 1957 there were 567 primary, 110 secondary, and 5 vocational schools on the island.

[32] *Singapore Annual Report, 1949, 1958.* Since population was growing rapidly, this probably did not represent a marked increase in the percentage of school-age children in school.

[33] ———. *First Education Triennial Survey, op. cit.,* 75–90.   [34] See pp. 25–26.

it united with Raffles College to form the University of Malaya.[35] The university's 1950 enrollment was 450; by 1957 this had risen to 1,700.[36] There were Faculties of Medicine, Science, and Arts, and Departments of Social Work and of Law. In 1958 the first classes began at the new Singapore Polytechnic. And 1955 marked the opening of Nanyang University, the first institution of higher education in Southeast Asia for those educated in the Chinese language stream. Although its degrees were not accredited, and did not serve as a suitable qualification for government employment, it had 900 students by 1957.

Thus, by 1959 graduates from Singapore institutions of higher learning were available as generalists for the bureaucracy and business, lawyers, medical practitioners, social workers, teachers, and scientifically trained personnel for industry. Foreign institutions had supplied Singapore with trained lawyers, doctors, teachers, architects, public administrators, and engineers.

Specialists in other fields were still lacking. By the end of the 1960's, Singapore was still completely without local specialists in such fields as marine and road engineering, sewerage, urban planning, sociology, or survey research, as well as those with other advanced technological and academic skills. However, rapid advances in education during the 1960's assure that it will be possible to create such skills in the 1970's.

The island's development was further favored by the desire of the government to retain the services of expatriates with needed skills. Because of the existence of comfortable living conditions, reasonably high sala-

[35] The Straits Settlements and Federated Malay State Government Medical School was founded in July 1905; in 1912 its name was changed to King Edward VII Medical School. In 1916 its license was recognized by the General Medical Council of Great Britain, and in 1921 its name was again changed, to King Edward VII College of Medicine. In 1929 it added a Department of Dental Surgery, whose license was recognized by the General Medical Council in 1947. A Department of Pharmacy was added in 1936. The University of Malaya was formed in October 1949, and it inherited the Faculties of Arts & Science from Raffles College, and of Medicine (including Dentistry and Pharmacy) from King Edward VII College. The governments of Singapore and Malaya cooperated on this project. In 1953 a new library building was completed, and in 1954 there began a building program for new halls of residence, administration buildings, lecture halls, and a science tower. See University of Singapore, *University of Singapore Calendar, 1967–68*. The Straits Chinese British Association (see footnote 25) was active in advocating all of these educational advances. See Sir Song Ong-siang, *One Hundred Years' History of the Chinese in Singapore* (London: J. Murray, 1923).

[36] *Singapore Annual Report, 1950, 1957.*

ries, and easy access to other areas of the world, Singapore had been more successful than most new nations in retaining the services of overseas staff and attracting new recruits to posts requiring specialized skills. Even so, recruits sometimes came only for a few months, and seldom stayed longer than four years. It is the pool of local skills that really counts, and these had many years of gestation behind them.

These skills existed only among the English-educated. This seemingly harmless fact, as we shall see, was not without serious repercussions—part of the price paid for rapid acquisition of the preconditions for planning.

ADMINISTRATIVE CAPABILITIES

> . . . individuals who are capable of uniting these people into administrative organizations which will have both the ability and motivation to conceive and carry out projects.

As was the case with most of her colonies, Britain endowed Singapore with a highly trained and modern constabulary [37] and a skilled judiciary. She also left behind her military forces after independence (until 1971) supplying the government with sufficient strength to meet any contingency that might arise to upset the established power structure or planning procedures. There were those, we shall find, who did not welcome the established procedures or their protection. This points to the importance of a trained constabulary as a precondition for planning. At the same time it raises questions as to whether a modern constabulary assists in adapting procedures to serve human needs or simply allows the procedures to continue whether they serve them or not.

Britain also left behind planning machinery—in this case more extensive than that created in most of her colonies.

The Public Works Department had its origins when Sir Stamford Raffles hired day laborers to fill the mangrove swamps on the site of the new city; by 1959 the Department had working divisions designing and building roads, bridges, drains, public buildings, and other amenities. The Harbour Board had been operating and adding to harbor facilities since 1913. Divisions of Agriculture, Fisheries, Veterinary Services,

---

[37] In 1963, the year that the British relinquished control of the police to Malaysia, Singapore had a regular police force of 6,012 and Special Constabulary of 1,001. This force included only nine Europeans. *Singapore Annual Report, 1963,* 200–202.

Cooperative Development, and Rural Development had made beginning advances toward providing services to the rural sector. The Botanic Gardens, established by Sir Stamford Raffles, had conducted the first experiments with rubber trees in Southeast Asia. A Gas Department, Electricity Department, Sewerage Department, and Water Department —operated by the City Council—provided public utilities.

The most impressive framework for development, however, was that created by the Singapore Improvement Trust. Beginning operation in 1927, it had as its initial purpose to counter urban blight by creating back lanes behind back-to-back shophouse blocks. Patterned after similar bodies in Bombay, Calcutta, Madras, Hyderabad, and other Indian cities, the Singapore Improvement Trust was destined to surpass its Indian counterparts in effectiveness.

The surveyors and engineers brought in to staff the Trust soon took an interest in a great variety of urban problems. They planned sewerage and new roads and purchased land for public purposes. They made land-use maps and began to serve as a development control agency for private construction. In 1936 they began construction of Singapore's first low cost public housing satellite town at Tiong Bahru (see Photo 2, No. 6). Other public housing was built elsewhere. These efforts were interrupted by the war but were resumed immediately afterward, and a Housing Committee was established in 1947.

In January 1952, Sir George Pepler brought a team of experts to Singapore to do a major survey of the island's planning needs. The reports of their findings were published in 1955 under the title of the *Master Plan*.[38] As indicated in later chapters, this report was to have an important influence upon Singapore's subsequent planning. An immediate result of the report (and of the work of the Housing Committee), was the beginning in 1954 of Queenstown—a completely planned satellite town containing public housing, schools, factories, and recreational facilities. Another result was the creation in 1957 of Singapore's first planned industrial estate, on Bukit Timah Road, by the Colonial Development Corporation.

By the time internal self-government began in 1959, the Singapore Improvement Trust had established planning control over private development, purchased over 1,500 acres of undeveloped land for housing and industrial development, and established 26 rural resettlement areas

[38] Colony of Singapore, *Master Plan: Report of Survey* (Singapore: GPO, 1955).

totaling over 5,000 acres.[39] It had constructed, or begun construction on, 21,364 units of public housing and created a complete administrative apparatus for this purpose.[40] It had opened the Payah Lebar International Airport, completed construction of a major highway and bridge leading along the ocean shore into the heart of the city, and drafted rudimentary plans for a wide variety of development projects for the island.

Britain was ready, too, to leave these apparatuses in the hands of Singaporeans. Malayanisation of the civil service was well advanced. In 1933, with the establishment of the Straits Settlements Civil Service, Asians were first admitted into the civil service of Singapore, though only at lower levels.[41] Before the war this process proceeded slowly. In 1946, Command Paper 197 stated that the public services "must to the greatest possible extent be staffed by local people." [42] A 1949 White Paper on Recruitment recommended absorption of civil servants into higher posts.[43] The Public Service Commission was established in 1951, with the right to give priority to local applicants. It created a unified scheme of service, with basic salaries of local applicants on a par with those of expatriates. In 1949 there were 102 local Division I officers.[44] By 1955 this number had increased to 284—all university honors graduates—out of a total of 740.[45] However, only 15 of the 153 su-

[39] Colony of Singapore, *SIT Annual Report,* 1958, 37.

[40] *Singapore Annual Report, 1958,* 141. Dwellings completed, end of 1958: Singapore Improvement Trust, 21,364 units; PWD, 9,166 units; City Council 4,680 units; Singapore Harbour Board 5,657. Total 40,867.

[41] Lee Yong Hock, "A History of the Straits Chinese British Association (1900–1959)," (B.A. Honours thesis, Department of History, University of Malaya, 1960), 54.

[42] Yeo Kim Wah, "Political Development in Singapore 1945–55" (Master's thesis, Department of History, University of Singapore, 1967), 45.

[43] *Ibid.,* 69.

[44] *Ibid.,* 72. Super-Scale Division I officers hold the highest civil service posts. Other Division I officers are just below them in rank.

[45] *Memorandum to the Malayanisation Commission* by the Federation of Unions of Government Employees, the Singapore Senior Officers' Association, the Graduate Teachers' Association, and the Singapore Teachers' Union, 1955, 7. Dr. Goh Keng Swee and other PAP leaders were among the members of this federation, which pressed hard for Malayanisation. By the end of 1955 there were 975 Division I posts, with 327 occupied by the locally domiciled, 362 by expatriate officers on the permanent establishment, 21 by expatriates on loan from Malaya, 88 expatriates on contract, and 71 employed on temporary terms, with 106 posts vacant. By the end of 1955 the government, the City Council, the Harbour Board, and the Singapore Improvement Trust together employed approximately

perscale Division I posts were held by local men.[46] The final report of the Malayanisation Commission in 1956, followed by the 1956 white paper on Malayanisation,[47] recommended that Malayanisation be extended to the highest levels. During 1957, 408 expatriates were asked to leave their posts.[48] By 1959 high percentages of local officers occupied all levels and agencies of the civil service.

These administrative capabilities, it should again be noted, existed principally among English speakers. The importance of this fact will become apparent in the next chapter. The fast educational and administrative advances were bought at the expense of creating a serious handicap in opportunities for social mobility among those who did not speak English.

Great Britain's reign in Singapore could have been the pride of Kipling's heart. By the standards of colonialism, and of British liberalism, her rule was progressive. She passed a torch burning brightly with the rudiments of public services and human amenities. Surely one might be critical. But not critical of this?

48,000 people, 98 per cent of whom were locally domiciled. *Singapore Annual Report, 1955,* 252–254.

[46] Colony of Singapore, Malayanisation Commission. *Interim Report* (Singapore: GPO, 1956), 12.

[47] Colony of Singapore, *White Paper on Malayanisation* (Singapore: GPO, 1956).

[48] *Singapore Annual Report, 1957.*

CHAPTER II

Political Capabilities: The Rise of the People's Action Party

> The Government needs enough stability to concentrate on development rather than simply on its own continuance in office. Its development goals must be acceptable to its principal political supporters. It must be in a position to mobilize the available resources, skills, and administrative capabilities.[1]

Governments often have available resources and skills but cannot use them to promote development. Their enemies are in a position to keep them from acting. Some of their supporters, or those who control the resources and skills, may be in that same position. Cleavages in the society (e.g., racial, religious, cultural, linguistic, class, generational, regional, urban-rural, status, traditional-modern) also can set tempers on edge and throw development programs into disarray. Such was the situation that prevailed in Singapore during the 1940's and 1950's.

There is another side of the coin as well. Many of the preconditions for planning discussed in the previous chapter came into being largely *because* of pressures generated by the political instability of the 1940's and 1950's. The creation of the University of Malaya and increases in scholarships to study abroad (see Chapter I, footnotes 25 and 35), the reform of Chinese education, Malayanisation of the civil service (see Chapter I, footnote 45), extension of suffrage and legislative representation, and advances toward self-government took place only after many political pressures upon the Colonial Government from a broad variety of local group interests. It was, ironically, necessary to reduce the intensity of these pressures in order to attain enough stability to institute the very programs they helped generate. Gradually, successive Governments succeeded in removing the sources of these pressures, and in calming

[1] See Introduction, p. xx. (Note: Throughout, I have capitalized "Government" when the Prime Minister and his Cabinet are meant.)

some of the social and economic tensions in the society. In the process of doing so, they may inadvertently have removed some of the vehicles needed to assure that the programs being instituted meet the specific needs of great numbers of people.

ROOTS OF DISORDER

When the British returned to Singapore at the end of World War II, they found turmoil. The island was virtually without food. The populace was jammed into deteriorating shophouses. Inflation spiraled yet businesses continued to pay prewar wages. In protest, workers soon started a series of crippling strikes.[2]

The British Military Administration responded with carrot and stick. Shiploads of rice were imported and distributed at subsidized prices. Unions were registered, and industrial arbitration measures instituted. A large volunteer corps was organized to patrol the docks. At the same time agitators were arrested and banished. Twenty-one unions were de-registered, and meetings and demonstrations were restricted for the rest. When the Communists then began the Malayan Emergency in June 1948, curfews, roadblocks, and police interrogations were added to the repertoire of coercive measures.

The government also took a step which served, ironically, to heighten conflict. It established a Legislative Council of twenty-three persons to advise the Governor. Dominated by Britishers (appointed by the British Military Administration) and some representatives of the Chambers of Commerce, the Council also included six elected members. Only the small part of the population who were English-educated were allowed to vote, however;[3] so, naturally, all six elected members were

[2] Labor organization began in Singapore during the 1920's. Before World War II there were 51 registered unions on the island. Immediately after the war the Communist-organized left-wing underground movement that had led the resistance against the Japanese reorganized those unions. See Charles Gamba, *The Origins of Trade Unionism in Malaya* (Singapore: Donald Moore, 1962).

[3] In 1957, 75 per cent of Singapore's 1,445,000 population was Chinese, 12 per cent Malay, 10 per cent Indian, and 3 per cent other races. As one can tell from the school attendance figures in the previous chapter, only a small percentage of the populace had been exposed to English education. In the first election, held in 1948, 13,458 persons voted. Suffrage was limited to British subjects (defined as living five years in a British territory, demonstrating some proficiency in English, declaring exclusive allegiance to the Crown and/or intent to reside permanently in the Colony) with one year's residence in Singapore.

English-educated. This cautious gesture toward local involvement was probably meant to quiet the situation. Instead, it stirred a hornet's nest:

Resentment had long been quietly brewing among Chinese-speaking Chinese. It had been a practice of British colonial Governments to select from English-stream secondary schools a chosen few English-speaking Chinese who would serve as middlemen in dealing with Chinese-speaking businessmen and man lower echelons of the civil service.[4] There were not similar opportunities for Chinese-speakers. Chinese schools received little government aid.[5] Even when Chinese-stream graduates could obtain relatively menial jobs as clerks and schoolteachers, their salaries were one-third to one-fourth those of their English-educated counterparts. After the war, the government was constructing new buildings and expanding programs for English-stream schools, with no commensurate help for Chinese-stream schools. Commerce was increasingly conducted in English. The Chinese-educated was keenly aware of being a member of a disadvantaged class. This was unsatisfactory to him even as a temporary condition. As the English-educated began to entrench themselves in the Legislative Council, with a prospect that the reins of government might be handed over to them, the Chinese-speakers began to worry that their condition might become permanent.

Hitherto, the British had been but dimly aware of these grievances. They were first openly discussed in English by a group of English-

---

[4] René Onreat, *Singapore, A Police Background* (London: D. Crisp, circa 1946) describes the complete social gulf separating the British from their local English-speaking cohorts. Garden parties, he said, provided the least embarrassing method for them to mingle occasionally. These had the advantage of being held outdoors, and of allowing everyone to get away fast. Even at these, the different racial groups tended to cluster together. E. M. Forster, *A Passage to India* (New York: Harcourt, Brace, 1925) describes the same phenomenon in India. Though never regarded as social equals by the English, they had no chance to learn about China in their schooling, but instead knew a good deal about the flora and fauna of the English countryside. They were often snubbed as well by the Chinese-speaking Chinese, who considered them more British than Chinese. Besides, for fear of losing their positions, they did not dare mix too closely with the Chinese cultural activities of their day, which were heavily encrusted with Kuomintang and Communist Party politics (see footnote 8).

[5] See Yeo Kim Wah, "Political Development in Singapore 1945–55" (Master's thesis, Department of History, University of Singapore, 1967), 188–203. The government-aided English-language-school student received twelve times more support than the government-aided Chinese-language-school student. There was no teachers' training for Chinese schoolteachers at the Teachers' Training College before 1955. Salaries in English-language schools averaged three times those in Chinese-language schools.

educated who formed the Malayan Democratic Union in 1946.[6] These men were placed in prison or exiled in 1950 and 1951.[7] Then in 1953, Chinese middle school students and teachers themselves began to articulate their resentments openly.[8] Some expressed themselves in blunt and militant terms.

[6] It is evident in retrospect that the Chinese educated would have to come to power and develop among themselves the skills and administrative capabilities needed to support a modern state, or the English speakers would have to find some way to absorb the Chinese-speakers into their own political movement. Those in political power had not yet grasped this truth in 1951. The members of the Malayan Democratic Union foresaw this, along with the further necessity to find a *modus vivendi* with the Malay community in the surrounding region (Indonesia and Malaya). The middle-class English-educated intellectuals who constituted the backbone of this organization wrote at length, advocating multilingualism in the schools as a means of reducing the dichotomy between English-speakers and Chinese-speakers; many of the 1955 education reforms discussed in this chapter were based on their writing. In 1947 they helped to crystallize opinion around raising income taxes so as to support education in all language streams. Their memo on housing suggested the Tiong Bahru, Queenstown, St. Michael's, and Prince Philip housing estates. But they were ahead of their time. Their efforts to form a coalition of Chinese-speaking Chinese, English-speakers, and Malays led to their arrests and exiles. For more on the MDU see Yeo Kim Wah, *ibid.*

[7] Some of these men have left Singapore permanently. Lim Kean Chye, a London-trained lawyer, has been active in left-wing politics in Malaya. D. V. Sharma moved to Peking to head the Malayan Liberation Front. John Eber (Harrow and Cambridge) became the publisher of the *Malayan Monitor* from exile in London. Others are now active in Singapore. Gerald de Cruz became an assistant director of the Political Studies Centre (see p. 48–49).

[8] This political activism had a long history. Sun Yat-Sen first visited Singapore in 1900, and his Kuomintang (KMT) movement was extremely active in Singapore from then until 1942. Communist organization in Singapore dates at least from the 1924–1927 KMT-Communist alliance in China. They had to operate secretly from the beginning. Early KMT branches were often disguised as schools for the poor. In the 1920's, KMT teachers were sent from China to Malaya to start and staff Chinese schools and spread KMT teachings. Communist-oriented teachers operated in night schools ("hsueh-hsih" tutorial programs operated by the Chinese Middle School Students' Union in 1955 were patterned after the night schools). Later in the 1920's, the British cracked down on KMT day-school teachers as well. After the outbreak of the Sino-Japanese war, Chinese teachers and pupils in Chinese-stream schools organized to raise funds to aid China by selling paper flowers or flags. There was a good deal of fervor about this, and those who did not buy were sometimes branded as "nationless slaves." In 1940 supporters of Chiang Kai Shek's "New Life Movement" sent some students to China for training, until the Director of Education put a stop to it. See Png Poh Seng, "The Kuomintang in Malaya," *Journal of Southeast Asian History,* 2 (March 1961), 1–32.

The experience for the Britisher was perhaps not unlike that of Southern gentlemen, used to being called sir, being confronted by their first black militants. But by this time Chinese-stream schools (over three hundred of them) had the largest overall enrollment of students on the island. And feeling over the issue ran deep. They could not be disposed of so easily as the few intellectuals in the Malayan Democratic Union.

To quell this renewed unrest, the government offered a plan to increase aid to Chinese schools. Strings were attached, however. In exchange for the aid, the traditional Chinese curriculum would have to be largely abandoned, and some courses would have to be taught in English. The plan was not acceptable to the teachers' unions.

Then another related issue interjected itself. By 1954 it was evident that Malaya would soon achieve self-government. The Chinese Chamber of Commerce began pressing the government more vigorously than before to decide on the citizenship status of Chinese in the future political structures both in Malaya and Singapore.

The successes of the British forces in bringing the Malayan Emergency under control was also proving to be a mixed blessing. Left-wing agitators were being freed to increase the pace of union organizing in Singapore.

In the face of all these pressures the government decided to act more boldly. It was announced that elections would be held in 1955 for a new Legislative Assembly to replace the Legislative Council; this new body would be numerically dominated by elected representatives. Six of the elected members would form a Council of Members, headed by a Chief Minister, which would consult with the British Governor on policy decisions. Proceedings would be conducted in English, but for the first time large numbers of Chinese-speakers would be enfranchised to vote in the election.

The results were electrifying—probably more so than those who conceived the plan had imagined they could be. Late in 1953, to help quell the growing disturbances, the government passed a conscription law. In May 1954 a group of Chinese middle school students organized a delegation to march on the Governor's Palace with a petition asking that students be exempted from service. This march was broken up by the police, and a number of those involved were arrested. A young Cambridge-educated lawyer named Lee Kuan Yew stepped in to defend them. He lost the court case, but in doing so accomplished something few English-speakers up to that time had been able to do: he established contact with the militant leadership of the Chinese-speakers.[9] Soon some of Lee Kuan Yew's political cohorts were integrated into the leadership of the unions that these Chinese-speakers had been organizing (see footnote 15). In October 1954 the new group of allies launched the People's Action Party with a mass rally. For the first time, English-educated and Chinese-educated leadership were joined together in organizing a mass political party.

The 1955 elections for the Legislative Assembly were hotly contested by six political parties and several independents. The parties of the left called for immediate internal self-government, abolition of the firm internal security regulations, relaxation of control on the unions, equal treatment for the different language streams in education, complete Malayanisation of the civil service, and a local citizenship. The party that had held the most seats in the previous Legislative Council carried on a far more conservative campaign. It called for independence in 1963, but supported a continuance of the Emergency Regulations, and basically stressed such economic issues as maintaining free port status, attracting foreign capital, and keeping income taxes low. On other issues, it remained quiet.[10]

There were 156,314 votes cast in the election. The parties of the right [11] took only 6 of the 25 seats. The People's Action Party, wishing to test its strength without the embarrassment of winning the election at this premature juncture, won three of the four seats it contested.[12] Two of the other parties of the left formed a coalition with a Eurasian,

[9] In *The Battle for Merger* (Singapore: GPO, 1964), 16, Lee Kuan Yew states: "Then one day in 1954 we came into contact with the Chinese-educated world. The Chinese middle-school students were in revolt against national service and they were beaten down. Riots took place, charges were preferred in court. Through devious ways they came into contact with us."

[10] Yeo, *op. cit.,* 316.

[11] Referring to the Progressive Party and the Democratic Party. The Progressive Party had held most elected seats on the two previous Legislative Councils (there had been a second election in 1951, with 25,065 English-speakers voting). The Democratic Party was formed by the Chinese Chamber of Commerce for purposes of the 1955 elections. Both parties coalesced around business and professional men. They erred in opposing one another in many constituencies—thus splitting more conservative voting strength. Together they received 70,810 votes.

[12] Lee Kuan Yew, Lim Chin Siong, and Goh Chew Chua won, while C. V. Devan Nair lost to a Labour Front candidate.

David Marshall, occupying the newly created post of Chief Minister.[13]

A dispute immediately arose between Marshall and the Governor over the meaning of the former's new post. Marshall interpreted the document that created his post [14] as meaning that the Chief Minister should have final say over internal affairs other than police matters. The Governor felt the wording made it quite clear that the Governor retained final say. Exasperated, the testy Chief Minister was soon calling for negotiations with Britain over self-government.

This was a battle that had probably not been anticipated. Also probably unanticipated, the inauguration of a local Government signaled the onslaught of the biggest battles yet on the streets. The Chinese middle school students and the trade unionists had now established large centralized action organizations.[15] Marshall wished to follow a less repressive course than previous Governments, and he legalized the student organization immediately upon taking office. Three weeks after he took office, one of the new mass unions under leadership of a PAP organizer

[13] Marshall led the Labour Front. This party, founded as the Labour Party by English-speaking business and professional people and white collar workers, had held 2 of the 9 elected seats on the previous 25-member Legislative Council. It reorganized shortly before the 1955 election to broaden its base. The PAP chose to field candidates in only 4 of the 25 races of the 1955 election. The other major party supporting the issues of non-English-speakers, the Alliance (an adjunct of the ruling party in Malaya), only contested for 17 seats and had support from the Chinese-speaking mass leadership; it generally steered clear of opposing Labour Front or PAP candidates.

[14] Colony of Singapore, *Report of the Constitutional Commission* (Singapore: GPO, 1954), 18–19. Appendix I supplies more detail on how the government operated during this period.

[15] The 55-man Exemption Delegation that led the march to the Governor's Palace in 1954 formed the Chinese Middle School Students' Union in October 1954. On March 30, 1955—one week before Marshall took office—they called a one-day strike in all Chinese middle schools to protest the government's failure to register them.

The Singapore Factory and Shop Workers' Union, formed April 22, 1954, under leadership of Lim Chin Siong (now a PAP member of the Legislative Council) and Fong Swee Suan, contained 30 unions by the end of 1955. It claimed an average 30 per cent wage increase for its members during 1955. See J. J. Puthucheary, "Growth and Development of the Trade Union Movement after the Election," *Fajar* No. 25 (November 30, 1955), 3. Lim and Fong were the Chinese-speaking leaders with whom Lee Kuan Yew and his friends established contact in 1954 to form the PAP. In 1955 three of the four SFSWU assistant secretaries (Devan Nair, J. J. Puthucheary and S. Woodhull) were English-speaking PAP leaders.

called a bus strike. On May 12, 1955, the anniversary of the previous year's march to the Governor's Palace that had sparked the inception of the PAP, the newly recognized Chinese Middle School Students' Union organized a march downtown to support the bus strikers. Feelings ran high, and tragedy ensued. In the course of the day a policeman was beaten to death, a voluntary corpsman burned to death, and an American journalist and a student killed. Nineteen were injured.

The Government (Marshall and the Governor were now more or less working together) responded by threatening to close the schools, and by expelling seventy students. Two thousand students then held a camp-in on the school grounds. Ten days later the camp-in was ended with a victory parade after Marshall announced the convening of an All-Party Committee to discuss Chinese education. Two weeks later 503 Chinese bodies joined together to participate in these negotiations. Elsewhere, workers joined together to organize a series of crippling strikes.[16] In addition, the student and union leaders were joining with the People's Action Party to organize mass rallies protesting the detention laws (and the detention of seventy persons in 1955), discrimination against Chinese education and culture, and continuance of colonial rule. David Marshall used the unrest as leverage to push the British more quickly toward calling a conference on self-government. Talks were called in London early in 1956. When they ended in disagreement,[17] David Marshall resigned. Another leader of his party became Chief Minister.

On September 18, 1956, the Government acted against the continuing agitation by banishing two teachers and a union organizer to Communist China and dissolving the Chinese Middle School Students' Union and two ancillary organizations.[18] Additional arrests and student dismissals on October 10 sparked a camp-in by 4,000 students and a series of protest rallies.[19] After thirteen days of this the Government an-

[16] The number of unions had increased from 91 with 48,595 members in 1950, to 136 with 76,452 in 1954, to 187 with 139,317 in 1955. By year's end 1955, a record of 946,354 man-days (vs. 47,316 in 1953) had been lost through 275 strikes.

[17] Leaders of the Liberal Socialist Party (an amalgam of the Progressive and the Democratic parties), the Labour Front (David Marshall), and the PAP (Lee Kuan Yew) attended.

[18] The Brass Gong Musical Society (which had organized unauthorized cultural concerts to play left-wing songs) and the Singapore Women's Federation.

[19] Three of these were organized by the PAP, and eight by another ancillary group in the movement, the Farmers' Association. Chinese-speaking farmers were also heavily involved in the Independence movement.

nounced that it was about to forcibly break up the camp-in. Within hours, the protesting groups had organized a massive march downtown. People turned out from all over for what was to be the crescendo of the Independence movement. The police and army turned out as well. Twenty-four hours later the students had been cleared from the schools by tear gas. The police had opened fire 81 times, and 67 were wounded (including 12 policemen). Eight demonstrators and 5 policemen died on the streets. Most of the radical leadership was placed under detention, and most of the cooperating organizations were deregistered. The battle for the streets was abruptly over.[20]

STEPS TOWARD PEACE

On the surface it might appear that the Government (the Chief Minister *cum* Council of Members, with the British Governor as final arbiter) had at last attained some stability. However, it was the demonstrators who actually won the day. The surface calm was partially premised on the understanding that this Government was (a) now going to attempt to remedy some of the outstanding grievances; (b) to be only a caretaker Government until the advent of full internal self-government; and (c) probably destined to be voted out of office by a party endorsed by the political leadership of the Chinese-speaking community. As a caretaker Government, it was not in a position to undertake any bold departures in the realm of planning. With uncertainty as to who would succeed it, businessmen were also hesitant to commit themselves on any new planning schemes.

Agreement was soon reached on Chinese education, thanks to the fact that the All-Party Committee (p. 24) had already been formed the previous year.[21] The compromise provided for government aid to, or

[20] See Colony of Singapore, *Singapore Annual Report, 1956.* Also Colony of Singapore, Legislative Assembly, *Singapore Chinese Middle School Students' Union* (Singapore: GPO, 1956); Colony of Singapore, Legislative Assembly, *The Communist Threat in Singapore* (Singapore: GPO, 1957). Among those jailed at this juncture and in subsequent months were key Chinese-speaking and more radical English-speaking leaders of the PAP.

[21] The Chinese Chamber of Commerce took an active part in these negotiations. The Chamber, containing the wealthiest Chinese-speaking businessmen in the colony, had long played an uneasy role in the politics of the Chinese-speaking community. Chinese businessmen had helped support some of the KMT schoolteachers in the 1920's. While KMT fundraising was taking place in the schools after the outbreak of the Sino-Japanese War (footnote 8), the Chinese Chamber

control of, most schools, equal aid to aided schools and students in all language streams, reductions in the gaps among teachers' salaries, acceptance of all language streams into the Teachers' Training College, the teaching of an extra language in all schools, and common textbooks and syllabuses.[22] Likewise, a compromise was reached on the citizenship issue; it provided citizenship to all persons residing in Singapore for eight years who would renounce other loyalties. A series of meetings in Britain with Singapore party leaders culminated in the decision to grant Singapore internal self-government in 1959. The Legislative Assembly passed a compulsory voting law for all citizens over twenty-one.

Still, with all this, the path was not yet clear for instituting the kind of governmental power needed to plan. A wide gap continued to separate those who would lead planning and those who held political power.

Singapore's development skills existed chiefly among the English-educated. Her investment and trade primarily involved the English-speaking world and its allies. Her governmental and administrative institutions all functioned in English. Yet to win an election, a political party had to attract the vote of the Chinese-speaker, and to remain in power a Government had to win a number of allies among the Chinese-speaking majority. To proceed with development, an English-speaking government would need to acquire Chinese-speaking supporters; a Chinese-speaking government would have needed to borrow the skills and resources of the English-speakers. Until such partnerships

---

of Commerce formed a drive to raise $228 million for China Relief; this caused some friction with the KMT and the Communists. Three months before Singapore fell to the Japanese the Governor asked the Chamber to organize a "Singapore Chinese Anti-Enemy Backing up Council." Both the KMT and the Communists were represented on this council; many of these same individuals later took to the jungle to form the resistance movement.

[22] See Colony of Singapore, *Report of the All-Party Committee of the Singapore Legislative Assembly on Chinese Education* (Singapore: GPO, 1956). Students would hitherto be barred from political activities. All schools would be administered on the advice of an Educational Advisory Board and would have their own management and disciplinary committees with clearly defined responsibilities (so they could be circumvented if they failed to carry out these responsibilities). The agreement left a finely knit balance between autonomy and government control, but generally gave the government the power to prevent future political organization in the schools and begin to modernize the curriculum. The arrest on September 26, 1957, and subsequent deportation, of the principal of Chung Cheng High School (where the 1956 camp-in was held) also helped to control disturbance.

could be cemented, there was little hope for pursuing a vigorous development program.

Such a partnership was not to be easily created. Its formation required the use of coercive tactics which go beyond those permissible for most city and national governments.

Lee Kuan Yew's alliance with Chinese-speakers was tenuous from the beginning. The first parting of ways came already in 1957. At the Second All-Party Conference in London, Lee Kuan Yew agreed that when Singapore achieved internal self-government in 1959 internal security would still remain in the hands of the British until merger with Malaya.[23] This would allow the British to prevent the Chinese-speaking wing of the PAP from taking control of the party should it come to political power. Thinking they saw handwriting on the wall, the Chinese-speaking wing decided to take control of the party immediately. At the 1957 Annual General Meeting of the People's Action Party, they succeeded in capturing six of the twelve seats on the Executive Committee. The English-speakers thereupon resigned, charging fraudulent procedures in the voting. In a raid on various left-wing elements a few days later, Internal Security officers conveniently detained five of the six Chinese-speakers newly elected to the Executive Committee, along with several officials in PAP branches. Returned to full command of the PAP, the English-speakers thereupon created a special class of cadre members who alone would be permitted to vote at annual meetings. This incident momentarily lowered popular support for the PAP.

To win the forthcoming 1959 Legislative Assembly election, each faction of the party needed the other, however.[24] The English-speaking

[23] Devised for handling security until merger with Malaya the Internal Security Council consisted of two Singapore Government representatives, two United Kingdom representatives, and one representative from the Federation of Malaya. This ensured that Chinese-speaking Chinese could not dominate the council's decisions.

[24] After the 1957 Annual General Meeting, some of the Communists seem to have turned their support temporarily to David Marshall, who formed a new Workers' Party to contest four of the 32 seats in the year-end City Council elections (which brought the city a PAP mayor, Ong Eng Guan, who was not closely identified with either wing of the party). Marshall's party won 3 of these 4 seats. Lee asserts (*op. cit.*, 27–28) that he re-established contact with the Communists in March 1958, and they told him they were dropping support for Marshall. Partial verification of this may come from the fact that when Marshall resigned from the City Council two months later and forced a by-election he received fewer than 100 votes. The Communists probably perceived that Lee was better at playing electoral politics than Marshall. They may not have given the PAP support in

and Chinese-speaking leadership rejoined forces in 1958, quickly organized powerful party organizations in all constituencies, and together
went forward to win 43 of the 51 seats contested in the election, taking
53.4 per cent of the total vote.[25] The party's greatest voting strength lay
in the Chinese-speaking areas. Lee Kuan Yew (as leader of his party)
became the island's first prime minister—with full authority over all
matters except internal security—after the British had obeyed his direc-
tive to release from prison eight PAP leaders who had been detained
over the years. The top Cabinet posts went to English-speakers. The
Chinese-speakers received political secretaryships and other relatively
harmless roles within his Government.[26]

Lee Kuan Yew immediately set out to tackle the social and economic
problems that had been building up during the period of political instability. Slums were worse than they had ever been, and a high percentage
of the populace lived in them. Foreign investment was stagnating. Road
repair was needed. Sewers and garbage collection required extension.
Unemployment was high, and salaries low. Harbor facilities needed repairs.

The government was soon to discover, however, that it still did not
have all the political capabilities it needed to promote development.

For instance, it was necessary to restore confidence among businessmen so as to generate investment capital. One necessary ancillary of
such a policy was to convince them that the government had the capacity to promote moderation in the demands of labor unions. Yet many of
the Chinese-speakers within the PAP were leaders of aggressive labor
unions, which supported the party largely because of its pro-union
stand. The leaders of a number of unions failed to heed requests by
government that they hold back on wage demands. So in 1959 and 1960
the government deregistered 106 unions [27] and sought to absorb the re-

---

every constituency during the campaign, but their influence must have contributed to the PAP win.

[25] The election was contested by 160 candidates from 10 political parties and
by 34 Independents. The ruling Labour Front had changed to the Singapore People's Alliance, opting more middle class support. The PAP received 281,891
votes.

[26] In Lee Kuan Yew, op. cit., 24–25, he maintains that this was deliberate policy on his part.

[27] Colony of Singapore, Singapore Annual Reports, and other sources. This is
more than the combined total of deregistrations or cancellations of unions between 1950 and 1958 (76) and between 1961 and 1966 (22 plus). One hundred
twenty-six unions were registered from 1955 through 1958; only 20 unions were

mainder into a new Trade Union Congress. These moves were not popular among many who had helped vote the PAP into power.

Also, in order to build new housing projects or industrial estates, it was necessary to clear people off the land on the sites of the projects. Often these people were poorer Chinese-speaking Chinese, and they did not wish to move. The Rural Residents' Association and Wooden House Dwellers' Association—both former allies of the PAP—helped them organize to prevent their resettlement.

Many businessmen considered the PAP to be Communist, prone to nationalize industry, and ready to take from the rich to give to the poor. Lowering these fears involved lowering the tone of the party's appeals. The fact that the government operated the radio stations, and later television, helped. Those who held these views within government could be induced to keep silent in the name of party unity. But some independent editors balked, as did some private organizations; they were asked to tone down their appeals. To cut back on the number of individuals voicing radical appeals, preventive detention was continued. Many of the most active former political leaders among the Chinese-speakers remained in prison.

If the working force were to achieve modern skills so as to compete for jobs, they would need modern educations. This implied abandoning many aspects of the classical curriculum in Chinese-stream schools— the very thing that many of the Chinese-speakers who had supported the PAP had been opposing.[28] It also meant continuing to discriminate in the hiring of Chinese-stream students by the civil service until their education was modernized.

---

registered from 1959 through 1963. In 1958 there were 218 unions with 129,159 members; in 1963 there were 112 unions with 142,036 members.

[28] Many of the militants had agreed to the 1956 All-Party Committee report on the premise that its provisions gave them some flexibility to work for their goals within the new system. For instance, the 1956 "Memorandum of the Singapore Chinese Middle School Students' Union on the All-Party Report on Chinese Education" agreed to the report. But it asked that there be as little change in the textbooks as possible, that one-third of the new curriculum change committee be composed of Chinese educationists, that there be more time for Chinese than English in the Chinese schools, and that the management committees have full power to appoint principals. Some of the individuals supporting the position in this memorandum subsequently obtained committee representation, and issues such as keeping more time for Chinese than English were won. By the beginning of the 1960's, however, they probably felt their power to win on issues like this slipping away.

What was necessary for economic development conflicted with what was necessary to hold the political party and its voting base intact.

Proof of this came in 1961. In July 1961 thirteen PAP legislative assemblymen broke with the party, leaving it a bare majority of 26 out of 51 in the Assembly. Since Singapore has a parliamentary system of government—the Government would be expected to resign in the event of a vote of no confidence—this immediately placed the PAP in a precarious position. On August 13, 1961, these dissidents formed the Barisan Sosialis, which held its inaugural meeting on September 17, 1961. At this juncture, the PAP lost a staggering 80.5 per cent of its total membership.[29] Nineteen of the 23 paid organizing branch secretaries of the party resigned. Thirty-five of the 51 branch executive committees resigned *en bloc*.[30] The Trade Union Congress dissolved, and the dissidents formed a union federation on their own. When the government introduced its new higher school examinations as part of the reforms in the Chinese middle schools, 40 per cent of the students scheduled to take the exams boycotted them.

FIRMING UP CONTROL

The Government was clearly not in a position to continue its approach to economic development, or even to remain in office, without

[29] The PAP had only 4,861 members in 1959. By the start of 1961 that number had grown to 11,632 members. In 1961, 5.1 per cent of members resigned or were expelled. In 1962, 75.4 per cent of 1961 members failed to pay their dues; 19.5 per cent did so, leaving only 2,270 former members in the party. Hence the turnover was substantial. These percentages were compiled by Miss Pang Cheng Lian for use in her masters thesis at the University of Singapore. At PAP headquarters, the files of application forms for all past and present members are kept in order of their membership numbers. Miss Pang transferred data from every fifth form onto punch cards. In this manner she transferred data from 2,207 forms of pre-1962 members; she also examined all the forms of the 597 who resigned or were expelled. Multiplying the 2,207 figured by five, and adding 597, she came up with the estimated total party membership in 1961 (just before the split) of 11,632. Anyone who paid dues in 1962 is still regarded as a PAP member, regardless of whether he or she has paid since. Multiplying by five the punch cards indicating dues paid in 1962 or since, she found the June 1966 membership figure was 14,830. The infusion of new blood came later, however. Only 720 joined the PAP in 1962.

[30] See Pang Cheng Lian, "The People's Action Party, 1954–1963," *Journal of Southeast Asian History,* 10 (March, 1969), 151–152. This article also reports that a number of cadre members (the party's ruling body) were expelled or resigned at this juncture. A PAP official insists that the number was less than 30 per cent, while a Barisan Sosialis official maintains that practically all the cadres left.

some immediate retaliatory measures and some long-range shift in the base for its electoral support.

The Prime Minister responded with a combination of cunning and coercion. His opponents accused him of attacking Chinese education and culture; of continuing detentions; of suppressing trade unionism; of continuing low wages, poverty, and unemployment; of putting up with the British presence; and of suppressing democracy. The Prime Minister did not answer the charges. Instead, he shifted the issue. His opponents, he charged, opposed merger with Malaya. This alone could induce the increased trade and economic interdependence on which Singapore's future prosperity would depend. He put this issue before the voters in a referendum in September 1962 and focused great attention on this debate. Of those voting, 71 per cent endorsed his position. Then in January 1963, 140 of the most active opposition leaders were detained. April saw the arrest of the Barisan Chairman, legal adviser, and ten of its assemblymen. The merger agreement between Malaya and Singapore was signed in London, July 9, 1963. The Prime Minister returned for a tour of all fifty-one constituencies.

On August 30, 1963, seven dissident unions—including the three largest—were asked to show cause why they should not be deregistered.[31] On August 31, in a surprise move designed to have a psychological impact against the argument that there should be independence before merger, the Prime Minister declared *de facto* independence for Singapore. On September 9 the Government froze the funds of the three largest dissident unions. Nomination day for the new election was set on September 13, and the day of elections was announced that afternoon.[32] On September 16, Singapore became part of Malaysia (with gala festivities scheduled), and Singapore's general elections were held on September 21, 1963.

[31] Three days before, members of these unions had engaged in organized booing of the Prime Minister at a political rally. They were accused of trying to exploit the rally for political purposes and of taking part in activities outside the normal functions of genuine trade unions. A more complete report on this election is found in F. L. Starner, "The Singapore Election of 1963," in K. J. Ratnam and R. S. Milne, *The Malayan Parliamentary Election of 1964* (Singapore: University of Malaya Press, 1967), 312–358.

[32] The top Barisan leadership was under detention. The party was informed on nomination day that it could not run individuals who could not show up at the nomination centers in person. On nomination day seventeen former detainees were rounded up by the police for questioning, to prevent any notions that they might have had about filing papers. Hence most of the candidates were second-echelon leaders of the party.

Almost exactly two years previous to this election the Barisan had been formed, to challenge the Government's approach to students, teachers, labor, poor farmers, and Chinese culture. For two years it had few means with which to present its side on these issues. Mass rallies could not be held without government approval. Finding printers and convenient circulation channels for its literature was difficult, and it could not use radio—which had been used extensively by the government. The Barisan had been invited to debate about entrance into Malaysia—an issue it did not wish to discuss. Now this party had only four days in which to conduct an election campaign. Its rallies were well attended. It was given seventeen and one half minutes of speaking time on each language channel of radio to present its case. In the forty-five-minute radio debates among all participating parties, speaking time was dominated by the Prime Minister. Still, the Barisan won 32.1 per cent of the vote (compared to 47.4 per cent for the PAP), and took thirteen seats.

The PAP was in a firmer position to act after the 1963 election. It had not, however, won a majority of the votes, and worked to consolidate its position further. In October 1963 came more detentions, including some Barisan assemblymen and candidates.[33] The dissident trade union federation was deregistered, along with some of its leading unions. The same month, a more moderate National Association of Trade Unions applied for registration. Later, most other dissident unions and organizations were deregistered. Concerted demonstrations by Chinese-stream university students late in 1964 and 1965 were dealt with severely by the police.[34] The Legislative Assembly was seldom called into session. In December 1965 four Barisan members of the legislature resigned in order to carry their struggle "to the streets." The

---

[33] Two other newly elected Barisan assemblymen fled to avoid arrest. Control over internal security was now in the hands of the Malaysian Government in Kuala Lumpur; it is unlikely that the Singapore Government expressed disapproval of these actions, however. Arrests like this are usually timed to coincide with moments of civil unrest. Deregistrations are also carefully timed and are generally accompanied by charges of financial or other sorts of malfeasance on the part of union officials.

[34] The government tended to be more gingerly in its handling of protest among English-speaking students—avoiding direct confrontations or mass arrests. A moderate political organization was formed among students at the University of Singapore, to counter the influence of a more left-leaning body. Suitability certificates from the Special Branch (internal security) were instituted as a requirement for entering all institutions of higher learning; this offered an opportunity to weed out potential agitators.

street demonstrations that took place sporadically over ensuing months occasioned more arrests.[35]

The Government's control of communications media has enhanced its position in these battles with its opponents. All publications of any kind must be approved by the Registrar of Societies. Regular publications of rival political parties have not been banned (though they have sometimes found it difficult to find printers); a number of nonparty or occasional left-wing publications have been banned, and there are strict controls over the import of publications from the People's Republic of China. All gatherings of ten or more persons must (according to the law books) be approved by the Registrar of Societies. Street demonstrations are seldom approved, and registered societies must adhere to strict rules as to membership, time of meetings, and the like. Public forums must also be registered, and not all are approved. Radio and television are under government control. They simultaneously broadcast in the several language streams, and carry speeches by government officials, regular news programs that report on national news, forums, and other programs with political content.[36] Prime Minister Lee can speak in five languages (he learned Mandarin, Cantonese. Hokkien, and Malay later in life with the aid of private lessons), is masterful with metaphors and homely syllogisms, and is as effective over the air as he is at his frequent public speeches. The Government seems to keep a close watch over and informal liaison with the press regarding their daily news output. Major daily newspapers have on occasion been sued or arraigned in court by the Prime Minister for printing statements that he felt to be untrue; at other times they have received public reprimands. In May 1971 four senior officials of a leading Chinese-language daily were detained on grounds that they were fostering communism and communalism, and an English-language daily was forced to close.[37]

[35] The most serious disturbances took place in October 1966, the week before President Lyndon Johnson's visit to Malaysia. The Barisan held an Aid-Vietnam show, which became a focal point for disturbances; the license was canceled for the last four nights.

[36] One program appearing periodically is the recantations of former detainees. Detainees are ordinarily allowed to leave prison only after a television appearance in which they renounce communism and foreswear future participation in politics. After their release, these men, whose previous experience often gives them an unusual degree of energy, idealism, and comprehension of what the Government wants of them, are frequently given jobs in the bureaucracy.

[37] Communalism means racial politics. The Chinese-language daily was printing uncritical news stories from western news sources about China, and reviving a plea (voiced by the Chinese Chamber of Commerce and other groups in 1954)

Community centers have also played a role in establishing government control. During the early 1950's the wives of British administrators and other groups in the city had created recreation centers for underprivileged youth. Left-wing organizations also created such programs—especially kindergartens, day care centers, and youth study groups (see p. 20); they used these groups for political indoctrination. When David Marshall became Chief Minister in 1954, one of his first priorities was the expansion of community centers which could counter the influence of the left-wing programs. He found 11 community centers already in existence, along with 19 children's social centers. By the end of 1954 the number of community centers had been increased to 25, a large new Children's Social Centre was under construction, and a Singapore Youth Council had been established comprising 35,000 members in 30 affiliated private youth organizations. By 1957 the Youth Council was occupying the terminal building of the former Kallang Airport. By the time the PAP took office 32 community centers had been organized under the Ministry of Labor and Welfare, with neighborhood advisory committees to manage them. The expansion of this program became a high priority item for the PAP, who had expanded the number of centers to 186 by 1967. The Barisan re-established the left-wing kindergartens and day care centers, as well as cultural concerts in the evening; the PAP duplicated these facilities at the community centers, along with many other programs designed to increase national consciousness.[38]

---

that the proceedings of the legislature be printed in Chinese as well as in English. (This sort of plea carries with it implications of a multilingual legislature, which could function in languages other than English and could accommodate participation by non-English-speakers). The English-language daily (*Singapore Herald*) was a new paper, which had been printing letters to the editor opposed to some PAP policies like conscription. In addition, some former PAP activists and other English-speakers opposed to a number of PAP policies had organized a new political party called the Popular Front; the *Herald* carried information about their activities and criticisms. Most alarming to the Government, perhaps, was the fact that the paper's circulation began to grow very rapidly after the Prime Minister criticized it. The Prime Minister accused it of carrying out the wishes of Hong Kong investors, publicly pressured the Chase Manhattan Bank to withdraw its loan to the paper, and then withdrew the paper's permit to print.

[38] The centers house a broad range of services; sports, community dinners, the kindergartens and day care centers, films on agricultural techniques, television viewing, recruitment centers for various government brigades, distribution points for welfare funds, birth control information, and more. Every community center (and every bus stop) receives a biweekly poster from the Ministry of Culture describing socially beneficial activities of the government.

The Prime Minister and his Cabinet also moved in other ways to broaden their base of support among the populace. They offered generous inducements to business investment. The civil service was given responsible new programs to administer. A great deal of construction activity began on government contracts. Private builders set to work on suburbs, providing middle class housing. High-rise luxury apartments also began to appear in abundance. Imports of consumer goods remained unrestricted. New luxury office structures were built in the central business district, with assistance from the government. New public housing was constructed for the lower and lower middle classes. Increasing percentages of young people were educated in the English language.[39] All this helped to increase support for the Government among the middle and lower middle classes.

In February 1967 the five Barisan members remaining in the legislature resigned, and the party withdrew completely from electoral politics.

In the parliamentary election of April 1968, the PAP was returned unopposed in 51 seats, and was challenged in the remaining seats by 5 Independents and 2 remnant members of a 1950's party, who were handily defeated. The Government no longer had to fear that the activities needed to promote its development program would weaken its political base. It had finally acquired the political capability to plan. It could probably keep this new capability, however, only so long as it could retain the cooperation of the business community, white collar workers, professional people, and some blue collar workers. Without their support, the economic development program could not easily continue, and it would be more difficult to prevent the emergence of popular dissident political movements.

[39] The percentage of students being educated in the English-language stream increased, from around 48.7 per cent in 1957 to 58.2 per cent in 1967. That is, 58.2 per cent of all children currently enrolled in primary and secondary school were attending English-language-stream schools in 1967. In the same period, from 1957 to 1967, the percentage of students in Chinese-stream schools declined from 45.7 per cent to 34.2 per cent. The percentage in Malay-stream schools rose from 5.1 per cent to 7 per cent and in Tamil changed from 0.5 per cent to 0.3 per cent. Mrs. Chew, "Demography," in Republic of Singapore, State and City Planning, *Notes for Consultant Briefing at Node One in the Plan of Operations* (Singapore: GPO, 1967). In 1966 there were 292,652 in English-stream, 172,224 in Chinese-stream, 36,351 in Malay-stream, and 1,760 in Tamil-stream schools. Of the Chinese heads of household in stratified random samples interviewed by my students in two Singapore neighborhoods (Queenstown and the oldest part of Chinatown), 74 per cent had at least one child in an English-stream school. R. E. Gamer, "Political Socialization in Three Working Class Neighborhoods of Singapore" (mimeo), July 1965, 5.

PART TWO

THE DYNAMICS
OF PLANNING:
KALLANG BASIN
RECLAMATION PROJECT

CHAPTER III

The People's Action Party and Urban Development

In this age of modern science and technology, two million people can achieve as much as 20 million people through rational organization and through determined and disciplined effort.

President Yusof bin Ishak, *The Mirror*
January 10, 1966 [1]

At its inception the People's Action Party considered itself a socialist party and supported trade unions and the abolition of inequalities of wealth and opportunities; it also advocated working within a free enterprise system and expanding trade and industry with the aid of government fiscal policy.

The dynamism of its leaders made people suspect even before it took power that the PAP Government would be an active one. Its leader, Lee Kuan Yew, has devoted himself to what he calls "the initiative, the drive and the thrustfulness of a young and vigorous society." [2] He is a man of great personal discipline, who seldom takes off a moment for frivolity. [3] Until Singapore achieves stable prosperity, he asks his fellow

[1] Republic of Singapore, Ministry of Culture, *The Mirror*, January 10, 1966. See footnote 6.

[2] *The Mirror*, October 10, 1966.

[3] A former close colleague of Lee Kuan Yew in the 1950's (J. J. Puthucheary) tells a parlor story (perhaps apocryphal) about a rare visit which he and Lee made to a bar after a hard day of work in the early days of the PAP in the 1950's. The colleague was pleased to see Lee relaxing for a change. Finally Lee took his eyes off the girls and turned. "These girls," he said, "will never be good Socialists."

When Governor George Romney visited Singapore early in 1968, Prime Minister Lee played a round of golf with him. While Romney was changing there was a break for a few minutes, during which Lee entertained a Romney aide by telling him stories about how as a young newsboy, Lee had gone to the Padang to hear Lord Louis Mountbatten receive the Japanese surrender. Since the whole day had been spent in pointed conversation related to the American presence in Southeast Asia, the aide was surprised at the seemingly irrelevant respite. The Prime Minister has a reputation for seldom straying from business. The following citizens to emulate his discipline and dedication to hard work for social uplift; nearly all his evenings since 1955 have been devoted to speeches urging his listeners toward a "multi-racial, tolerant society which is prosperous, ever surging forward." [4]

Before 1959, PAP leaders frequently asserted that they would be vigorous in promoting housing and industry. During the 1950's one of the founders of the party—Dr. Goh Keng Swee—conducted an academic survey to ascertain the dimensions of the housing shortage.[5] This study showed that over a third of the population lived in badly deteriorating shophouses, while another third lived in huts made of wood, old boxes, rusty corrugated iron, and the like. There was a strong public demand for housing. The party committed itself to an extensive public housing program.

On other development issues, it had little to say. Its opening message to the Legislative Assembly [6] in July 1959 said little about urban devel-

---

week, however, Lee was using the Mountbatten stories in London, in his efforts to persuade Prime Minister Harold Wilson not to speed up the British withdrawal from Singapore. Lee had been practicing for the next round.

[4] *The Mirror,* January 17, 1966. I once heard him comment on an overresponse to his pleas. He told a university audience that when developing nations react to events they sometimes tend to overreact. As an example, he cited his Vigorous Society campaign to develop physical fitness in the schools. "Now, whenever I go to the schools I see all the little children jumping around." He probably prefers to see little children jumping around during calisthenics than in the midst of adult activities. During a speech he was giving at a community center checkers tournament I noticed some children playing a game of tag on the fringes of the gathering. The Prime Minister paused in his speech and asked these children to stop running around and be more "disciplined" and "national minded." He paused for a very fast game of checkers after the speech.

[5] Goh Keng Swee, *Urban Incomes & Housing: A Report of the Social Survey of Singapore 1953–54* (Singapore: GPO, 1956). See also C. W. A. Sennet, *Report of the Housing Committee, Singapore, 1947* (Singapore: GPO, 1948); Colony of Singapore, *Master Plan: Report of Survey* (Singapore: GPO, 1955), 26.

[6] Government of Singapore, *Legislative Assembly Debates State of Singapore, Official Report, First Session of the First Legislative Assembly, Part 1 of First Session,* Vol II, 6–18. This was the Yang di-Pertuan Negara's Speech to the new Assembly. As part of the transition to internal self-government in 1959, the post of the British Governor was abolished. Since Singapore has a parliamentary form of government, patterned after the British system, and since Singapore was planning to join Malaya (whose states are ceremonially headed by traditional royalty), the post of Yang di-Pertuan Negara—ceremonial head of state—was created to replace that of the British Governor. Inche Yusof bin Ishak, a journalist and early supporter of the PAP, became the first to occupy this position. When Singapore later became a republic after breaking away from Malaysia, the title of this post was changed to President.

opment. In outlining its policies, the new Government reasserted its strong resolve to expand the public housing program. Aside from this, the only specific development programs mentioned were creating out-patient clinics [7] and constructing public water standpipes, electrical services, and side roads and drains in rural areas.

The PAP inherited a financially solvent government (see Chapter I). Berthing, harbor, and servicing charges for foreign ships provided revenue relatively independent of local taxation. The United Kingdom offered the new Government sizable long-term aid in financing public housing and industrial estates. Hence the cost of public housing—often a bone of contention among economic elites—could be absorbed without disturbing taxpayers in any marked manner. Insofar as aid to industry produced new jobs, this would be a popular program. Aid to industry would also calm the fears of many industrialists and bureaucrats who had been disturbed over the radical sound of some of the PAP rhetoric. Hence, as immediate program objectives, public housing and industrial estates [8] could be expected to enjoy broad public support. As Chapter VI indicates, they fit well into the long-range objectives of the PAP as well. With these potentials in mind, Dr. Goh Keng Swee, now Minister of Finance, called on all government agencies to submit proposals for development projects.

Proposals were readily forthcoming. Some of them were quite old.

THE ORIGINS OF URBAN DEVELOPMENT

The Singapore government had, of course, been involved in public works projects since the time of Sir Stamford Raffles. Discussed in Chapter I, such projects were to continue under the PAP Government without a great deal of reorganization or shifting of techniques. Gas and sewerage services expanded markedly.[9] So did electrical services.[10]

[7] By 1967 there were 31 such clinics. There were in addition 62 maternal and child health centers (compared to 53 in 1958) and 62 dental clinics (compared to 5 in 1958). The 17 maternity and other hospitals have been expanded, and equipment improved.

[8] See pp. 151–158 for a further discussion of reasons why these programs could be expected to draw broad public support.

[9] By the end of 1966 there were 71,240 gas customers, vs. 14,723 in 1958. By 1967 there were 201,052 sewer fittings, vs. 35,218 in 1958. Nearly all the new gas customers were in public housing, whereas some 100,000 of the sewer fittings must have been installed outside public housing.

[10] Singapore's electrical power generating capacity increased from 105,700 kilowatts in 1958 to 415,000 kilowatts in 1967. The new Pasir Panjong Power station

Construction of new school buildings speeded up, and school enroll-
ments continued to rise.[11] Several hundred miles of roads were paved,
and some new road construction began during the first few years of
PAP rule.[12]

The most notable PAP development projects—public housing, industrial estates, and urban renewal—involved more than simply continuing established programs, however.

Urban development projects were first mooted in the 1920's by colonial administrators in the Singapore Improvement Trust.[13] Influenced
by liberal philosophies among English town planners of their time, they
drew up schemes for sanitation, for providing sunlight to shophouses by
widening back lanes, for housing and industrial estates, parks, and for
other such endeavors. There was especially great interest among these
administrators in creating public housing. Finally in 1932, after much
encouragement from within the Singapore Improvement Trust, the Colonial Governor authorized that body to build public housing.

Although the housing shortage was by then already acute, the Trust's
initial efforts in this direction produced few tangible results. From 1932
to 1951 fewer than 3,000 permanent-type units of housing were con-

---

had achieved a 150,000 kilowatt capacity by 1959 and helped considerably in
registering this increase. At the end of 1966 there were 214,000 registered consumers of electricity vs. 86,621 in 1958.

[11] By 1966 there were 502,987 students attending school (approximately 150,-
000 above 1958). Republic of Singapore, *Singapore Year Book, 1966.* By 1967,
94.1 per cent of the primary school age population were attending school, and 39
per cent of secondary school graduates were going on to tertiary education (either
vocational or academic). Mrs. Chew, "Demography," in Republic of Singapore,
State and City Planning, *Notes for Consultant Briefing at Node One of the Plan
of Operations* (Singapore: GPO, 1967). The percentage of secondary schools offering technical/vocational (vs. academic) programs rose from 2.1 per cent to
12.6 per cent in 1966. In 1966 there were 370,809 in primary schools, 115,432 in
secondary academic schools, and 16,656 in technical, vocational, and commercial
schools.

[12] Lim Leong Geck, in State and City Planning, *op. cit.,* reports 142.13 miles
of major arterial roads, 67.95 miles of collector roads, 453.40 miles of paved
local roads, and 475.52 miles of unpaved kampong roads, making a total of 1,138
miles of roads on the island. Colony of Singapore, *Singapore Annual Report,
1947,* 112, reported 275 miles of paved roads on the island at that time. I could
not find a record of how much road was paved between 1947 and 1959, but there
does not seem to have been extensive activity on road paving during this period.

[13] See Chapter I, pp. 14–15. An interesting parallel to this is to be found in
Chapter 2 of Daniel P. Moynihan, *Maximum Feasible Misunderstanding* (New
York, Free Press, 1969), with regard to the genesis of the war on poverty in the
United States.

structed.[14] About 1,000 of these were contained in the four-story concrete and brick structures of the new satellite town of Tiong Bahru (Photo 2, No. 6). Many of the remainder were single-family units built of concrete with tin roofs.

In 1952 construction of public housing took on a quicker pace. During that year the satellite town of Queenstown (see Map 3) was recommended, and in 1953 ground was broken for this project. The government instituted a system of loans to the Trust for public housing. A new type of reinforced concrete and hollow block multistory structure was designed, which was relatively inexpensive and highly durable. Between 1952 and 1958, 11,141 flats [15] were built in structures of this type. Over 3,000 additional units were constructed in two-story structures with tin roofs. By 1959 the Singapore Improvement Trust had completed several hundred shops, 12 large market buildings, and a total of 23,019 dwelling units.[16]

These efforts only scratched the surface, however. They provided housing for around 100,000 out of a population of a million and a half,[17] which was increasing in size at the rate of about 60,000 a year. Over two-thirds of the population continued to live in grossly deficient housing, as indicated earlier in this chapter. The rate of private construction was approximately the same as that of the Singapore Improvement Trust; private dwellings were primarily for the middle class. Hence it was imperative that the supply of public housing be vastly increased.

Construction of public housing by the Singapore Improvement Trust fell far below their targets. A principal hindrance to construction was the presence of squatters [18] on land the Singapore Improvement Trust had been purchasing for public housing since the 1920's. It was difficult to move these individuals, so sites had to be chosen that were for the most part unoccupied. The Queenstown site was a former military base, combined with a former low wet area. The other major housing estates

[14] See State of Singapore, Housing and Development Board, *50,000 Up* (1964), 20; *Singapore Annual Reports*.

[15] *Singapore Annual Reports*, 1952–1958.

[16] Housing and Development Board, *op. cit.*, 24. This figure includes some one-story thatched-roof emergency units that were not permanent.

[17] In 1957, Singapore island had a total population of 1,445,929. State of Singapore, Statistics Department, *Report on the Census of Population, 1957* (Singapore: GPO, 1964).

[18] A squatter is an unauthorized occupant of land he does not own.

—Kallang Airport, St. Michael's, and Farrar Park—were built on land converted immediately from other public uses (an airport, a wireless receiving station, and a public park).

In 1958 the Singapore Improvement Trust set up working parties to seek additional sites for public housing. Their attention became focused upon three areas, shown on Map 1: Chua Chu Kang, Woodlands, and Toa Payoh. Initially, the first two seemed more attractive, since they were only sparsely encumbered by squatters. The roads linking them to the city were narrow and deteriorating, however, and difficulty was encountered in purchasing the land.

By the end of the year attention had narrowed to Toa Payoh, adjoining Kallang Basin (see Map 4 and Photo 6). This tract of 607 acres had been purchased by the Singapore Improvement Trust between 1951 and 1954. A 1954 Working Party found 21,000 persons living there, "working land which we consider to be the most fertile on the island" and "an important factor in the Singapore food supply." They recommended a small amount of public housing and industries for the site, with the bulk of the tract reserved for farming. Toward the end of 1958, however, the Trust rethought the matter. A March 1959 report suggested that in view of the difficulties in finding other sites, 70,000 to 100,000 persons should be accommodated at Toa Payoh in an emergency housing scheme. Some additional acres should be used for an industrial estate.

During the 1920's a number of larger manufacturers—among them Ford and General Motors, two breweries, and a pineapple plant—had considered siting factories in Singapore but decided against the move. A principal factor in their decisions had been the unavailability of land suitably close to labor, transportation, and services. Some officers of the Singapore Improvement Trust took an interest in this problem and sought out a potential site for an industrial estate.

Northeast of the city—adjoining Toa Payoh—was a thousand-acre stretch of land known as the Kallang Basin, which lay for the most part below the high tide line (see Maps 1 and 4; Photos 4, 5, 6). Because it provided access by water to the sea, the periphery of the area had invited sawmills and fishermen's huts. Some squatters had constructed huts on stilts and were growing water vegetables, while some others had established squatter's colonies on drier portions of the interior. Several acres were covered with rubber trees. The city gas works, and a coal and petroleum station, were also located here.[19] Otherwise, the land—covering about a square mile—was largely unsettled and unused.

Late in 1931 the Manager of the Singapore Improvement Trust submitted to the Colonial Secretary a scheme for developing the Kallang Basin. It called for constructing a series of navigable canals and two lagoons that would serve several large factories. There would be 205 acres of small factories, 116 warehouses, and 158 acres of shops and dwellings. An extension of the Malay State Railway Line would be built to serve the industrial complex from the landward side.

This scheme was not implemented. The depression had tightened investment funds. On April 28, 1933, the Colonial Secretary wrote to the Chairman of the Singapore Improvement Trust that "the Finance Committee of the Legislative Council has expressed the view that the Kallang Scheme should not be proceeded with at present on the grounds that it is too grandiose and that there is no real necessity for it." Some members of the Singapore Improvement Trust agreed. The Treasurer saw no convincing evidence that the town required "further factory sites or workmen's dwellings" or that the Basin presented a hazard to health. "Why not let the manufacturers reclaim their own land?" Another Trust member saw no guarantee that the reclaimed land would ever be desired by factories, and he suggested that the scheme boiled down to "wild land speculations."

The most serious objections, though, centered around planning concepts for the city. The Legislative Council had spent S$80 million to build port facilities and to reclaim from the sea nearly a square mile of land extending along the shore line to the south of the old city (see Photo 1). With space available in the southern part of the city for docks, factories, and houses, there seemed no pressing need to duplicate such facilities elsewhere. And the Basin already contained several factories.

After World War II, however, an end to colonialism—and mercantilism—was more clearly at hand. The island needed an independent economic footing which would at the same time provide it with permanent financial links with Britain. There was more openness to the idea of industrial estates. Already in 1947 the Singapore Improvement

---

[19] The Lee Rubber Company (known over time by various names) subsequently established a rubber mill in the Basin in the 1930's, which became its largest industry.

Trust began to set aside some potential factory sites.[20] The 1955 *Master Plan* reported Kallang Basin to be again under consideration:

The Aljunied Road District "contains one of the main 'problem' areas of the City, i.e., the Kallang Basin. . . . The new Esplanade road [was] made necessary by traffic congestion on Kallang Road. . . . A scheme for filling the swamplands in the Basin, rendering them suitable for factory land, is at present under consideration." [21]

But this was still just talk. The years 1957 and 1958 saw the beginning of industrial estates for small industries at Bukit Timah, Alexandra, and Tiong Bharu. Yet, as with housing, there was still a shortage of sites for industries when the People's Action Party took power on June 3, 1959.

ORGANIZING FOR ACTION

The 1960–1965 development budget that was presented a few months after the PAP took power gave an early indication of the party's priorities. It included S$194 million for public housing (US$1.00 = S$3.00), S$194 million for industrial estates and economic planning, S$150 million for public works, and S$150 million for school construction, rural development, and health facilities.

Dr. Goh Keng Swee froze all housing construction while the Singapore Improvement Trust was reorganized into a new Housing and Development Board. The Board kept much of the SIT personnel, while adding new staff—especially architects. It was becoming increasingly necessary to clear squatters from land before new public housing could be built. Dr. Goh felt that the problem of squatters on land scheduled for public housing would be minimized if the housing were built at greater density. The SIT had generally built its structures two to seven stories in height and left considerable green space between buildings. This provided pleasant open spaces, but sometimes the density in these estates was lower than in squatter-occupied areas. Dr. Goh called for ten-story structures, to be built closer together. He suggested that the structures be constructed on land currently being used for building public housing, but at the new higher densities. The new structures could then house the squatters they displaced and still offer ample room for additional inhabitants.

[20] *Singapore Annual Report, 1947.*   [21] *Master Plan: Report of Survey,* 63.

In 1960 construction began on the new types of structures, and spread quickly. Between 1960 and 1965, 54,423 units of public housing were constructed [22]—twice as many as during the preceding twenty-seven years. Work was continuing at a rate of 12,000 units a year.[23] At the same time the Family Planning Program was bringing a marked reduction in the birth rate.[24] Together, these programs ended the housing shortage within a decade. By 1968 nearly three-quarters of a million people lived in flats occupying a total area of only 2.2 square miles [25] (see Map 3).

The new Government acted with equal deliberate speed on industrial estates. Finding no scheme yet mooted for industrial space on a scale that would meet the anticipated demand, it set aside some 15,000 acres of land on the southwest corner of the island for the Jurong Industrial Estate (see Map 1). By the end of 1966 over 3,000 acres of land had been cleared at Jurong, and major wharfage, water, and sanitary facilities were complete. Closer to the city, several industrial estates of from seven to sixty acres were begun or completed for small and medium-sized industries. The thousand-acre Kallang Basin Reclamation Project, to be discussed in the next chapters, was also under way. In addition, the Government developed programs for attractive loans and tax incentives to new industries, relatively unrestricted transfer of profits abroad, holding the line on wage increases, vocational training, and fiscal and political stability. Thanks to all this, industrial investors around the world turned a favorable eye on Singapore.[26] By the beginning of the 1970's, most of the space in these estates was committed to industries.

[22] Housing and Development Board, *op. cit.,* 36, 65. Each housing estate included markets, shops, and other facilities.

[23] *Ibid.,* 68.

[24] Between 1957 and 1965, Singapore's crude birth rate dropped from 42.7 per thousand to 29.9 per thousand, reducing the population increase to 2.3 per cent per annum. See Quah Kay Seng, "Government Economy, Development Funds, and Public Housing Costs," in State and City Planning, *op. cit.* Abortion was legalized in 1967.

[25] Ooi Jin-Bee, "Singapore: the Balance Sheet," in Ooi Jin-Bee and Chiang Hai Ding (eds.), *Modern Singapore* (Singapore: University of Singapore, 1969), 6.

[26] During the early months that the PAP was in office, some members of the new Government investigated the possibilities of setting up nationalized industries. They concluded that problems in obtaining skilled management, technical information, dies, parts, marketing and financing arrangements, and the like made it impossible to do so. Singapore has set up semipublic organizations to operate public utilities and the shipyards. Her industries are all private.

In addition, during the 1960's Singapore began an urban renewal program designed to raze major portions of the old city (see Map 2) and replace these areas with new hotels, office buildings, stores, and apartments. Along the eastern coastline, the Bedok Reclamation Project (see Map 1) created 1,000 acres of new land.

The Government's success in organizing the bureaucracy to create these projects must partially be attributed to the energy of Prime Minister Lee and his colleagues. At least in the early years of his regime, Mr. Lee took an active interest in the workings of every department, suggesting penalties for those who did not produce to his satisfaction and rewarding those who did. He still spends considerable time making visits, sometimes surprise ones on notice of an hour or so, to institutions, community centers, and constituencies.[27] He has given the Criminal Practices Investigating Squad full power to investigate bureaucratic irregularities, including those reported by the public, and has fired even top members of his Government whom he has suspected of being implicated in corrupt activities.[28] He helped introduce a Political Studies

[27] When his party came to power, civil servants, who were predominantly English-speaking, were fearful that PAP ascendancy would weaken their position vis-à-vis that of the Chinese-speaking populace. To emphasize the perilousness of their position, and probably to please the Chinese-speaking wing of the party, he immediately chopped extra benefits from the salaries of civil servants (reinstated in 1963) and told them that in the future reward would be related to performance. It is widely believed among civil servants that the Prime Minister keeps a notebook in which he makes a record of thousands of minor irregularities that he observes: broken light switches, refuse on the roads, laxity on the job. His office sees to it that personal reprimands are delivered for all of these. It is common to see feverish scurrying to clean grounds, floors, and windows, paint walls, and to make minor repairs around institutions that have been informed that a visit from the Prime Minister is imminent. He can be pungent in his criticisms. While he is generally polite, most Singaporeans have seen on television or from an audience his ability to rattle the nerves of a questioner, force an opponent into retracting a statement, or talk circles around a critic. Hence stories about his dealings with the civil service are easily believed, though many of them may not be true. One that sticks in my mind—recounted to me by a secondary school pupil who says it occurred in his classroom—concerns a visit by the Prime Minister to a classroom during one of his surprise visits to schools. After listening for several minutes to an ineffectual presentation by the teacher, he called the teacher aside, and within earshot of all the students, said, "Why don't you retire?"

[28] On November 3, 1966, Tan Kia Gan—1959, Parliamentary Secretary to the Ministry of Home Affairs; 1961, Minister of National Development; 1963, Chairman of HDB; then, Chairman of the Tourist Promotion Board, and representative of the government on the Board of Malaysian Airways—was dismissed by the government from all statutory boards. The government appeared to believe that Boeing had made some attempts to bribe in connection with the purchase of

Centre where civil servants are given special courses to acquaint them with the broader political significance of their activities.

Another explanation for the speed with which Singapore has been able to proceed comes from looking at her bureaucratic structure. As in the case of preconditions and programs, this structure slowly evolved over time. Appendix I goes into specifics about this evolution. The organization that has emerged is ideally suited for fast implementation of programs. Chart 1 shows Singapore's bureaucratic structure as it was constituted in January 1968; Chart 2 shows an ideal type of planning structure that is sometimes suggested for improving planning. A comparison of these two charts offers a clue to one of the reasons for the speed with which Singapore develops:

If a bureaucratic agency in Singapore has a development project that it wishes to construct, it passes this proposal—usually in the form of a short memorandum—along to its ministry, which, if agreeable, sends it in turn to the Ministry of Finance. There a small staff [29] reviews the proposal to see that it fits into the general objectives of the Government

---

aircraft. The government statement said, "Investigations have not disclosed evidence of a nature to satisfy a court of law that there was a connection between Mr. Tan Kia Gan and the proposition. . . ." But there was some suspicion arising from Mr. Tan's silence about certain activities of which he was probably aware, and the government felt this raised sufficient questions of propriety to warrant dismissal. See headline stories, *Straits Times* and *Eastern Sun,* November 4, 1966.

[29] The organizational structure within which this staff operates has changed over time. From 1959 to 1963 they operated within the Economic Development Division of the Ministry of Finance. In 1963 the Economic Planning Unit was established to contain their operation. Late in 1963 the EPU was placed under the purview of the Prime Minister's Office, then moved to the Ministry of Law in mid-1964, and back to the Ministry of Finance in November 1964. Early in 1968 most of this staff was transferred to the Budget Branch of the Treasury Division of the Ministry of Finance, to carry on their operation there. (The Economic Planning Unit was retained, with a new staff, to carry out research on problems like international monetary crises, and international shipping.) Despite these changes in organizational format, the procedures for budgeting capital projects varied little throughout this period, and there was considerable continuity in staff as well. On January 1, 1967, the Economic Planning Unit was staffed by five senior officers, and four executive officers. Its Deputy Secretary had a degree in engineering; the other four senior officers had honors degrees from the University of Singapore—three in economics and one in physics. One of these had a master's degree in Economic Planning from Williams College in Massachusetts. The four executive officers were all arts graduates—three from the University of Singapore and one from an Australian university. Most of this staff was transferred to the Budget Branch in 1968.

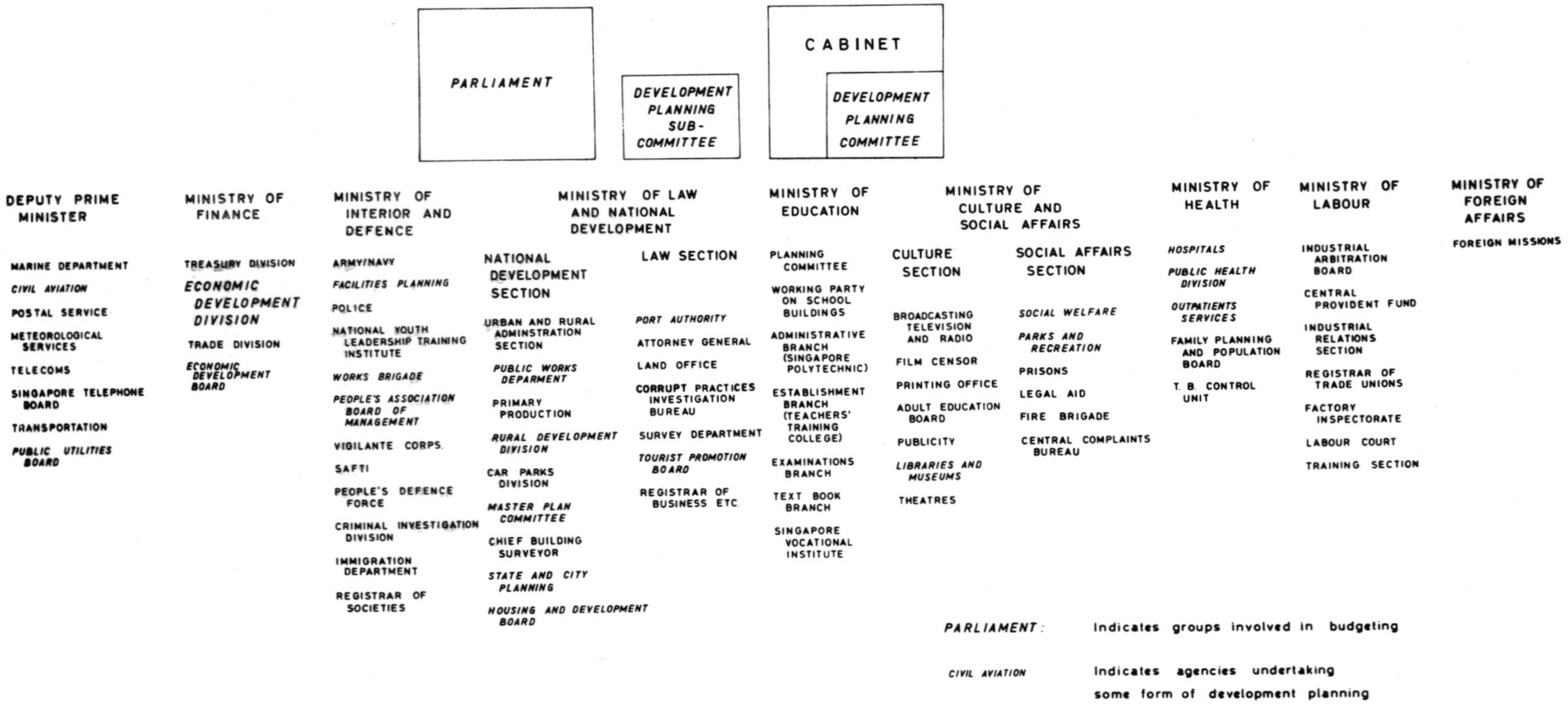

CABINET

PARLIAMENT

DEVELOPMENT PLANNING SUB-COMMITTEE

DEVELOPMENT PLANNING COMMITTEE

DEPUTY PRIME MINISTER
- MARINE DEPARTMENT
- CIVIL AVIATION
- POSTAL SERVICE
- METEOROLOGICAL SERVICES
- TELECOMS
- SINGAPORE TELEPHONE BOARD
- TRANSPORTATION
- PUBLIC UTILITIES BOARD

MINISTRY OF FINANCE
- TREASURY DIVISION
- ECONOMIC DEVELOPMENT DIVISION
- TRADE DIVISION
- ECONOMIC DEVELOPMENT BOARD

MINISTRY OF INTERIOR AND DEFENCE
- ARMY/NAVY
- FACILITIES PLANNING
- POLICE
- NATIONAL YOUTH LEADERSHIP TRAINING INSTITUTE
- WORKS BRIGADE
- PEOPLE'S ASSOCIATION BOARD OF MANAGEMENT
- VIGILANTE CORPS
- SAFTI
- PEOPLE'S DEFENCE FORCE
- CRIMINAL INVESTIGATION DIVISION
- IMMIGRATION DEPARTMENT
- REGISTRAR OF SOCIETIES

MINISTRY OF LAW AND NATIONAL DEVELOPMENT

NATIONAL DEVELOPMENT SECTION
- URBAN AND RURAL ADMINISTRATION SECTION
- PUBLIC WORKS DEPARTMENT
- PRIMARY PRODUCTION
- RURAL DEVELOPMENT DIVISION
- CAR PARKS DIVISION
- MASTER PLAN COMMITTEE
- CHIEF BUILDING SURVEYOR
- STATE AND CITY PLANNING
- HOUSING AND DEVELOPMENT BOARD

LAW SECTION
- PORT AUTHORITY
- ATTORNEY GENERAL
- LAND OFFICE
- CORRUPT PRACTICES INVESTIGATION BUREAU
- SURVEY DEPARTMENT
- TOURIST PROMOTION BOARD
- REGISTRAR OF BUSINESS ETC

MINISTRY OF EDUCATION
- PLANNING COMMITTEE
- WORKING PARTY ON SCHOOL BUILDINGS
- ADMINISTRATIVE BRANCH (SINGAPORE POLYTECHNIC)
- ESTABLISHMENT BRANCH (TEACHERS' TRAINING COLLEGE)
- EXAMINATIONS BRANCH
- TEXT BOOK BRANCH
- SINGAPORE VOCATIONAL INSTITUTE

MINISTRY OF CULTURE AND SOCIAL AFFAIRS

CULTURE SECTION
- BROADCASTING TELEVISION AND RADIO
- FILM CENSOR
- PRINTING OFFICE
- ADULT EDUCATION BOARD
- PUBLICITY
- LIBRARIES AND MUSEUMS
- THEATRES

SOCIAL AFFAIRS SECTION
- SOCIAL WELFARE
- PARKS AND RECREATION
- PRISONS
- LEGAL AID
- FIRE BRIGADE
- CENTRAL COMPLAINTS BUREAU

MINISTRY OF HEALTH
- HOSPITALS
- PUBLIC HEALTH DIVISION
- OUTPATIENTS SERVICES
- FAMILY PLANNING AND POPULATION BOARD
- T. B. CONTROL UNIT

MINISTRY OF LABOUR
- INDUSTRIAL ARBITRATION BOARD
- CENTRAL PROVIDENT FUND
- INDUSTRIAL RELATIONS SECTION
- REGISTRAR OF TRADE UNIONS
- FACTORY INSPECTORATE
- LABOUR COURT
- TRAINING SECTION

MINISTRY OF FOREIGN AFFAIRS
- FOREIGN MISSIONS

PARLIAMENT : Indicates groups involved in budgeting

CIVIL AVIATION : Indicates agencies undertaking some form of development planning

Chart 1. Singapore's bureaucratic structure, January 1968

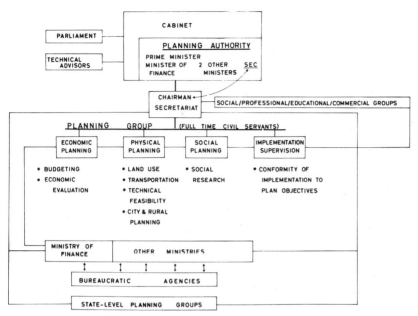

Chart 2. Planning structure: An ideal type, based on Louis Walinsky's model

and that its price tag does not seem out of line. Then the proposal is passed along—perhaps with some minor revisions—to the Minister of Finance. The Development Planning Committee indicated on Chart 1 consists of the Minister of Finance and other Ministers; [30] it rarely formally meets. The Minister of Finance, in his capacity as chairman of the Development Planning Committee, lists the proposals he receives (and their projected cost) on a document called "development estimates." [31] Periodically these estimates are brought before Parliament (after Singapore became a Republic in 1966 the name of the Legislative Assembly was changed to Parliament). Because the PAP has a majority

[30] The Minister of National Development, and the minister from which the project in question emanates.

[31] Republic of Singapore Development Estimates 19**. Before 1966 this was called Development Estimates of the State of Singapore for the Year 19**. In 1960, and again in 1965, the Ministry of Finance drew up five-year plans. These were simply catalogues of project ideas emanating from various agencies—some of which were already in the development estimates and others of which had not yet been submitted. No attempts were made to relate the projects to one another. Before 1959 documents such as a 1949 white paper on education that proposed constructing 170 schools over a ten-year period served this purpose for individual sectors.

in Parliament, and the members are subject to party discipline, the document always passes. The Minister of Finance is free to finance the projects listed on it, or not to finance them, as he sees fit.

The project is then in the hands of the agency that proposed it. If— as in the case of the Housing and Development Board, the Economic Development Board, the Singapore Port Authority, and the Ministry of Interior and Defence—the agency owns land, it is free to build the project on its land. Should it need to use other public land, it will turn to the Master Plan Committee [32] in the National Development Section of the Ministry of Law and National Development. This committee rarely turns away such applications. (During 1966 it turned down 6 out of 70 applications for use of state land; in 1967, 8 out of 60.) Once layouts have been drawn up, they are also submitted to this committee (regardless of who owns the land) for approval as to heights of buildings, distances from roads, and the like. When detailed building blueprints are complete, they are submitted to the Development Planning Sub-committee,[33] which makes a final check to see that costs have been kept down. The projects are then constructed by the agency that submitted it, the Public Works Department, or the private contractor submitting the lowest bid. Each agency supervises the construction of its own project. Should the site require new sewerage, water, roads, electrical service, or

---

[32] Consisting of the Chief Planner, the Commissioner of Lands, the Director of Public Works, and the Head of the Urban Renewal Section of the HDB. This committee was formed in 1960; it meets monthly. Initially it also included the Manager of the Public Utilities Board, the Director of Primary Production, and the Surveyor-Planner of the Economic Development Board. These were dropped from the committee in 1965. Prior to 1959 a Planning Co-ordination Committee handled the conflict resolution functions of the Master Plan Committee. In this earlier period the Singapore Improvement Trust handled land allocations for public and private projects; the siting and planning of industrial estates; most road design; housing estates; the siting of public works, rural resettlement areas and schools; and many other projects. Hence coordination was considerably easier. With the advent of semi-, and later full, self-government, it was necessary to subject these activities to greater ministerial control. As the size of projects increased, it was also necessary to increase the functional specialization of agencies. Much of the coordination within the Singapore Improvement Trust was carried out through informal working parties; these too became more difficult as bureaucracy grew in size and became composed of lifetime career bureaucrats who must be loyal to their particular agencies.

[33] This committee (created in 1960) consists of the Director of Public Works, a representative of the Economic Development Division of the Ministry of Finance, the Permanent Secretary of National Development, and the Chief Planner; it meets every Tuesday.

bridges, arrangements for this are worked out later with the agency that normally constructs such services.

Private developers wishing to initiate projects can consult zoning maps to determine the areas in which they are permitted to build. They submit both ground layouts and building blueprints to the Development Control Committee functioning within the Chief Building Surveyor's Office.[34] This committee checks to see that the plans conform to building specifications and zoning regulations [35] and that they do not lie within an area potentially designated for public purposes.

These procedures are simple and straightforward. They leave individual agencies with a good deal of freedom to implement projects. There are times, however, when one might wish that the procedures were a bit more complex. I am thinking not simply of instances in which one agency's programs do not mesh with the programs of another,[36] or where public complaints to an agency go unheeded,[37] or one agency

[34] The Chief Building Surveyor's office maintains a large staff to check blueprints of private builders. The Development Control Committee, consisting of the Chief Building Surveyor or his representative (Chairman), the Chief Planner, the Director of Public Works or his representative, the Assistant Director of Medical Services (from the Ministry of Health), and two representatives from professional organizations (the Malayan Society of Architects and the Malayan Society of Engineers). This committee was created within the Singapore Improvement Trust in the 1930's and transferred to the Chief Building Surveyor's office in 1960.

[35] During the 1930's the Singapore Improvement Trust became responsible for development control. Large cadastral sheets were used to record all developments, public and private. Between 1953 and 1955 a team brought in from England by the Singapore Improvement Trust surveyed many of the island's problems. In one of their projects, they produced maps using colors to zone the entire island into dense residential areas, lower density residential, shophouses, commercial, green belt, industrial, institutional, and so on. These maps are still used in zoning for private development. They have been revised to record public developments that did not accord with original designations.

[36] During the Kallang Basin Reclamation Project earthfill material occasionally clogged drains. In such instances, the Public Health Division wrote to the HDB to report the problem, and the drains were usually cleared out promptly. When mosquitoes bred in stagnant pools caused by polders that had been built by remaining inhabitants to give them access to their homes, the HDB could do little to rectify the situation. These problems were handled by letter and telephone. It is interesting that of all the liaison committees listed in Appendices III–V, only the Urban and Rural Services Committee (discussed on p. 199) is designed for coordination among agencies on the implementation of projects.

[37] During the Kallang project, the fence of a sports club was torn down by mistake. It was promptly replaced, with a new gate added as well. But little could be done about citizen complaints about the dust raised by the fill trucks. And a temporary bridge built for the access road to Kallang Basin was constructed in such

needs forewarning of what another is doing.[38] In addition, in the midst of a plethora of individual development programs it is possible for major environmental problems to arise almost without anyone having foreknowledge of them. If no agency is in charge of keeping track of the densities at which population is being distributed, living conditions can become crowded and chaotic, and roads may gradually fill with increasing traffic until major bottlenecks occur and elaborate remedial procedures are called for. Noxious wastes can pollute the air and water. Increasing numbers of workers may be separated by increasing distances from their job sites.

It is problems like these that bring reformers to call for planning procedures like those outlined in Chart 2. The principal difference between it and Chart 1 is the existence of a group standing between the ministries and the Cabinet in the planning process. Such a group—whether it is private or an independent government agency (as Walinsky advocates) [39] or indirectly attached to one of the ministries—might be in a position to look into such questions in the context of all developmental planning in the state, and improve coordination. As Chapter VI explains, Singapore is experimenting with such a group. At the time the Kallang Basin Reclamation Project began, it had no such experiment.

OVERLOOKED QUESTIONS

Overcrowded residential areas, traffic bottlenecks, noxious wastes, and work location are serious questions. In the next two chapters we

---

a way that it blocked the flow of the stream and caused flooding of a small nearby factory. Although the factory personnel and other dwellers alongside the bridge wrote frequent letters of complaint over a period of eighteen months, nothing was done to remedy the situation. Inconvenient design or not, replacement of the bridge would have held up the reclamation and been costly. As in the case of the examples in footnote 36, changes in the organization of planning would probably have had little effect on these situations.

[38] The sewerage section of the Public Works Department, and those who plan school buildings in the Ministry of Education, need information on future densities to plan efficiently. The drainage section of the Public Works Department is affected by many planning decisions. The Welfare Department is affected by nearly every planning decision. These agencies are frequently unaware of major development programs until implementation is under way, which makes long-range planning difficult for them.

[39] See pp. xxi–xxii, 50–51. Chart 2, which I designed, illustrates the sorts of proposals made by Walinsky and others interested in structuralizing coordinated planning. See pp. 242–246 in the Bibliography for other books and articles that discuss such organizational problems and proposals.

shall see that they were raised in connection with the Kallang Basin Reclamation Project, but not seriously considered. There are other questions, also difficult to deal with in the absence of some broader planning mechanism like that suggested in Chart 2, that are seldom even raised. They, too, should be considered an important part of any inquiry into the workings of urban development:

Will the development activity result in greater prosperity and tolerant social interaction among people? Is it contributing to stable labor conditions and economic progress? Is it equalizing opportunities for people of differing rank, race, religion, or sex? Are rewards becoming better correlated to effort and output?

Is the activity catering to the most urgent needs and desires of people? Is it helping to create stable social and economic development?

How is it affecting the conditions that caused such political instability a few years ago? How is it affecting the frustrations of today's citizens, and tomorrow's?

Is it improving the quality of people's lives?

It is tempting to reel off statistics about what has been constructed, or what programs are in operation, or how many votes one has received, or how many people use one's services, and assume that somehow this will answer such questions. But it will not.

Or it might be argued that it is better to do something than to do nothing, so such questions do not matter as long as one is doing something. Yet the choice is seldom between doing something and doing nothing. The choice is between doing one set of things and doing another set of things, of doing a lot of one thing at the expense of doing only a little of something else. What you do a lot of at the expense of doing only a little of something else needs to be justified in human terms.

Or a government can intimate that it is aiding the poor. It can be intending to aid the poor by spending a lot of money on them. How does it know it has actually aided them?

If a city or nation is going to make the best use of its resources, and avert social crisis in this era when people's lives are constantly being affected by change, it needs to ask itself questions like these. It needs to think about how it might possibly improve planning so as to better cater to human needs.

One of the striking aspects of the case study which follows in the next two chapters is that questions like these were not raised. (Or, when they were, they were answered with glib indifference to the facts). In the course of presenting the case study, I raise some of them, together with queries as to whether favorable answers to them might be more likely in the presence of a more elaborate planning structure. In Chapter VI, after having probed the Kallang Basin Reclamation Project, we shall explore the possibilities for such a structure.

CHAPTER IV

Kallang: Dealing with Those Who Stood in the Way

> A government is likely to be faced with many obstacles before it arrives at finished programs: from those who have sufficient resources and skills to prevent programs from being implemented, and from those whose resources and skills are needed. At times, the line between these two groups is a narrow one. Together they can subtly divert programs away from popular needs.[1]

Before the Kallang Basin Reclamation Project could proceed, the Government had to assign the project to some agency in order to remove those occupying the site and to purchase part of the land.

BUDGETING AND BUREAUCRATS

When the Ministry of Finance announced in April 1960 that it was budgeting S\$40 million [2] in the first five-year plan for an industrial estate in Kallang Basin, it had little information about the Basin, its inhabitants, its relationship to surrounding areas, or its relative suitability as an industrial estate. The process of selecting an agency to implement the project served to further inhibit the collection of such information. The site adjoined the most densely settled part of the city, while other sites were potentially available that were relatively free of congestion and occupants. It was chosen without knowledge that it was the best available site for such a purpose.

After announcing its interest in a Kallang Basin project, the Ministry of Finance asked the Housing and Development Board to submit a report on the feasibility of such a scheme. This report was submitted in June 1960. The report discussed a 1954 proposal of certain techniques for depositing earth-fill into the land below high tide level. It suggested the sorts of equipment that might be needed for such earth-fill and

---

[1] See Introduction, pp. xxii–xxiv, for a discussion of this problem.

[2] US\$1.00 = S\$3.00. See explanation on footnoting in Chapters IV and V, p. 231.

Chart 3. Chronology of the Kallang Basin Reclamation Project

1960

April	Ministry of Finance first budgets S$40,000,000 for an industrial estate at Kallang Basin.
June	First HDB report on reclaiming Kallang Basin.

1961

January	HDB begins land fill at Bendemeer Road.
March	HDB proposes leveling hills of Toa Payoh to reclaim Kallang Basin.
May	Development Planning Committee authorizes HDB to proceed with Toa Payoh and Kallang Basin projects—then quickly rescinds decision.
	Public Works Department and HDB both submit new engineering proposals on Kallang Basin.
July	Left wingers break from PAP.
August	Barisan Sosialis formed.
	Industrial Promotion Board becomes Economic Development Board.
	Chief Planner and HDB hold meeting about Kallang Basin.
October	HDB begins first abortive attempt to resettle Kallang Basin.
November	Commissioner of Lands gives HDB former Singapore Improvement Trust land in Kallang Basin.

1962

May	Planning Department and Economic Development Board agree on HDB plan for Bendemeer Road industrial resettlement estate.
	Planning Department and Economic Development Board form Ad Hoc Working Party on Kallang Basin.
June	HDB issues rejoinder to Ad Hoc Working Party report.
July	Irrigation expert's report.
September	Referendum on entry into Malaysia.

1963

February	140 left-wing leaders arrested: "Operation Cold Storage."
May	HDB formally placed in charge of Kallang Basin Project.
June	Malaysia Agreement signed.
	First bulldozers into Toa Payoh.
September	Merger with Malaysia.
	PAP defeats Barisan Sosialis in election.

1964

January	Resettlement commences in Kallang Basin.
April	Kallang Basin reclamation begins.
	PAP contests in Malayan General Election.
June	Malay Action Committee formed.
July	UMNO Convention.
	Lee Kuan Yew meets with Singapore Malay leaders.
	Rioting.

1965

January	"Malaysian Malaysia" campaign ends. PAP attempt to cooperate with Alliance.

	First coordination meeting on Kallang Basin among HDB, Economic Development Board, and Planning Department.
March	First meeting of Kallang Basin Coordinating Committee.
August	Singapore leaves Malaysia.

1966

March	Last meeting of the Kallang Basin Coordinating Committee.
June	First meeting of the Committee to Study the Physical Condition and Economic Viability of Each Factory in Kallang Basin.
October	Last meeting of the same.

dredging operations and proposed a series of canals and roads to serve the industries. The estimated price tag for dredging and filling and for building roads and bridges was S$41,450,000. There was no discussion of the relative merits of clearing all the land or of placing industries in this particular location. The report simply gave some suggestions as to how this could be accomplished.

It was obvious that a major project of this kind would take time to unfold. Meanwhile, there was a pressing need for industrial resettlement sites. While the above report was being written, the Government placed the Lands Manager of the HDB in charge of industrial resettlement for all industries displaced by other development projects, because he had been in charge of industrial resettlement under the Singapore Improvement Trust. By giving him this assignment, however, they subtly passed industrial resettlement to the HDB itself. He immediately surveyed— not all land on the island to see which might be best for industrial resettlement purposes—but the land that might be currently available to the HDB for this purpose. Most was far from basic services. As it happened, the only site that lent itself for immediate development as a resettlement estate was Bendemeer Road.[3] This was located in the corner of Kallang Basin (see Map 5). The HDB Building Department drew up a plan to locate 12 single-story and 23 two-story factory units here.

The HDB soon found itself in controversy with the Commissioner of Lands, however, over ownership of the Bendemeer Road site and of other former Singapore Improvement Trust property within Kallang Basin. Citing legal technicalities, the commissioner insisted that most former Singapore Improvement Trust land within Kallang Basin should revert to the State, rather than be transferred to the new HDB.

[3] The land at nearby Kampong Ampat was not yet fully acquired and, though the Lands Manager recommended it be used as soon as possible, it contained only seven acres. A trend had begun there of allowing manufacturers to construct their own facilities. This meant that it could accommodate only a few industries.

The Planning Department also raised objections to the proposed industrial estate at Bendemeer Road. They suggested that it was premature to plan an industrial estate so near the Serangoon Road/Lavender Street junction, since this was probably already the most congested corner of the city.[4] They also suggested that the proposed designs for road access would cause congestion.

Both the Commissioner of Lands and the Planning Department had already raised these objections when the HDB learned in December 1960 that 400,000 cubic yards of earth fill material would be available from excavations for a new power station. Despite the objections, the Board decided to use this fill to reclaim more land behind Bendemeer Road.[5] A disastrous fire at Bukit Ho Swee followed by an emergency housing scheme there provided additional material. By January 1962 the Board had reclaimed thirty-two acres of swamp behind Bendemeer Road. Meanwhile, nothing else was happening with regard to the overall Kallang Basin scheme.

Then, in March 1961, interest was revived. The HDB presented two plans for developing a housing estate at adjoining Toa Payoh. One called for leaving the rolling hills there intact. The other called for leveling the hills so as to provide enough earth-fill to reclaim most of nearby Kallang Basin. The latter scheme so caught the imagination of senior officials of the Board that they took a trip through the Basin in a small launch. It apparently also appealed to the Minister of Finance. On May 2, 1961, the Development Planning Committee decided to approve the plan by which the HDB would reclaim Kallang Basin using earth-fill material furnished by the hills of Toa Payoh.

On May 20, 1961—three weeks later—the Minister of Finance reversed his decision, however. He had learned in the interim that a Dutch engineering firm might be interested in the project.[6] Besides, no detailed survey had been conducted on the feasibility of the engineering plan. The Ministry of Finance also indicated that it might be desirable

[4] See Maps 5, 6. The traffic survey for the 1955 *Master Plan* had shown Serangoon Road to be by far the most heavily traveled road on the island. The Lavender Street junction was especially bad because this road formed the most direct path around the southern edge of Kallang Basin, and because of the emergence of heavy trucks from the sawmills and foundries located there.

[5] The Commissioner of Lands had suggested that they might proceed on land improvements there "at your own risk."

[6] This firm subsequently lost interest.

to consider alternative commercial and industrial uses for the Basin before physical planning and engineering designs were considered.

During the ensuing two years considerable additional information was to be gathered regarding the feasibility of the engineering plan. No additional information would be gathered, however, regarding alternative commercial and industrial uses.

Some of the information was quick to appear. In the three-week period in May 1961, before the Ministry of Finance reversed its decision, the Public Works Department submitted a report in which they suggested that the basic improvements in Kallang Basin might be completed for S$25 million (vs. the S$41,450,000 mentioned in the earlier HDB estimate). Two days after the reversal the HDB submitted a report containing new information. The land below high tide did not amount to 500 acres or 440 acres as previously assumed, but rather 387 acres. Without further land acquisitions it would be feasible to reclaim only 230 acres. There would be sufficient fill from Toa Payoh to accomplish this. They estimated that the filling could be completed for only S$2,450,000. The report provoked no reaction.

There was one consolation to the HDB about the brief period in May 1961, during which it was authorized to proceed with the Kallang Basin project. At that time the Commissioner of Lands indicated that he was prepared to consider handing over the former Singapore Improvement Trust land in Kallang Basin to the HDB. In November 1961 he did so. After the Industrial Promotion Board was reorganized into the Economic Development Board in August, it may have been agreed that this was the most expeditious strategy.

A breakthrough also soon came for the proposed industrial resettlement estate at Bendemeer Road. In May 1962 the Planning Department and the Economic Development Board agreed upon a revised plan presented by the HDB for an eight-acre resettlement estate there. In September 1962 the Development Planning Committee approved this plan. Also, in April 1962 the HDB completed an agreement by which the British forces would construct a bridge across Serangoon Road if and when a full Kallang Basin reclamation project were approved.

At this point other agencies began to worry about possible implications of a full Kallang Basin reclamation project. In May 1962 the Economic Development Board and Planning Department formed an Ad Hoc Working Party on Kallang Basin.

This was only the second time since the 1959 change in governments that officers from two or more departments had held a formal meeting about the Kallang Basin project.[7] The first meeting had been held in August 1961, after repeated inquiries from the Chief Planner regarding the intentions of the HDB. It was agreed at that meeting that the Bendemeer Road resettlement estate might proceed and that any additional proposals of the HDB would be reviewed along with others upon the arrival of a team of experts from the United Nations.

When that "team" arrived in April 1962, it proved to consist of one man—an expert not on reclamation, as previously assumed, but rather on irrigation.

At any rate, in May 1962, this irrigation expert (together with some United Nations experts on shipping and town planning who happened to be in the city) was able to join a "team"—the Ad Hoc Working Party on Kallang Basin. This Working Party—emerging from the Economic Development Board and the Planning Department—issued a report. This report suggested that first priority be given not to Kallang Basin, but rather to the site of the former Kallang Airport (see Map 4). It wanted this site to be used as a lighterage and coastal traffic port that could serve as a replacement for the Singapore River harbor downtown and that would allow for replanning in that area. Later, the westernmost 300 acres of Kallang Basin might be developed for light industries and might contain an expressway linking downtown with portions of the island to the northeast. After this road was completed—easing the traffic problem—the remaining 600 acres might be developed for labor-intensive industries without bulk handling or noxious discharges.

The Working Party also suggested that formulation of Kallang Basin proposals take into consideration more than engineering aspects and the investment cost. It was important, in addition, to consider the effects of the project on general town planning, zoning, and traffic and communications—in short, "overall Singapore needs." The timing and priority of implementation should be seen as important factors.

All these suggestions were ignored. In June 1962 the HDB issued a rejoinder to them that, as usual, dealt only with engineering and costs. It suggested that the Working Party had presented no new engineering

[7] A possible exception is the June 1961 agreement between the HDB Senior Civil Engineer and the Chief Engineer (Bridges and Drains) of the Public Works Department over a drainage plan for the Kallang River. See p. 126 for the tragicomic finale to that plan.

proposals, pointing out that the Working Party did not seem even to be aware that only 387 acres—not 900 acres—were beneath high tide level and in need of filling. Costs would be lower if the HDB, acting freely, carried out the project. If the Economic Development Board were placed in charge of the project, the HDB would have no part in it beyond giving the Economic Development Board permission to cart away Toa Payoh earth fill; otherwise, the HDB should be in complete charge.[8]

The Ad Hoc Working Party on Kallang Basin did not meet again. When the United Nations irrigation expert issued his own report a month later, the HDB reply was the same. It mentioned only engineering and cost aspects. The Senior Civil Engineer of the Board commented that "all the details of method given are those which were given to Mr. *** by myself in discussion." "Mr. ***'s proposals as to how to deal with mangrove swamp I suggest with due respect be left until the job has to be tackled, since no specific course can be predicted as if in a textbook." "Even an earth-lined canal (or river) has also been reaffirmed."

The irrigation expert's report came in July 1962. Some time after this the Minister of Finance apparently made up his mind to act. Late in 1962, when the *1963 Development Estimates* appeared, they contained the following items next to the heading "Kallang Basin Reclamation":

Plan Cost:	S$43,124,000
Revised Plan Cost:	S$28,500,000
Estimated Expenditure to December 31, 1962:	S$ 500,000
Estimated Expenditure in 1963:	S$ 5,000,000

Despite this, by February 15, 1963, no specific delegation of responsibility had been made on the project. On that date the Chief Architect of the HDB sent a memo to the Chairman of the Economic Development Board inquiring what was to be done with the earth material soon to be removed from Toa Payoh. He suggested that the Building Department of the HDB be responsible for coordinating with the Planning De-

---

[8] Moves of this "empire building" nature often arouse intense animosity among Singapore civil servants in other agencies and departments.

partment on the overall Kallang layout, with the Public Works Department on roads and drainages, and with the Economic Development Board on the layout of the industrial estate.

Upon receipt of this memo, the Chairman of the Economic Development Board wrote a letter to the Development Planning Committee suggesting that the HDB be placed in charge of the Kallang Basin project.

In May 1963 the Development Planning Committee acted. The HDB was placed officially in charge of the Kallang Basin Reclamation Project. It immediately authorized the expenditure of the S$5 million from the *1963 Development Estimates* for the project, and on June 10, 1963, S$1 million for initial bills was forwarded to the HDB.

This was the end of the Cabinet's role in planning the project until the phase when industrial buildings would be constructed. Reclamation, and the design and construction of roads, bridges, and housing estates could now proceed on the site without further permission. Each year the project would be included in the budget estimates without review. As it happened, the total estimated cost for the project was lowered each year; but authorizations for annual expenditure were always higher than the sums spent. The HDB was free to begin implementation, without other bureaucratic agencies standing in its way.

At the time of approval by the Development Planning Committee only one aspect of implementation had been thoroughly explored—the engineering techniques which would be used to reclaim the land below high tide level. Unexplored were:

The present uses to which the Basin was being put

The pattern of land tenure

The size and density of the population in the area of the Basin

Potential relationships between the reclaimed Basin and the surrounding road system

Relative advantages and disadvantages of using the Basin as an industrial estate

Other possible locations for an industrial estate of this type

Other uses to which the Basin might be put

Possible advantages of leaving portions of the Basin intact

Optimal phasing and timing of projects in the area

Potential effects of resettlement upon the inhabitants of the Basin

The social and economic needs of those inhabitants or of those who would be using the new facilities of the Basin.

No meeting had yet been held among all the principal agencies participating in the project. Welfare, health, education, and recreation agencies were not participating in the project.

Who lived in the Basin? What did they do for a living? What would they do for a living after they had been resettled? How much money did their families earn? How much money would their families earn after they had been resettled? What did their earnings have to buy? What would their earnings have to buy after they were resettled? Where did they get their food? Where would they get their food after they were resettled? How much income and proportion of the gross national product was derived from small cottage industries in the Basin and from agriculture in Toa Payoh? How could this income be replaced after resettlement? What industries might wish to use the new industrial estate? Would it be well suited for them? Would it have been preferable to locate the housing estate on less valuable farmland, or the industrial estate in a less congested area? Or would it have been preferable to place the development of the two areas elsewhere in the order of priorities?

What was life like for the people in the Basin? Would their life be better as a result of the reclamation project? Were they extorted by criminal elements? Was there reason to believe that there would be less (or more?) extortion as a result of the reclamation project? How did they get along with their neighbors? Was there reason to believe that they would get along better (or as well?) as a result of the reclamation project? Were they good citizens? Was there reason to believe that they would be better (or worse?) citizens as a result of the reclamation project? Did the young people in the Basin study their homework? Was there reason to believe that they would study as much after the reclamation project? What were living conditions like in their houses? Would their living conditions be better as a result of moving? Were the inhabitants content with their existence? Was there reason to believe that they would be as content after the reclamation project?

These were questions that had not yet even been explored, and to which there were no obvious answers.

The organization of the project up to this point had inhibited such an exploration. To analyze such basic human problems, the government would have had to rely on the facilities of various bureaucratic agencies. It did not seek out such information. Instead, it maintained for itself a free hand for placing the project in charge of the agency most capable of implementing the reclamation efficiently. It did so at the cost of receiving information that could have helped it to assess more fully the implications of its decisions.

It was natural that the agencies would not have devoted themselves on their own to such fundamental questions about the human factors behind the project. Most agencies had barely enough staff for the tasks to which they were assigned, not to mention for those to which they were not assigned. An agency that wished to gain the ear of the Ministry of Finance needed to present information on how to implement the project most cheaply and expeditiously—not information on the human problems involved in the project.

RESETTLEMENT AND THE RESETTLED

Having succeeded in placing the project in the hands of the authority that appeared to be most capable of effectively implementing reclamation, the Government and bureaucracy had next to deal with a group literally standing in the way of the project—those who occupied the land. Until political capabilities were sharply honed, it was not easy to deal with this group. Once these capabilities were honed, it may have been too easy to deal with them. It was possible to move them without looking into the human problems that the move entailed.

The land in Kallang Basin was partly privately owned, and partly owned by the state or by government agencies. A good deal of the private land was occupied by families who paid a small rent to the landowner or his agent for the privilege of constructing a simple wooden house on a portion of his property. Many of the families who occupied state-owned land paid a small monthly rental fee for a temporary occupation license. Others had simply constructed themselves a house without permission; these are the people known as squatters.

It was long-established government policy in Singapore to compensate those who needed to be resettled during urban development projects, and to offer them alternative housing. Before 1959 the relatively small number of families that were resettled were often offered plots of ground in rural resettlement areas; the SIT established 26 Rural Resettlement areas comprising 5,000 acres (see pp. 14–15). When the PAP Government began the Jurong Industrial Estate, it was necessary to displace some small Malay settlements. Villages of similar construction had been built for them on a nearby island, and they were moved there. As construction picked up on the new housing estates, these offered space for resettlement. All families being resettled receive S$300–S$350 for moving expenses. In addition, if they can prove they own the structure in which they are living (or built it themselves), they receive at least S$1.00 a square foot compensation for this, plus compensation for certain other improvements (trees, vegetables, sheds, water tanks, etc.) that they can prove they built or planted.

Even with this assistance, people are often not pleased to be moved. Most of the houses of Kallang Basin were of simple wood construction. Some were in good condition and attractively decorated; others were badly run down. Most were fairly large inside, however—some consisted of several rooms. Outside, there was often room for a fruit tree, a vegetable patch, and some chickens or a pig. Rodent and insect infestation was a serious problem. Few houses had running water, though outside standpipes were available. Sewage disposal was inadequate. Yet many of these people had lived in this part of town for many years and shared in some community life with their neighbors. This was especially true in the case of Malays, who traditionally have a tightly knit community structure. Some lived here because their jobs were near by; others carried on small manufacturing pursuits or storekeeping operations right in their houses. Land rent was very low—seldom rising above S$10.00 per month and often far below this. One can understand why people might have mixed feelings about leaving.

The authorization to proceed with the Kallang Basin Reclamation Project came in May 1963. A reference to Chapter II will remind the reader that this authorization occurred in the midst of important political events. The People's Action Party was fighting for its political life against the breakaway Barisan Sosialis. Mr. Lee returned from signing the Malaysia Agreement in June 1963. On his tour of the constituencies, and during the election campaign immediately following, he was to stress the progressive social reforms of his government. Tangible evidence that a major project was in the works north of the city would be valuable campaign material. But "Operation Cold Storage," the arrest of the 140 left-wing leaders, came only in February 1963. Before that time the Ministry probably did not dare to risk starting a major move on resettlement. The Barisan Sosialis and the Rural Dwellers' Association probably could have led an effective campaign of resistance among those being affected by resettlement.

In 1961 and 1962 the HDB had had a taste of the difficulties in-

volved in trying to resettle people during a period of political instability. In October 1961—frustrated over the delay in receiving authorization for the Kallang Basin and Toa Payoh projects—the Board decided
to press ahead with these projects without authorization.

The first resettlement plan drawn up by the HDB's Resettlement Department had proved to be overly optimistic. It divided the entire Kallang Basin into four sections and proposed clearing the people from
each section at intervals of three months. To facilitate the clearance, the
Board's Chief Architect wrote the Lands Manager a memo on December 14, 1961, suggesting that the latter "survey all Temporary Occupation License holders on land owned by the HDB in the Basin. This
could be done by mailing a standard form to all the tenancy holders
asking them to indicate the number of families, number of persons, and
their ages."

The officers soon discovered the inadequacy of this suggestion. Re-
plies did not materialize. On December 27, 1961, the Board's Chief
Architect wrote to the Senior Engineer suggesting that resettlement
might be facilitated at that time by "cutting down the unoccupied
[sic] [9] hills in Toa Payoh and bring this fill to Kallang Basin" in order
to "create a psychological effect in urging the squatters to move out."
He also suggested that the Board "must adopt a more realistic attitude
and assume that any heavy concentration of the huts will remain in the
Basin and filling will only occupy those areas more or less free of huts."
On February 2, 1962, the HDB Architect-Planner suggested creating a
"restrictive resettlement area within the site."

Meanwhile the resettlement officers were not having an easy time. On
February 14, 1962, the resettlement officer assigned to Kallang Basin
reported that he had served 119 eviction notices. Eighty-one of the affected families had indicated to the census takers that they would be interested in HDB flats; only eight, however, had subsequently accepted
these flats. Most complained that the flats assigned were too far away
and that the rents were too high. An additional partial explanation of
their hesitancy comes from a news item in *Sin Chew Jit Poh* of January
8, 1962, reporting a meeting of the Kallang Basin Villagers presided
over by the Chairman of the Ad Hoc Committee of Kallang Basin Villagers and attended by the President of the Rural Dwellers' Association.
The meeting called upon the villagers to support the Association against

[9] There were no unoccupied hills in Toa Payoh. All the hills in Toa Payoh
were under cultivation.

the "cunning scheme designed to destroy the unity of the people" and to give full support to the Rural Dwellers' Association, which stood "for the protection of their interests and welfare." The meeting passed resolutions demanding reasonable compensation and arrangements for livelihood after resettlement, delegating authority to the Committee leaders to negotiate with the HDB regarding resettlement problems, and appealing to other Kallang Basin settlers to join.

By March 1962 the Board had for the time being abandoned any notions about resettlement in Kallang Basin and Toa Payoh. Thus ended the HDB's first attempt at mass resettlement.

In June 1963, freshly authorized to proceed with the Toa Payoh and Kallang Basin projects, the HDB began again at the attempt to resettle. This time—with the detentions of left wingers—the needed political capabilities were more firmly established. The Senior Civil Engineer of the HDB describes the drama which began that month:

. . . the major obstacle to commencing work at all in the Toa Payoh area was the presence of squatters.

A flight was made over the area for the purpose of taking aerial photographs and to observe directly the nature and extent of the problem and it can only be described as formidable.

Within the area of the photograph the Resettlement Department established that there were 4,072 families in all, and that they were living in 1,-900 huts and shacks. Of the total number of families, 3,759 were ordinary squatters who had a livelihood either in Singapore or by keeping a few chickens or pigs around their huts.

Of the remaining 313, two hundred and eight were genuine farming (small holding) cases, 63 had small shops and 42 were minor factory owners.

Despite the enormity of the difficulties, it was decided to make a start on the previously surveyed haul road, since some 80 acres of higher ground, just south of the large temple which was to remain as a focal point, was free of encumbrance.

. . . With these items in favor therefore the Board took its first dozer into the site in June, 1963, and boldly pursued its policy. However, the squatters through whose lands the initial haul-road was planned, were happy to receive compensation for crops, provided their living accommodation was not interfered with at that stage.[10]

The first day of the bold pursuit was hectic. The dozer and the Senior Civil Engineer were met below the temple by a large crowd of the local

[10] J. T. Stevens, "The Development of Toa Payoh New Town—Singapore" (unpublished manuscript), 8–9.

farmers, whose spokesmen demanded that they be left in peace. They blocked the path of the machine. In the afternoon the Permanent Secretary of National Development was summoned. He gave some explanations to the group about what the project meant, and accompanied resettlement officers from door to door. To build the access road it was not yet necessary to remove houses—only to pass through vegetable gardens. The resettlement officers made a quick assessment of the value of the vegetables being destroyed and paid the inhabitants cash-on-the-spot for these vegetables. A number of the farmers were also promised eventual accommodation in bungalow-type houses to be built on the nearby Kim Keat Road Estate. For this purpose, the HDB subsequently constructed 194 bungalow-type houses at Kim Keat Road—the only houses of this type it has ever constructed on the main island of Singapore.[11] In this manner the resettlement officers proceeded down the road from farm to farm; as soon as the agreement was completed at one farm the bulldozer scraped its pathway through the vegetables while the resettlement officers talked with the next farmer.

By the time this road was built and initial plans for further resettlement were drawn up, the September 1963 elections were over. Assured at last of its continuing position in office, the PAP soon deregistered the Rural Dwellers' Association.[12] After this, organized opposition to resettlement among Chinese and Indians could not easily be established, since the chief troublemakers could be hunted out and arrested.

Sporadic resistance continued; but it was of a sort that could be readily controlled. On January 1, 1964, the resettlement of Kallang Basin began. As it proceeded, some resistance was met among Chinese settlers. Although many of the occupants had simply come to the Basin and built houses on land they did not own, it is HDB policy to compensate all resettlement cases for the houses and improvements they are forced to abandon if they had been paying a temporary occupation fee. One man had developed approximately five acres of the Basin into a farm with 2,200 pigs, which he operated with the aid of six sons. He had begun his farming operation before World War II and had built extensive improvements on this land which was not his. Now he was being

[11] It constructed some other houses of this type on the southern islands for the resettlement of Malays from Jurong—the most delicate operation up to 1963. Until January 1, 1964, bona fide farmers were provided with houses on Rural Resettlement plots. Other than these two exceptions, all other resettlement accommodation has been provided in standardized blocks of flats.

[12] See Chapter II, p. 32.

asked to move. Throughout 1965 he carried on correspondence with the Resettlement Office, complaining that he was able to obtain only two acres of resettlement land and that he disagreed with the assessor's measurements of his pig sties, houses, and ponds. He eventually bought land from private sources, hired a lawyer to ask for time extensions on moving, and succeeded in delaying his move for several months. In many other instances settlers refused to move until the last minute, and the authorities were forced to carry through with their threats of demolition printed on the notices asking people to abandon their premises. For instance, between November 15 and 27, 1965, eighty huts were demolished while the settlers protested vigorously. A reserve unit of policemen stood by to prevent any incidents. None of this resistance was enough to stand in the way of continuing the resettlement, as had been the case in Toa Payoh two years earlier.

Just as merger with Malaysia in September 1963 had weakened the power of the left-wing Chinese, however, so did it add potential political power to that 12 per cent of the island's population which was Malay. Immediately after Merger, the PAP began to make overtures to Tengku Abdul Rahman's United Malay National Organization (UMNO). Malaysia was ruled by the Alliance—an amalgam of UMNO with the Malayan Chinese Association,[13] under the prime ministership of Tengku Abdul Rahman (commonly referred to simply by his title of nobility as the Tengku). The PAP apparently wished to replace the Malayan Chinese Association as UMNO's partner in the Alliance. After the 1963 Singapore elections, Lee Kuan Yew, as a gesture of friendship, allowed the Tengku to select one of the two Singapore senators which Lee was entitled to select for the upper house in the Federation. In April 1964 the PAP fielded eleven candidates against the MCA in the Malayan parliamentary elections. It was badly defeated in all but one district. Instead of being pleased, UMNO responded with outrage to this attempt to split the Alliance. It decided that it in turn would make an active entry into Singapore politics.

Some glimpses into the problems of resettling Malays during this pe-

---

[13] The Alliance is an unusual sort of political party; it is two parties in one. The two parties ordinarily do not run against one another in the same constituency. In areas with a preponderantly Chinese population, the MCA generally fields the candidate; in predominently Malay areas, UMNO generally does so. In Parliament they form a more or less continuous coalition. They have kept a majority in Parliament, although other political parties hold some seats in that body.

riod will serve to indicate the sorts of power that can temporarily accrue to groups during periods of intense political cleavage. This power was sufficient to cause the government to listen to the Malays, and to win for them some minor policy concessions, but not sufficient to effect any major or permanent changes in the programs affecting them.

In January 1962, when the HDB made its first abortive attempt to resettle Kallang Basin, it sent letters to the inhabitants of Kampong Beng Wan (adjoining Bendemeer Estate), ordering them to move in three months. With the help of a Malay living in another part of the Basin they arranged for an interview with the Chairman of the HDB at which they asked him to withdraw the demand for removal. According to them [14] the Chairman was baffled to learn of the order because he did not know that this land was required for development.[15] Nothing then happened for over two more years.

In July 1964, however, the inhabitants of the kampong approached the Malay Action Committee (discussed below) asking for help. They said that in June 1964, after a long silence, they received a letter saying that the kampong was no longer required by government and asking them to pay their land rent of S$5.00 a month as usual (US$1.00 = S$3.00). However, with other resettlement proceeding in the Basin, they were apprehensive lest they soon be required to move. Hence on July 8, 1964, they sent a letter to Tengku Abdul Rahman, informing him of their situation.

Just north of Kallang Basin, at Mt. Vernon Road, a group of Malays had cleared a patch of jungle in 1956 to build themselves a kampong. The construction had been a community (gotong royong) project, and each house had cost between S$1,000 and S$1,500. There were 400 in the community, but none of the houses had received a house number.

In 1960 they built themselves a surau (small combination mosque/religious school); in 1963, shortly after the general election, they constructed an addition to the surau. On April 7, 1964, as they later reported to the Malay Action Committee,[16] two Chinese officers from the Lands Department fastened up notices ordering that the new portion of the surau be demolished. They were unhappy about the atti-

---

[14] Malay Action Committee "Report of Inquiries and Grievances Committee of Malay Action Committee," (mimeo), October 7, 1964.

[15] It is conceivable that he did not know, in view of the experimental nature of this initial resettlement attempt.

[16] See Footnote 14.

tude of these officers, who, they said, walked into the *surau* with their shoes on (a religious taboo) and spoke roughly to the inhabitants.[17]

The week before the Malayan General Election in April 1964, Prime Minister Lee delivered a speech in Geylang Serai (the area of the island containing the heaviest concentration of Malays) aimed at assuaging some of the Malay resentments and frustrations revealed in these two incidents.[18] He reiterated the Government's pledge to respect the rights of Malays guaranteed in the Malaysian Constitution and promised that a new block of flats would be built for Malays, beneath which two-thirds of the stalls would be reserved for selling Muslim food. He pointed out that Malays served on the Housing Board [19] and the Public Services Commission. He stressed that the government was prepared to consider any "practical and realistic suggestions" to raise the living standards and economic life of Malays.

During June 1964 the Government quietly issued invitations to 144 Malay organizations to send representatives to a meeting to be held on July 19, 1964, to discuss the problems of Malays.[20] This meeting triggered a profound social and political crisis:

On June 28 the Singapore branch of the UMNO announced a convention of its own on the "Situation of Malays in Singapore," to be held on July 12. It also formed a twelve-man Malay Action Committee, including representatives of the Pan Malayan Islamic Party [21] and other

[17] *Ibid.* These reports refer to several such incidents on private land as well. At Radin Mas, in the south portion of the city, some Malays reported that they had cleared jungle on private land to build houses. Three times the landowners, with the support of the police, had demolished these houses; three times they had been rebuilt. They claimed to have written to the Yang di-Pertuan Negara about their plight, and in 1961 Singapore's Prime Minister and Deputy Prime Minister had written to them, promising to consider their position. They heard nothing more, however. Then on May 25, 1964, at 3:30 P.M., thirty Chinese carrying wrecking tools came to the kampong with a bulldozer and attempted to knock down the houses. The inhabitants strongly opposed the move, and in the quarrel that ensued a Malay woman and two Malay men claim to have been struck. They said they reported the incident to the police station.

[18] *Straits Times,* April 19, 1964.

[19] The group that governs the operations of the HDB (see Appendix VI). On January 1, 1964, the Secretary of the Malay Chamber of Commerce wrote to the Minister for Social Affairs asking that Malays be appointed to statutory boards. See Singapore UMNO, "Appointments of Malays to the Statutory Boards" (mimeo). This is from the files of Singapore UMNO.

[20] *Straits Times,* July 18, 1964.

[21] An intensely Muslim party whose greatest support is in predominantly Malay Trengganu and Kelantan.

relatively extremist Malay groups.[22] The Singapore UMNO urged the
government to introduce legislation to guarantee Malay employment, to
establish special Malay settlements, to lower the rents of HDB flats for
Malays, to ensure the wide use of the official National Language
(Malay) in government departments and bureaus, to give free transportation to all Malay students, and to establish schools for Malays from
the primary to the university level.[23]

At this, the government disclosed its invitations to the 144 organizations to attend the July 19 meeting. On July 2, 1964, *Utusan Melayu,*
an influential Malay daily, charged that the Government's meeting was
designed to split the Malay community. On July 3 the Minister for Social Affairs, Inche Othman Wok (a Malay), denied this intent; on July
10 it was announced that "no political parties were involved and political issues would be kept out." [24] Nonetheless, the July 12 UMNO convention, attended by about 150 organizations, condemned the forthcoming meeting and urged that it be boycotted.[25] Meanwhile, some UMNO
leaders who had come in from Malaya for the convention went to the
Malay rural villages on the island, delivering hot-tempered speeches de-
nouncing the PAP.

The Government's meeting on July 19 was attended by 300 Malays
representing (or belonging to) 101 of the 144 invited organizations.[26]

In his address, Prime Minister Lee indicated that the Indonesians
were attempting to foment racial strife in Singapore as part of Confrontation.[27] On June 5, Radio Indonesia had stated that the Chinese Government in Singapore was "deliberately forcing the Malays out of the
city, so that the Chinese can be in control." He suggested that the Singapore UMNO was exacerbating this propaganda by charging that Malays were being deliberately expelled from along Crawford Street in the
N1 Urban Renewal District (see Map 5 and Photo 5). Yet the 200
Malay families there, he stated, were only 10 per cent of the total who
would have to move. "We have done nothing which is dishonorable or
wrong to the Malays," he stated, "and we are prepared to have our record put under the closest scrutiny." He defined three problems: education, employment, and housing.

Education, he suggested, is the most important problem. If this can

[22] The Singapore government had already charged these groups with aiding Indonesian terrorists.

[23] *Straits Times,* July 30, 1964.   [24] *Ibid.,* July 6 and 10, 1964.

[25] *Ibid.,* July 14, 1964.   [26] *Ibid.,* July 20, 1964.

[27] Early in 1963, Indonesia had announced a military Confrontation against
Singapore and Malaya, as a protest against the formation of Malaysia.

be solved, all else can be solved. Some of those attending the meeting urged the government to give free transport allowance to all Malay students living three or more miles from school and requested new Malay schools to replace old ones; Mr. Lee promised to refer the question of school transport to the Minister of Education and indicated that a Malay technical school was being planned. The Minister of Education indicated that all Malays who can obtain admission to the University of Singapore and the Polytechnic are given S$1,500 bursaries.

The problem of employment, he said, is a direct result of weaknesses in education. Very few Malays attend secondary school, and fewer still attend universities. The Works Brigade (similar to the WPA and Job Corps in the USA) started off with 30 per cent Malays; now 80 per cent of Works Brigade employees are Malays, for they are finding it difficult to get jobs. "There are just not enough jobs as messengers and peons and other unskilled jobs." He would never allow the introduction of a quota system for Malays, such as they had in the rest of Malaysia; this had been clearly understood when Singapore entered Malaysia. Malays would have to find jobs on the basis of merit. Every effort would be made, however, to train Malays for top positions. When a delegate asked that recognition be given to Malay shorthand, Mr. Lee replied that Malay shorthand writers do not possess basic educational qualifications, and "it is a drain of public money employing people who do not work." Someone complained that only 16 per cent of employees at Jurong were Malay; the Prime Minister reminded him that only 12 per cent of the population was Malay, and that 77 per cent of the Economic Development Board's 80 (manual labor) employees at Jurong were Malays. He said he had already called the three Chambers of Commerce and the Singapore Manufacturers' Association to a meeting to discuss the employment of Malays.

With regard to housing, the Prime Minister indicated that it was out of the question to set aside special licenses or land reservations for Malays; they would have to accept flats along with others. One representative urged him to build flats and sell them to Malays on an installment basis; Mr. Lee said that the proposal was a good one, but that the housing needs of the Malays would first have to be studied by the HDB. When another delegate urged easing the qualifications for flats, he stated that the same qualifications must apply to all races. But he was considering the construction of some lower-rent flats for Malays only, to be allocated on the basis of a means test.

The Prime Minister had spoken in a straightforward manner; but many present were probably offended by what he said. Malays are especially sensitive about their racial group being considered an employment risk.

The following day the Singapore UMNO charged that the Government was not implementing special rights for Malays. This was reported in the newspapers on the morning of July 21, 1964. That afternoon 25,000 Malays processed through the streets in honor of the Prophet Mohammed's birthday. During the procession some fist fights broke out between Chinese and Malay youths; the earliest of these seem to have occurred in the N1 Crawford District scheduled for Urban Renewal (Map 5, Photo 5). The riot which followed made even the 1956 confrontation seem tame. Before the night was out at least 18 persons had lost their lives, and over 200 others were injured; the city was placed under curfew for four days. The scenes of heaviest fighting had occurred in Geyland Serai and in the area around the gas works, where N1 intersects with Kallang Basin.

In the aftermath of this tragedy the Government formed a voluntary multiracial organization to patrol the streets at night and report any irregularities to the police.[28] It also created goodwill committees (later, Citizens' Consultative Committees) [29] in each district to promote racial harmony. To compete, UMNO set up its own goodwill committees. In August 1964, Tengku Abdul Rahman came to Singapore and announced that the federal government would cooperate with the Singapore government to formulate programs for the Malays.

The Tengku blamed the riots on Djakatikusumo, the former Indonesian Ambassador to Kuala Lumpur, who had been visiting kampongs and pitying the exploited Malays.[30] Prime Minister Lee indicated that he had told the Tengku that he would go to the end of the world to help him. When the Tengku asked to send down federal officials to set up programs for Malays, "I said, 'Yes, go ahead. Do anything you like,' because we are quite confident that at the end of the day, he will be just and fair all round." [31]

[28] The Vigilante Corps. A prototype of this had been established in 1948 and 1949 to control left-wing union activity in the harbor areas.

[29] See Chapter IX.

[30] *Straits Times*, August 20, 1964. The PAP pointed out continually the following year that during July the National Secretary-General of UMNO had come to Singapore from Kuala Lumpur to engage in similar activities.

[31] *Straits Times*, August 21, 1964. In 1967, Mr. Lee told a university audience that until 1965 he "ate satay until I was sick to my stomach" in his dealings with

Then on the evening of September 2, 1964, rioting broke out again, both in the areas where it had previously occurred, and in some additional ones. Another curfew was quickly imposed and the Singapore and federal governments once more blamed the action upon the Indonesians, whose radio broadcasts were continually harping on the theme that Malaysia was a plot by the Chinese to suppress the Malays.[32]

At the UMNO General Assembly held in Malaya on September 6, the Tengku still stressed the Indonesia explanation. But he also commented that Indonesian agents could not bring on so serious a situation if a subsoil of misunderstanding did not exist. He traced the cause of tension to uneven development of the communities and a sense of dissatisfaction with the pace of progress toward greater equality of economic status and opportunity. He promised a more energetic approach in this direction.[33] At another speech later in the month he said that perhaps the Malays in Singapore had felt neglected and had thought that under Malaysia they were entitled to more consideration than they had received. "On top of all that, they were being driven out of their homes which they had owned to make way for new flats and so on." [34]

In mid-September 1964, discussions were held between a team from Kuala Lumpur headed by the Deputy Prime Minister of Malaysia and a ministerial team from Singapore headed by Lee Kuan Yew.[35] It was agreed that a cooperative housing society would be formed for Malays to purchase or rent flats at reduced premiums; the Ministry of National Development agreed to make available over 2,000 housing units for this society. The two governments would cooperate in offering loans, training, and scholarships to Malay businessmen and in developing small handicraft industries for Malays.

A war on poverty had begun.

The Singapore Government now decided to make a concession on resettlement. The HDB was asked to avoid, as much as possible for the time being, the resettlement of Malays in Kallang Basin. And those who needed to be touched, the Government determined to handle with kid gloves.

An example will illustrate the wary approach. At the beginning of

---

the Malays, but he got nowhere. Satay is a popular Malay dish often served at social gatherings.

[32] *Ibid.*, September 3, 5, 1964.

[33] *Ibid.*, September 7, 1964.   [34] *Ibid.*, September 21, 1964.

[35] *Ibid.*, September, 18–19, 1964.

1958, a community of Malays built 24 houses at Jalan Kolam Ayer, just off Woodsville Circus at the northwest corner of Kallang Basin.[36] In April 1959, they received notices from the Lands Office asking them to knock down their illegal houses. They informed the Minister of Lands and Housing (a Malay) about this, and he advised them to be patient. A month later the PAP took office. At the end of 1960 they received summonses to court, which ordered that each individual pay, each month, S$7.00 land rent and S$17.00 deposit.[37] Only twelve subsequently made these payments, while the other twelve did not. Then, on September 8, 1964, the occupants of all these houses received notice to move by October 1, 1964, so that the land could be transferred to the HDB for the reclamation project. They immediately formed an action committee and on September 28, 1964, sent a letter to Prime Minister Lee asking for a delay.

Jaacob Mohamad, Parliamentary Secretary to the Prime Minister, invited them to a meeting in his office on November 9, 1964, along with two representatives of the Malay Action Committee of UMNO. According to the minutes taken by the latter representatives, the Parliamentary Secretary explained to the Kolam Ayer settlers that he had been trying to protect their interests. He indicated that he had already met with UMNO representatives over this matter, and after that meeting the villagers had indicated that they were prepared to move on a month's notice. He explained that the area was involved in a national development project and that the inhabitants would be required to move at the latest by February 1965.

Two of the settlers spoke at full length, asking for new homes more suitable than flats.[38] Jaacob explained that they could be offered only

[36] Malay Action Committee, "Report of Inquiries and Grievances Committee of Malay Action Committee" (mimeo reports, October 7, 1964, and November 25, 1964). This is from the files of Singapore UMNO.

[37] Deposits are frequently required on houses occupying state land. They consist of a fixed sum, payable monthly along with rent, and are refundable if the occupant is required to leave the land.

[38] In their October 7, 1964, report the Malay Action Committee proposed that the northern portion of the N1 Urban Renewal area be developed into housing for Malays. They proposed building four-story blocks for licensed *hajis* that would contain single bedrooms grouped around a large hall suitable for meetings or overnight accommodation of visitors. In the ordinary blocks, the flats on the ground floor would have access both through the front and back doors, while those on the upper stories would have stairs at the back, so that it would be easier for women to go out and come in freely if their husbands had guests in front. Also, unlike the HDB flats, these would have bathrooms separated from the lavatories, to make it possible to carry out ritual cleansing properly.

regular HDB flats, either at Tanjong Rhu or MacPherson Road, and he apologized that he could give each family only S$300 removal allowance. But he said that because of a request he himself had made to government they were being offered a compensation of S$1.00 per square foot on their houses—the first time that such compensation had been paid to illegal houses on government land. He asked that a reply be received soon from the settlement and expressed thanks for the clear way in which the Malay Action Committee had conducted the proceedings. The following week the inhabitants voted unanimously to accept the government's offer. Tact produced results.

In January 1965, however, came a new phase in Singapore-Kuala Lumpur relations with the inauguration of the PAP's Malaysian Solidarity Convention and the "Malaysian Malaysia" campaign, whose purpose was to challenge the supremacy of the Alliance Party in Malaysia. There followed six months of vituperative politics, which culminated on August 10, 1965, with the ejection of Singapore from Malaysia.

In the wake of this campaign the Malay Action Committee and the UMNO Goodwill Committees quietly disappeared, and all hopes among Malays for influencing the course of the island's development vanished. The sole monument to this period is the HDB's eleven-story, 485-unit, Geylang Serai Housing Estate, completed in 1965. The Malay Cooperative Society, as is the custom on such matters in Malaysia, filled the units with UMNO partisans, instead of allocating them on the basis of merit (however that might have been done). The Singapore government thereafter decided not to repeat this experiment. Malays, like everyone else, are offered accommodation in HDB flats, all blocks of which are filled on a multiracial basis.

The government had gained the upper hand in coercing all those who might block resettlement. In so doing it cut off virtually all further suggestions for changes in its housing and urban renewal policy.

After 1965 there was still one major avenue of recourse for those being resettled: the Citizens' Consultative Committees. These committees are successors to the good will committees of 1964. There is at least one in every constituency. Members are chosen by the PAP Member of Parliament for the district (or the losing PAP candidate in the previous election), and the lists are vetted by the Prime Minister. The Member of Parliament attends every meeting. While most members are chosen from among those not previously active in politics, most committees in fact contain a small percentage of PAP members. Unlike opposition parties, the committees are not well designed for challenging the rules or trends of development, but serve only to aid citizens in obtaining the fullest benefits from the existing rules. The only incidence since 1964 of a successful attempt to change the rules of resettlement, occurring during the late days of opposition party influence and the early days of the Citizens' Consultative Committees, serves to illustrate how the new process works.

Late in 1964 the HDB decided to develop the area around the Siglap Fire Site.[39] When in January 1965 a resettlement officer of the Board approached settlers on a particular piece of recently purchased land to make initial census, he was refused information by most of them.[40] The Citizens' Consultative Committee for the neighborhood offered some assistance in talking to householders, and the census was completed. However, none of the householders chose to move voluntarily, and eviction notices were served for July 31, 1965. At this point the officers of the Citizens' Consultative Committee began to meet with the householders regarding their grievances over compensation and resettlement. They used the PAP Member of Parliament as an intermediary.

The matter finally came to a head on June 26 when one hundred residents held a special meeting at the Youth Association building. Two bulldozers working just outside the settlement had accidentally severed the pipe furnishing the settlers with water. For seventy-two hours the broken tap had been flooding the ground around it. Furthermore, though legal eviction was over a month away, bulldozers were already getting mud on roofs and blocking entrances to houses.

The Member of Parliament, called in on the meeting, asked the HDB to rectify the situation immediately and to pay compensation to a widow who had lost four ducks to a bulldozer. He also asked for a meeting between himself, officers of the HDB Resettlement Department, and the Citizens' Consultative Committee.

At this meeting, which took place on July 1, 1965, the citizens were guaranteed the right to first preference when flats were completed on this same land one or two years hence; in the interim, they were offered temporary housing in flats located some distance away.

The point of keenest controversy, however, was over the question of whether people who could not produce adequate proof that their houses

---

[39] This is located inland from the eastern edge of the Bedok Reclamation Project (see Map 1), which was starting at that time.

[40] This case comes from HDB files.

were built before World War II could nonetheless receive a compensation of S$2.50 per square foot for their housing (the HDB paid this higher rate, usually reserved only for those qualifying as genuine farmers, to nonfarming households that could prove that their houses were built before World War II on private land).[41] The Member of Parliament promised to review this matter with the Ministry of National Development. Subsidiary issues centered around whether certain borderline cases should be classified as farmers (which would determine whether they were entitled to a Rural Resettlement plot or merely a HDB flat). There was also the problem that these people had been paying their private landlord S$1.00 a month rent. Now the HDB had purchased the land and was charging them S$2.00 a month (the HDB's minimum rent). Ironically, this meant that those willingly accepting the Board's tenancy were paying twice their former rent, while the recalcitrant ones appeared to be paying nothing.

The week following the meeting the Resettlement Department produced a listing of documents suitable for proving that one's house was built before the war. The list did not include tax assessment receipts, since these are easy to forge. Subsequent investigation showed that several settlers had only tax assessment receipts to prove the age of their houses. However, the Board stood firm on this point, and also refused to change its previous classification of "bona fide" farmer, for fear of creating untenable precedents or of appearing weak to those settlers who were still holding out on their cooperation in the hopes of gaining still further concessions. Despite considerable hesitancy on the parts of the Lands and Resettlement Officer, the Board did finally make one concession. It agreed to charge them S$1.00 a month rent instead of S$2.00.

Of course, all this took time, and the original deadline for vacating premises had to be moved back by over three months. Most citizens finally voluntarily acquiesced and accepted their compensation and resettlement. As demolition time drew near it was reported that some outside agitators (probably the Barisan Sosialis) were present in the neighborhood, counseling villagers to burn HDB cars and bulldozers. Demolition crews were provided with heavy police escort, and some settlers continued resistance until the last remains of their houses had been destroyed.

[41] The reasoning seems to be that if the family has lived in the house for that many years the deprivation is greater than if it lived there only a few years.

The villagers had won a dollar a month and a three-month reprieve.

Realizing the seriousness of a situation in which there were no channels of effective interest representation on matters such as these, after the Barisan boycott and resignations from Parliament, the PAP instituted another policy to fill this void. Its members of Parliament would get up and address questions to ministers regarding inadequacies in their ministries. An exchange of this nature on December 12, 1966, illustrates the methods—and limitations—of this policy.

The PAP Member for Bras Basah rose to speak on farm policy. The Singapore Livestock Farmers' Association had conveyed to him a message in which they complained that the government's resettlement policies were forcing farmers to move from land they had developed for years; the new Rural Resettlement plots to which they were resettled were usually too small to achieve both hygiene and decent productivity. They pointed out that increased productivity would mean a savings in foreign exchange reserves.

The Minister of National Development replied by stating that "you give them one acre and they want five." Singapore had not sufficient land to go round. The farmers behaved as though the state land they occupied were theirs, when they receive it practically as a gift. Despite this, unsuccessful or disinterested farmers let out part of their land to successful farmers and get a "big fat fee" for the transfer. The government tried to register farmers in 1965 to find out who were genuine farmers and who were bogus farmers [42] so that it could devise means to help farmers, but it had met with opposition over this from the farming populace. The alternative to resettlement would be to have no development projects, and the farmers would not want this to happen.

As is usual with such Parliamentary exchanges, no meeting between the Singapore Livestock Farmers' Association and representatives of the Ministry resulted, and no policy review was instituted by the functional agencies concerned. The criticism in Parliament serves more as a means of insulating the Cabinet from its critics than as an instrument for negotiating grievances.

Resettlement was well under control. Serious discussion about the merits of resettlement policy was at an end.

---

[42] That is, to separate those who receive most of their income from farming from those who receive only part of their income from farming, so that the latter will not receive assistance with their farming or special treatment in case of resettlement.

LAND ACQUISITION AND LANDOWNERS

The other delicate problem in connection with the Kallang Basin
project was land acquisition. Here, the government was dealing with the
middle and upper classes. Between 1961 and 1963 it was essential that
the PAP pick up all the votes it could from this sector and avoid any
moves that might cause them to form a right-wing party. Hence it was
difficult for the government to initiate any toughening of the 1955 land
acquisition laws. From 1963 to 1965 the new problem arose that Singapore did not wish to pass land acquisition laws that would appear
harsher than those in the rest of Malaysia. Only in December 1966 did
Parliament pass a law that allowed the government to institute acquisition proceedings before it presented detailed zoning of projects, to enter
land within seven days of instituting acquisition proceedings, and to assess the land at rates prevailing before government improvements began
in the area. Until this time they tread more softly so as not to further
widen political cleavages. Yet even then the government remained timid
about aggressive land acquisition programs. Land cost and acquisition
procedures remain more formidable obstacles than resettlement to flexibility in planning.

The year 1962 marked the first attempt to purchase land within the
Kallang Basin. On March 23, 1962, the HDB's Chief Executive Officer
authorized the Lands Manager to proceed with negotiations for buying
new land in the Basin. He had a specific objective in mind. If a bridge
were to be constructed over Serangoon Road to allow trucks to transport the earth-fill from Toa Payoh to Kallang Basin, there was only one
point at which the crossing could be made without demolishing shophouses or passing through densely settled squatter villages. As it happened, the land on the Toa Payoh side of this crossing point was
occupied by some sport associations, who had not objected to the
Board's inquiries about using their land. The pathway on the Kallang
side, however, was obstructed by Bendemeer Estate, formerly a moderately large rubber estate. It was fronted by a large home (Bendemeer
House; see Map 4), which for some decades had been a landmark of the
area. Its owner, who had recently passed away, had been the leader of a
political party which had opposed the PAP during the 1950's. The
HDB was about to deal with legal restrictions on its proposed activities
on this estate, restrictions which the government did not have the politi-

cal power to remove, in the face of its need for the support of the middle class during its struggle with the Barisan Sosialis Party.

In February 1962 the HDB approached the trustees of the estate of this deceased man to ask permission to use the land for an access route. The trustees indicated that the terms of the will forbade them granting such permission. The Board's Lands Manager pursued the matter further with the trustees, but without success. By July 1962 the HDB Chief Executive Officer decided that compulsory acquisition of this land might be necessary. If this were to be done, however, the Lands Manager was told by legal counsel that the Board would have to designate a permanent purpose for the land and obtain planning approval for this usage. This meant that the Board must either zone a permanent road on the site and acquire a narrow strip of land, or zone the entire estate for industry or housing and acquire the entire property.

The Economic Development Board was approached to determine whether it would like to acquire the land for industrial purposes, but it replied that it had no funds available for such an acquisition. As a result, in October 1962, the Chairman of the HDB agreed to acquire via eminent domain a fifty-foot-wide strip of land for an access road, unless the trustees decided to sell the strip voluntarily. They refused to sell. No further action was taken for another eight months. When in May 1963 the HDB was finally placed in charge of the Kallang Basin Reclamation Project, the Chief Executive Officer asked the Lands Manager to make further inquiries regarding the possibilities for compulsory acquisition.

In June 1963 the HDB Lands Manager estimated that the cost of a strip of land for an access road through this estate would be S$200,000 at current market prices. Legal counsel suggested that the entire cost of this strip would have to be borne by the Kallang Basin Reclamation Project, even though the roadbed would not be usable for either housing or industry. Furthermore, no overall road design had yet been produced for the Basin, and it was by no means certain that this was a practical place for a permanent road.

In the face of this, the Chairman of the HDB decided later in June to consider acquiring the entire twenty-seven acres of the estate. On July 3, 1963, he wrote to the Chairman of the Economic Development Board informing him of this intention, and on July 4 was informed by the latter of his agreement to the plan.

The Lands Manager now estimated the value of the entire twenty-seven acres to be S$2,800,000, and the Deputy Chief Valuer of the Property Tax Division of the Ministry of Finance commented that this seemed to be a reasonable price—perhaps even slightly low. Compulsory acquisition proceedings began in September 1963.

The HDB asked the trustees for permission to enter the land pending completion of the acquisition proceedings. The trustees refused permission, and in October 1963, when the Board undertook to enter the land despite the refusal, they were threatened with a trespassing summons. The earthmovers withdrew, pending negotiations with the lawyers.

Nothing further could be done, however, until the Prime Minister's Office gave permission to gazette the acquisition proceedings; this came on November 14, 1963. On November 22, *Gazette* notification was published.[43] At the Collector's Inquiry held on December 23, 1963, the owners' valuer claimed S$6,408,000 for the land. On January 1, 1964, the government filed in court an originating summons allowing the Board to deposit S$2,800,000 initial payment with the Court and take possession of the land pending a final settlement.

It was then discovered that the money which the HDB had thought it would use for this acquisition was depleted, and no further funds were available. Consequently, the Board had to turn to the Economic Development Board for an advance. On January 10, 1964, the latter advanced a check for S$2,800,000, and on January 17, 1964—twenty-three months after its initial request to enter the land—the HDB took possession of the Bendemeer Estate.

The following day—as the next chapter indicates—the construction of the Bailey Bridge across Serangoon Road began.

It was now necessary that all the land below high tide level (see Map 6) be acquired by the state or the HDB. A minor beginning on this had already been made in September 1961—two months before the Board was given formal possession of the former Singapore Improvement

---

[43] Under the procedure established by the 1955 Land Act, the government could compulsorily acquire land by printing its intention to do so in the *Gazette*. The government assessor then assessed the land at what he considered to be the current market prices. The owner could then appeal, and the Court of Appeals might raise the award somewhat. While the appeal was pending, the government could file in court an originating summons allowing it to take possession in the interim. Before the acquisition proceedings could be gazetted, however, the agency in question must have obtained approval to develop the land for some specific permanent purpose. This law was superceded by a new one in 1966 mentioned earlier in this chapter.

Trust land in the Basin. At that time the largest landholder in the Basin, the Lee Rubber Company (see Map 4), approached the HDB with an offer to sell three lots comprising 7.5 acres. On March 22, 1962, the Chairman of the HDB authorized the Board's Lands Manager to proceed with negotiations for two of these lots plus four others in the possession of the rubber company, on the basis of paying five cents a square foot for land below the high tide level and twenty-five cents a square foot for that above it. However, the uncertainty of plans caused these negotiations to lag. On April 25, 1963, the Senior Civil Engineer instructed the Lands Manager to put negotiations in abeyance for fifteen months until policy for the area had been clarified.

After the fill trucks began to move in April 1964, however, plans for land acquisition also began to move again. On October 16, 1964, a report of the HDB Lands Office indicated that

more than half of the land below the high tide level belongs to either the Government or the Housing Board [compare Maps 6 and 7]. The Lands Department of the Board has taken action to acquire all the remaining land below the high tide level to facilitate the reclamation. If it is considered necessary to acquire more land for the development of Kallang Basin, action will be taken by the Housing Board.

On October 29, 1964, the Lands Department asked for the right to institute acquisition proceedings for 47 lots, comprising 95 acres (30 above water), owned by 19 different owners, at an estimated cost of S$4,790,000 (S$1.16 a square foot overall). On October 14, 1964, the department had already asked for two other lots, and in December for 44 additional ones, comprising 55 acres, for S$3,600,000.

This brought to the fore the question of land prices. Between 1962 and 1964 land prices on the island had risen steeply, as it appeared that political stability would produce an ideal climate for building. Kallang Basin, partly because of this general change in climate and partly because of the existence of the government project in the area, had been affected by this increase in land prices. An October 6, 1964, memo by the HDB Lands Officer suggested that in Kallang Basin fair prices for land below high tide level ranged from fifteen to eighty cents per square foot and for land above high tide level, from S$1.20 to S$3.00 per square foot. This represented increases of three to eight times above 1961 estimates. The Chief Executive Officer of the Board expressed the opinion that these estimates were unrealistic and asked for more detailed papers on each plot. The Lands Office, with only two assessors responsible for HDB lands on the entire island, did not feel itself in a position to prepare lengthy reports on each lot. Nonetheless, in January 1965, the Chief Executive Officer approved the S$3,600,000 request.

There thus began the most extensive land acquisition in which the HDB had yet been involved. In January 1966 came the first major awards—S$1,503,798 to five owners at an average of S$1.33 per square foot for 42 acres. Included in this were the 7.5 acres originally offered to the Board in September 1961. At that time the Lands Manager had suggested making a preliminary offer of eight cents a square foot for these lots; the owners had asked twenty to twenty-five cents a square foot. The Board now paid S$1.56 a square foot for this 7.5 acres, including buildings (a timber-treating factory, a sawmill, and 40 huts); [44] the owners asked S$2.36 a square foot. During the latter half of 1966 the Board acquired an additional 49.8 acres.[45] (See Map 7 for acquisitions, 1963–1967.)

In December 1966 the new acquisition law mentioned at the beginning of this section came into effect. The government would not again have to wait so long or pay quite so much for land acquisition; its potential flexibility in planning was thereby increased. Without the Barisan Sosialis threat or Malaysian political competition as bargaining points, the landowners were not in a position to challenge the new law. Yet even under the new procedures, land acquisition remains a major potential expense in development. This probably accounts in part for the tendency to site new projects on land already owned by the state or government agencies.

During a six-year period the government was successful in removing

[44] Unencumbered land would be worth more. In this case, the government would have to tear down the factory structures and resettle the occupants before it could use the land.

[45] During this period the government had also acquired other land in the Basin. Included in the October 29, 1964, requests for permission to acquire land was the Pulau Minyak Kampong (this was the site which the Board had considered developing as the Geylang Road Industrial Site in 1960). On November 4, 1964, a fire swept through this kampong, destroying 160 huts. Fire victims were given relief funds and offered immediate accommodation. The Commissioner of Lands immediately instituted acquisitions proceedings for all the land on the fire site and in the remainder of the kampong. On April 10, 1965, the government took possession of this thirteen-acre tract of land. The Commissioner of Lands also bought other occasional pieces of land in the Basin, all of which would be available for resettlement and reclamation.

grounds for obstruction of the reclamation project by those who were initially in a good position to prevent its implementation. Part of the price the government paid can be measured in land costs. Another part is less tangible: a loss of information, and possibly of support.[46] The Senior Civil Engineer of the HDB felt that, from an engineering standpoint, leveling the hills of Toa Payoh into Kallang Basin was a convenient and relatively inexpensive way to proceed. The government had little opportunity to determine whether, in addition, this was the most suitable way to proceed in terms of social, economic, and physical planning problems.

[46] Daniel Goldrich, Raymond B. Pratt, and C. R. Schulter studied four marginal communities around Santiago, Chile, and Lima, Peru. Some settlers in these communities had been subjected to severe police and bureaucratic harassment in the early stages of settlement. They found this portion of the sample to be more politically passive than the rest, but also more politically alienated. The authors conclude from their interview data: ". . . extreme depoliticization will result from severe sanctions being levied against lower-class people relatively inexperienced in politics. . . . The effect can 'help' a government by reducing demands and therefore stress, but there is also a loss in the capacity to mobilize support." "The Political Integration of Lower-Class Urban Settlements in Chile and Peru," in Irving Louis Horowitz, *Masses in Latin America* (New York: Oxford University Press, 1970), 211–212.

MAPS AND ILLUSTRATIONS

MAP 1   90

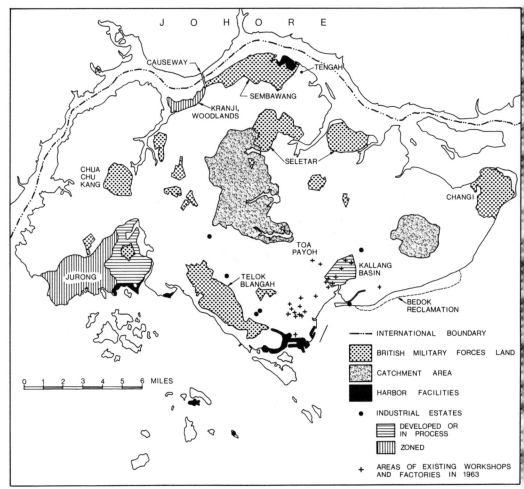

The Republic of Singapore, 1968. Information on this map was supplied by State and City Planning. The locations of workshops and factories employing ten or more persons were charted during an EDB survey in 1963.

MAP 2

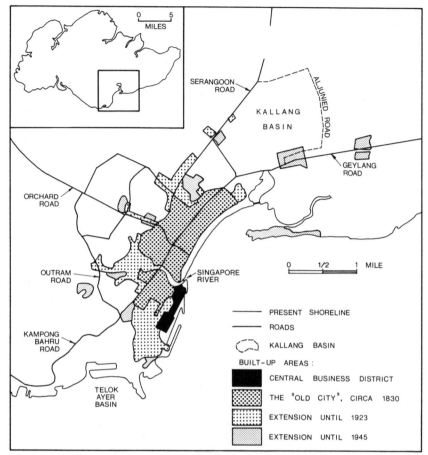

Built-up areas of Singapore, 1819–1945. Built-up areas are those covered more or less contiguously by permanent buildings, except warehouses, factories, and wooden houses. Maps consulted: Lieutenant Jackson's town plan, 1822; Fraser and Neave Map, 1923; Sheet 3L/12, Hind Series, 4th ed., 1945.

MAP 3   92

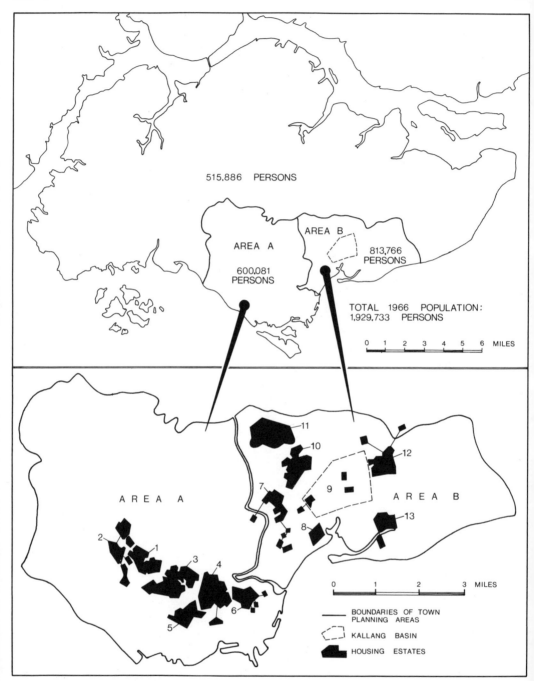

Location and population of Singapore Housing and Development Board estates, 1966 and 1972. Based on an outline map and chart produced by the HDB in May 1966, and on their estimates for future building.

Key to Housing Estates on Map 3

Name of housing estate	1966 population	1972 population (projected)
Planning Area A		
1. Queenstown	28,500	28,500
2. Queenstown	64,500	64,500
3. Clementi Road		
Alexander Hill		
Hock San Brickwork		
Alexandra Road	75,000	120,000
Bukit Merah		
Henderson Road		
Redhill		
4. Bukit Ho Swee		
Havelock Road		
Kampong Tiong Bahru	88,500	88,500
Kampong Silat		
5. Telok Blangah	——	80,000
6. S1		
York Hill		
Upper Pickering Street		
Cantonment Road	6,000	32,000
	262,500 persons	413,500 persons
Planning Area B		
7. Albert Street		
Selegie House		
Stamford	18,500	18,500
Farrer Park		
Tasek Utara		
Winstedt Court		
8. North Precinct One (N1)	——	27,500
9. Kallang Basin		
Jalan Besar	18,000	170,000
Lavender Street		
10. St. Michael's		
Kim Keat Road	39,000	39,000
Temple		
11. Toa Payoh	——	250,000
12. MacPherson Road		
Upper Aljunied	74,000	74,000
Lorong Tai Seng		
13. Kallang Airport		
Tanjong Rhu	50,000	50,000
	199,500 persons	629,000 persons
Rest of Island (not shown on map)		
14. Geylang Serei	4,000	4,000
15. Upper Changi Road	5,000	5,000
16. Jurong	8,500	8,500
	17,500 persons	17,500 persons
TOTAL	479,500 persons	1,060,000 persons

These population figures were arrived at by multiplying the number of flats, and projected number of flats, in each estate, by six. This would seem to be a reasonable estimate. The HDB usually estimates on the basis of 5½ persons per flat. The 1966 Household Survey shows a mean of six persons per flat. Population figures for the upper portion of the map come from the 1966 Household Survey, as do the lines delineating Planning Areas A and B.

MAP 4   94

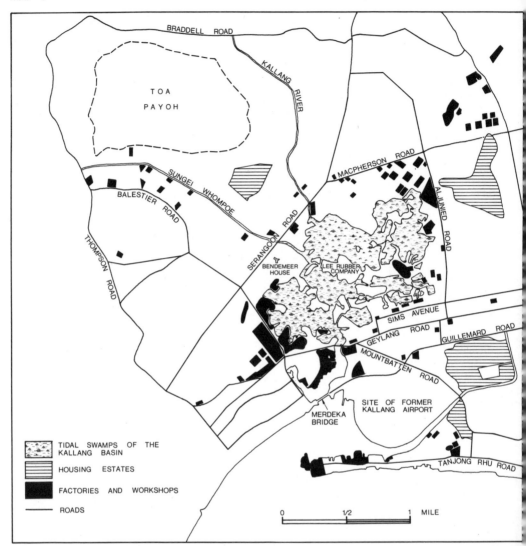

Kallang Basin area, 1963. From Series L905, Sheets 2 and 4, Troop R.E. Far East, 1959. Industrial locations were surveyed by the EDB in 1963, including only factories and workshops employing ten or more persons.

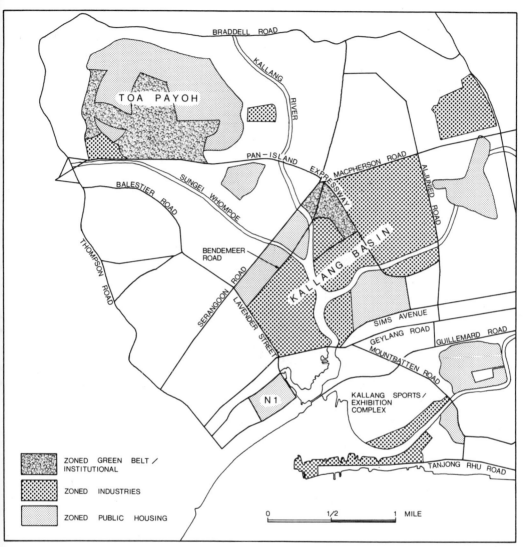

Housing and industrial estates zoned for Kallang Basin area, 1972. From maps furnished by the HDB. Compared with Map 4, this map shows some of the major changes in the Kallang Basin area between 1963 and 1972.

MAP 6   96

Kallang Basin: High tide line and location of buildings, 1962. From map produced by the HDB in 1962.

Land ownership of Kallang Basin, 1967. From map produced by the HDB in 1962.

MAP 8   98

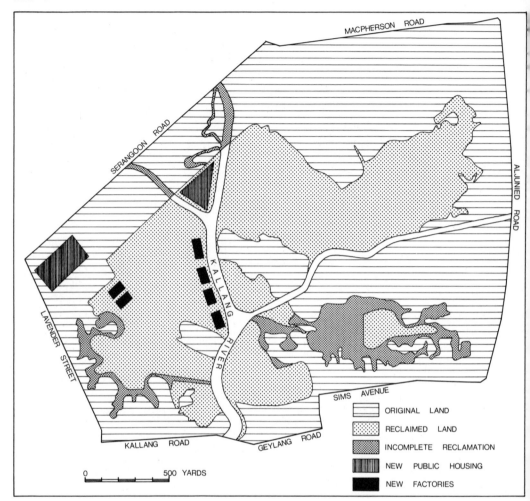

Stages of reclamation and new construction in Kallang Basin, April 1968. From maps furnished by the HDB and the EDB; and from on-site inspection and aerial photographs.

Key to identification numbers on photographs

1. Fullerton House, the central business district post office
2. Old Telok Ayer Market. The shore line once bordered it
3. Supreme Court building
4. Padang (spacious lawn) in front of City Hall, which now contains the Prime Minister's office. Buildings and grounds were laid out by Sir Stamford Raffles
5. Bukit Ho Swee Housing Estate, constructed on the site of a disastrous 1961 fire
6. Tiong Bahru Housing Estate—Singapore's first, begun in 1936
7. South Precinct One (S1) Urban Renewal site
8. First three new public housing blocs on North Precinct One (N1) Urban Renewal site
9. Crawford Street gas storage tank of gas works
10. The first two Kallang Basin flatted factories
11. Bendemeer Road Housing Estate
12. St. Michael's Housing Estate
13. MacPherson Road (South) Housing Estate
14. Payah Lebar International Airport
15. Tanjong Rhu
16. Kallang Airport (Guillemard Road) Housing Estate
17. Toa Payoh
18. Lee Rubber Company (called by various other names over the years)
19. First four warehouse-type factory structures on reclaimed Kallang Basin land
20. Factory resettlement site, containing early pilings
21. First HDB public housing on reclaimed Kallang Basin land
22. Squatter and build-your-own housing

Photo 1. Government buildings (*foreground*), the Singapore River, and the central business district (*looking south*)

Photo 2. The Tiong Bahru Housing Estate, built in 1936 (number 6)

Photo 3. The MacPherson Road (South) Housing Estate, built in 1961

Photo 4. Looking north / northeast over the central business district

Photo 5. North Precinct One (N1) Urban Renewal site, looking northwest

Photo 6. Kallang Basin, looking northwest

Photo 7. Kallang Basin, looking northwest

CHAPTER V

Successes and Failures
in Planning Kallang

> If capabilities are used to achieve objectives which are peripheral
> to the needs of the society, the effort expended to develop them
> may be considered wasted.[1]

The HDB, having overcome the most serious obstacles, quickly set to
work to complete the reclamation and open the ground for housing and
industry. It accomplished a good deal in a short time. The industrial
and housing estate it produced is providing needed jobs and housing for
Singaporeans. Yet, while the project created, it also destroyed—not
only things that were, but also the possibility of things that could have
been. This, too, is part of the measure of its usefulness.

RECLAMATION: SPEEDY IMPLEMENTATION

The reclamation was completed posthaste.

On June 10, 1963, the HDB received its check for the initial bills on
the Kallang Basin Reclamation Project. On June 14 an advertisement
was placed in the press calling for tenders from private construction
firms for hauling the earth from Toa Payoh to Kallang, and the lowest
bid was accepted on August 21, 1963. The road from Toa Payoh to
Kallang Basin was completed by January 1964. On January 18, 1964
—the day after the Court authorized the HDB to enter Bendemeer
Estate—work began on the Bailey Bridge across the Serangoon Road.
By April 4, 1964, the Bailey Bridge was complete, and work on the filling was able to start. Filling proceeded steadily from then on at the rate
of five acres per month. By April 1968 all but 120 acres had been filled
(see Map 8 and Photo 7).

In mid-1963 two resettlement officers were assigned full time to Toa
Payoh. They found 4,072 families there. The great majority of these
were resettled by the end of 1966. On January 1, 1964, the same pro-

---

[1] Chapter VI discusses this problem.

cess was begun in Kallang Basin. By December 1965, 1,188 families had been resettled from Kallang Basin, leaving 1,682 still to be moved —mostly from land peripheral to the reclamation (see Maps 6 and 8). The land fill operation was never slowed by the presence of housing structures.

On October 1, 1964, tenders were called for dredging and creating a new channel of the Kallang and Whompoe rivers within the reclamation site. By the end of 1966 most of the dredging that could be completed was complete.

CREATING A GROUND PLAN:
ACTIVE COORDINATION

In order to create a ground plan for the newly reclaimed area, it was necessary to draw upon the skills, resources, and administrative capabilities of several agencies.

On February 21, 1964, the Permanent Secretary of National Development wrote to the Chief Executive Officer of the HDB suggesting that

in the light of Urban Redevelopment, your officers dealing with Urban Renewal should look into the replanning of the whole Kallang Basin including existing land, reclaimed land and land adjoining the Renewal Precinct N1 to provide a comprehensive redevelopment plan for the next precinct for renewal. In so doing, since so much of the land involved is likely to be for small industries, your officers should work closely with the Economic Development Board and the Planning Department.

The Permanent Secretary suggested that the scheme for Kallang Basin should include land for small industries, standardized industrial structures on various-size plots, roads, community facilities, and housing.

Shortly after this a new Urban Renewal Department was formed within the HDB, with the Architect/Planner as its head. This same individual was already in charge of designing the layout of Toa Payoh. In January 1964, he had indicated his intention to plan Kallang Basin and Phase 1 of Toa Payoh together. Now the layout for Toa Payoh, Kallang Basin, and N1 were all his responsibility (see Maps 4 and 5).

It was nine months, however, before he began to work closely with the Economic Development Board and the Planning Department. The relations were somewhat strained. On October 20, 1964, he sent to the Chairman of the Economic Development Board a proposed road layout for Kallang Basin. On November 26, 1964, the head of the Traffic Unit of the Planning Department put out a memo expressing disagreement with certain features of this plan. So on January 19, 1965, the Economic Development Board (represented by its Chairman, Lands and Estates Manager, and Surveyor/Planner), the Architect/Planner of Urban Renewal, and the Chief Planner met to discuss the road proposals.

Yet on March 2, 1965, the Architect/Planner wrote to the Chief Planner. He expressed displeasure that the road plans he had received from the Chief Planner were different from those the latter had forwarded to the Economic Development Board. He indicated that he had asked the Permanent Secretary of National Development to put Urban Renewal in complete charge of all Kallang Basin roads not "affecting the overall island network." The Chief Planner, in reply, agreed to this proposal. But he expressed surprise that there should have been a difference in the two plans. He wondered whether these differences might be related to the scale of the two maps.

The Chief Architect of the HDB now felt that there was need for more formalized liaison on the Basin. On March 16, 1965—twenty-two months after the beginning of implementation of the Kallang Basin Reclamation Project—he convened the first meeting of a Kallang Basin Coordinating Committee. It was attended by representatives of the Ministry of National Development, the HDB, the Public Works Department, the Economic Development Board, and the Planning Department. The principal concern at the meeting was to delineate areas of responsibility. The minutes of this meeting and the three that followed it indicate the scope of the coordination which ensued.

It was agreed that the circulatory roads would be a joint venture of the HDB, the Public Works Department, and the Planning Department. The three agencies had differing opinions on the subject. The Planning Department's road proposals were designed to run through the downtown area (linking downtown and suburbia), while the Public Works Department considered this too expensive, and the HDB preferred a ring road to circle the city (linking together housing estates).

It was also decided that two-thirds of Kallang Basin would be zoned for industry; the land in the south and west portions of the Basin would be zoned as residential. The HDB would be coordinator for development of the area. It would carry out the physical implementation of the proposals. "It was also suggested that there be a planning authority for this project, but since the latter is a relatively small one, it was felt that this would be unnecessary." (This was an interesting observation, since Toa Payoh, N1, and Kallang Basin, which were supposed to constitute a comprehensive redevelopment plan, were bound to have a major physical and demographic impact.) [2]

The Economic Development Board indicated its desire to allocate industrial sites as soon as possible. The southwest corner of the Basin, behind the Bendemeer Road Industrial Estate, was chosen as the first area. The Public Works Department consented to undertake the construction of essential services. HDB also brought up their plans to acquire 159 acres of land in the Basin. After considerable discussion, the group decided that all lands to be affected by the project should be acquired. The meeting was adjourned with the understanding that further meetings would be convened as they were needed.

The Senior Executive Engineer (Sewerage) of the Public Works Department had inadvertently not been invited to the first meeting of the Kallang Basin Coordinating Committee. He was invited to the second, held on June 15, 1965. At this meeting he indicated that it would take two and a half years for him to complete the sewers. He would need to know projected population densities before drawing up plans, and exact road blueprints before laying the pipes. Road plans had been drawn up and agreed upon among the three agencies in the interval between the meetings. [3]

A third meeting of the Coordinating Committee on September 25, 1965, continued discussion of the road plans.

During November 1965 plans continued for the roundabout at highly congested Woodsville Circus, [4] with considerable give and take between the Planning Department and Urban Renewal. Then, in February 1966, the Surveyor/Planner of the Economic Development Board indicated that the road plans agreed upon in June 1965 by the Planning Department and Urban Renewal would not be convenient for his industries from an internal point of view. He asked for discussions. The sewerage engineer also indicated that, considering the continual changes in

[2] A comparison of Maps 2, 3, and 5 gives an indication of the importance of this area. Note the high percentage of the total population that it contains.

[3] The Economic Development Board's Surveyor/Architect submitted some plans, which were subsequently revised by the Traffic Unit of the Planning Department, and accepted by Urban Renewal with slight modification.

[4] On Map 4, the intersection of Serangoon and MacPherson Roads.

road plans and the absence of factory plans, it would be impossible to proceed with detailed design of the sewer system, and it would be risky to lay the main sewers along the route of the trunk roads before it was certain that the roads were going to occupy the ground currently designated. During the fortnight which followed, the Surveyor/Planner of the Economic Development Board, the Chief Planner's Office, and Urban Renewal carried on liaison to agree on some final plans for the roads.

The fourth and last meeting of the Kallang Coordinating Committee, on March 2, 1966, was principally devoted to reporting the accomplishments of the project. Urban Renewal presented a map of the Basin, which was subsequently sent to the Master Plan Committee for formal appending to the Master Plan in May 1966. The various zones of the Basin contained the following acreages:

Proposed industries	387.11	acres
Committed industries (existing)	105.08	”
Proposed public housing	278.29	”
Committed residential (existing)	8.94	”
Open space and institutional buildings	63.51	”
Proposed roads	135.80	”
Proposed river	50.19	”
TOTAL	1,028.92	acres

Although there were some additional refinements in zoning later in 1966, these acreages remained approximately the same. The original plan was to devote the entire Basin to industry. At the March 1965 meeting it was decided that only two-thirds be zoned industrial. Now public housing had been allocated the remaining third.

The committee agreed that the HDB would build the public housing on the site, while the Economic Development Board would build the industrial buildings. The HDB had acquired 200 acres; the responsibility for any further acquisition that might be necessary would now be undertaken by each individual authority. As the former Bendemeer Estate land was momentarily being used for military training, the first housing projects would begin in front of the extended Bendemeer Road and on the land bounded by the Whompoe and Kallang rivers (see the triangle of public housing on Map 8, and Photo 6, No. 21). The Economic Development Board would begin immediate plans for the land on the east side of the Kallang River.

The Public Utilities Board representatives (who were attending a Kallang Basin Coordinating Committee meeting for the first time) foresaw no difficulties with regard to gas and electricity, and the Public Works Department indicated that it would soon begin planning main water routes.

The task of building the various roads was divided among the participating agencies.

It will be seen that the layout up to this point was planned by the Architect/Planner of Urban Renewal, within the limits of the authority vested in him. The planning consisted of producing a colored map which indicated zones, and of drawing a series of roads on a map of Kallang Basin. In the latter instance he had the assistance of the Surveyor/Planner of the Economic Development Board, and of the Chief Planner's Office, in deciding alignments and designing the flyovers and roundabouts. Three different philosophies became enfused in this road planning. The HDB showed some enthusiasm for a ring road [5] to circle the island. The Chief Planner's Office stressed the need to link the populous old city (Map 2) areas with the outlying areas, using some straight roads in addition to a ring road. The Surveyor/Planner felt that detailed road plans needed to wait until it was known more definitely what sorts of industries would occupy the Basin and what their transportation needs would be. The compromise involved building a portion of a ring road (Pan-Island Expressway, Map 5), and a wide piece of straight road aiming toward the old city (Bendemeer Road, Map 5), while postponing the detailed planning of roads until industries were committed. There were no immediate specific plans for extending

[5] On June 15, 1963, the Chief Planner wrote to the HDB suggesting a meeting about Kallang Basin with Professors S. Kobe, O. H. Koenigsberger, and C. Abrams, who were in the city for the project discussed on pp. 140–146. A July 31 meeting was held with these experts and representatives from the Planning Department, the HDB, and Public Works; they were asked to return in a week (August 7) to present road plans for the island. At the August 7 meeting these experts proposed a ring road for the island—obviously part of the overall scheme discussed in Chapter VI. Dubbed the Pan-Island Expressway, it included the stretch shown on Map 5; this stretch had first appeared in Colony of Singapore, *Report on the Master Plan* (Singapore: GPO, 1955). While the Ministry of Finance did not show an interest in the satellite towns proposed by these experts (Chapter VI), it did show an interest in this expressway that was designed to link them, and there was considerable talk about this idea in subsequent years. Meanwhile, the portion actually constructed through Toa Payoh and Kallang Basin ended in heavily congested areas, which made it difficult to extend the road beyond these points.

these roads; it was hoped that future planning would find a means to link them to other areas.[6]

PLANNING FOR INDUSTRY:
EFFECTIVE ADMINISTRATION

The Kallang Basin and Toa Payoh were made available at an auspicious time. In 1967 the political situation in Hong Kong seemed to be showing signs of instability, and many manufacturers there sought new operating locations. Some of these came to Singapore. Manufacturers in Europe, the United States, and Japan were also looking for new factory sites abroad, to keep up with expanding markets and rising labor costs. The Economic Development Board began an active campaign to advertise Singapore's progress and her many incentives (see pp. 47, 150ff.) to foreign investors. Prime Minister Lee spent increasing time in the United States and Europe, talking to business groups. The campaign brought results. Jurong Industrial Estate was becoming quickly committed, and there was demand for additional industrial space elsewhere on the island.

During 1966 and 1967 the HDB and Economic Development Board constructed six flatted factories,[7] to join two others already operating. Two of these were located in Kallang Basin (see Photos 6 and 7, No. 10). By the end of 1969 an additional flatted factory had been completed in the Basin, and two others were nearing completion. Forty-seven industries were housed in the flatted factories. Four large warehouse-type single-story factories were constructed above the Kallang River, housing an additional twelve factories (see Photo 6, No. 19). In addition, four prefabricated factories just north of Geylang Road housed some seventy-six industries resettled from urban redevelopment areas. Altogether the 135 light industries occupying these eleven new structures employed approximately 6,000 persons as the decade of the sixties drew to a close. A new electronics factory at nearby Toa Payoh employed an additional 500 people.

[6] The widened Bendemeer Road emerges on the southwest into a portion of the city destined for urban renewal. The area has been divided into zones (N1, Map 5, is the first zone), with each zone being designed separately. This approach will not serve to add comprehensiveness to road planning. As Map 3 indicates, this is an especially congested portion of the city.

[7] Multistory structures, usually renting space to two or more manufacturers on each story—common in Hong Kong.

This still left a good deal of reclaimed land for further industrial expansion. A long waiting list, containing many foreign enterprises wishing to invest in Singapore, assured that this space would be filled. The objective of providing new jobs near to the city population had been accomplished.

RESETTLING FAMILIES:
INCOMPLETE INFORMATION

The Kallang Basin project was successful in providing new land for housing and industries. Nonetheless, an assessment of the success of the project should include some consideration of what happened to the families and industries which were displaced by the project. It would also seem relevant to consider whether this location was well suited to the new factory structures.

No one was assigned to find out what happened to the individuals who were displaced by the Kallang Basin project.

Between January 1, 1964, and December 31, 1964, 620 families were displaced from Kallang Basin. Of these, 535 indicated to the resettlement inspectors that they would accept rehousing in HDB flats. Three were offered Rural Resettlement plots. Eighty-two said they would find their own accommodations. Between January 1, 1965, and December 31, 1965, 568 more families were displaced from Kallang Basin. Of these, 343 said they would accept accommodations in HDB flats, while two were offered Rural Resettlement plots. One hundred forty-nine indicated that they would find their own accommodations (a higher percentage than in 1964).

The 1964 resettlement cases were offered flats in St. Michael's Estate, Kallang Airport Estate, Kim Keat Road Estate, Queenstown, Bukit Ho Swee, and MacPherson Road (South), while later on, most families were offered accommodations closer by at Bendemeer Road and Toa Payoh (see Map 3). These flats were available for immediate occupancy.

That is all that is known about these people. No record was kept of how many of these families actually accepted the flats they were offered, or of their record of tenancy, or of what happened to those who did not accept HDB flats.[8] The Welfare Department kept no record of the movements of these individuals.

[8] Though the Resettlement Department had no idea of the whereabouts of these individuals after they were evicted, it did retain the forms filled in by the

A number of settlers in Kallang Basin raised water vegetables and a small amount of livestock. Most settlers in Toa Payoh raised a few livestock and plots of garden vegetables, which yielded five crops a year. Thus these families could supplement their meager food budgets by eating food that they raised themselves. In addition, some could earn extra income from selling surplus crops. The government only considered those families to be genuine farming cases, entitled to a Rural Resettlement plot, if they derived a substantial portion of family income from farming. Of the families resettled from Toa Payoh, 208 were classified as genuine farming cases. As indicated above, only five of those in Kallang Basin were so classified. This left 4,942 in Toa Payoh and Kallang Basin who were only offered HDB flats and who would simply have to cease raising crops and animals. Since no data were collected on the nutritional and economic contributions of this activity, it was impossible to tell what impact this might have on their diets and family budgets.

Rural Resettlement plots are often located on swampland. Furthermore, in dividing this land so that all parcels would contain two acres, the Resettlement Department of the HDB has often ignored topography. A plot might be located on the ridge of a hill, or in swamp entirely surrounded by swamp, or in the line of traffic from other plots. Once a plot is assigned it comes under the jurisdiction of the Primary Production Department, which has no authority to reassign land. So the resettled farmer must make do with what he gets. The policy of furnishing him with a house on the plot was discontinued after it was discovered that some recipients had given up trying to farm and were simply renting out the house; so he must build himself a house, as well as a pond or a water facility.

Then, if he knows how to establish contact with the Primary Production Department, he might call on them for some low cost material for building drains, and for some spraying and innoculations. Though the soil and the problems of re-establishing arable land are probably new to

---

Resettlement Inspectors during the initial survey before resettlement procedures began. These one-page forms recorded: the number of persons occupying the dwelling; their occupations and usage of the premises; their estimated income, ages, schools attended, and the relationship of the members of the household to one another; an indication of the sort of resettlement accommodation to which each family unit would appear to be entitled; the locality and types of premises for which they might indicate a preference; number of square feet of floor space in the structure being demolished; and a listing of other improvements on the property. Once the family was paid its compensation and moved from the property, these forms were stored in Resettlement Department files.

him, they can furnish him with little technical advice. The cost of their fertilizer and plowing has often been more than the market price. Many resettlement farmers interviewed during a 1967–1968 academic survey indicated that they had had no contact with the Primary Production Department. Many were eager for information on the new soil, for they found it less productive than the soil on their former farms and did not know the techniques needed to adapt to it. Many had not yet been able to resume efficient farming.

In this situation it is some consolation to know that one's daughter can receive free medical attention should she become ill or that there is a community center a mile away to walk to for some relaxation after a hard day's work. It is not a great deal of consolation.

Most of those resettled from Kallang Basin and Toa Payoh probably moved to HDB flats, however. The HDB builds its rental flats in five sizes, renting for S$20, S$30, S$40, S$60, and S$100 per month, plus water, gas, electricity, and small maintenance fees. (US$1.00 = S$3.00). All flats contain a kitchen and a bath/lavatory room plus either one, one-and-a-half, two, three, or four additional rooms. Initially the Board built approximately 30 per cent one-room, 40 per cent two-room, and 30 per cent three-room units.[9] In 1965 it introduced the one-and-a-half room flat, especially to accommodate resettlement cases who had been paying next to nothing for rent and could not afford higher rents despite their large families. Around 40 per cent of its construction from 1966 to 1969 was in this and the one-room size. A one-room flat contains 240 square feet of floor space including kitchen, bathroom, and often a terrace; a two-room flat, 425 square feet.[10] The structures housing the flats are normally seven to fifteen stories in height and contain 100–200 flats apiece. These structures are built close together.

In October 1966 the Economic Research Centre of the University of Singapore conducted an island-wide survey.[11] They found that 38.3 per

[9] State of Singapore, Housing and Development Board, *50,000 Up* (Singapore: 1965), 32.

[10] Other sizes are: 1½ rooms, 330 square feet; 3 rooms, 550 square feet; 4 rooms, 780 square feet. See Teh Cheang Wan, "Public Housing," in Ooi Jin-Bee and Chiang Hai Ding, *Modern Singapore* (Singapore: University of Singapore, 1969), 178–179. Some blocks containing larger flats were set aside for sale, so that families of moderate income (not over S$1000 per month) could purchase their own flat. Individuals earning not over $800 a month could purchase such a flat.

[11] Republic of Singapore, Ministry of National Development and Economic Research Centre, University of Singapore, *Singapore Sample Household Survey, 1966, Report 1* (Singapore: GPO, 1967).

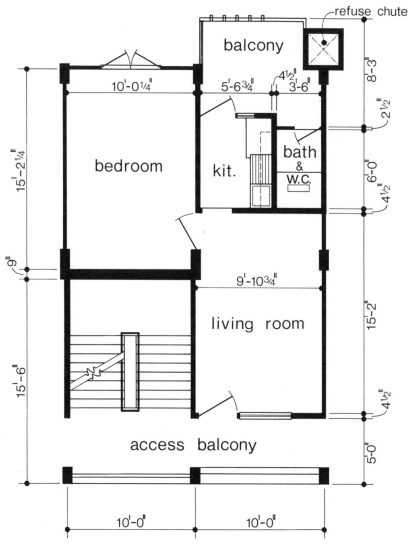

Chart 4. Typical plan of an HDB two-room flat

cent of the island's households, and 34.6 per cent of households living in HDB flats, contained six or more members. It would not be surprising if many families of more than six persons are living in one-room and one-and-a-half room flats under cramped conditions, and at higher rents than they paid in their older, more unsanitary, but often roomier structures in Kallang Basin (see pp. 67–69). In addition, the undetermined number of individuals who did not accept HDB housing would have found it difficult to secure other squatter or low rent accommodation. Squatter and build-your-own areas are noticeably becoming more crowded and restricted in size (e.g., notice Photo 2, No. 22) as urban development programs expand.

In addition, during high tide the water in Kallang Basin rose high enough so that small fishing boats, moored beneath the stilted houses, could be floated out to sea. One could observe these boats in great numbers. The houses and boats are now gone,[12] and there is no record of the present whereabouts or employment of those who used them. It is possible that they did little fishing in the first place, though this is not known either.[13]

Only once was any kind of study conducted on this sort of problem. This was a study by a geographer working on a master's thesis at the University of Singapore.[14] In 1966 he did intensive research into the problems of thirty-six contiguous families scheduled for resettlement in Kallang Basin. There was no way of knowing whether these families were typical, precisely because no similar research was conducted anywhere else in the Republic. Nor is there special reason to believe that they were atypical; their wooden houses and their racial background

[12] According to HDB Resettlement Department records, only eight self-employed fishermen were resettled from Kallang Basin. These went to HDB flats or found their own accommodations.

[13] The few Malays originally resettled to make way for the Jurong Industrial Estate were provided with offshore bungalows that were ideal for fishing. Since that time, there has been no program for resettling fishermen. There are practically no other uninhabited coastal areas available for fishermen, though in 1966 there were 4,001 licensed fishermen in the Republic. Fortunately, many of them can build *kelongs* (wooden platforms) offshore; but boat mooring and transportation will become an increasing problem and expense for them. To cater to fishermen, in February 1968, the Economic Development Board opened a modern fishing facility at Jurong. It consisted of a giant warehouse and a huge concrete pier. It provided no place for small fishermen to moor their boats, however, nor did it provide a nearby place for them to live. In 1966, 59 per cent of the 1,710 licensed fishing boats were small unpowered craft, and 60 per cent of the fishermen were inshore fishermen. These inshore fishermen accounted for 20 per cent of the total annual catch (Republic of Singapore, *Singapore Year Book,* 1966), but for 60 per cent of the breadwinners. As these small fishermen lose their boats, they will have to seek other means of livelihood. The Bedok Reclamation Project (Map 1) cut off a number of fishing settlements from their access to the water.

[14] A report on this research: Ian Buchanan, "The Fringe Dwellers," in SPUR (ed.), *Singapore Planning and Urban Research Group, 1968–1971* (Singapore: Eurasia Press, 1972), 13–23.

were similar to those of settlers all over Kallang Basin. Some of his findings are disturbing, and may indicate the wisdom of finding out whether others may face similar problems.

For instance, he found that 10 of the 36 families contained 9 or more members. These were also the families with the lowest per capita income. Twenty-two of the 36 families had incomes lower than S$42.00 per month per adult (plus S$21.00 for each child). In 16 of the 36 households the food budget was below seventy-five cents per day per adult (plus thirty-eight cents for each child)—the minimum diet standards set by the Singapore medical profession. These families paid either no rent, or rent under S$10.00 per month.

Seventy-five cents per day is a modest food budget by Singapore standards—necessarily involving a high percentage of rice and noodles in the total intake. A family containing a father, mother, and six children, earning S$42.00 per adult and eating on seventy-five cents per day per adult while renting a one-room HDB flat for S$35.00 per month (including utilities and maintenance fees) would still have S$62.50 per month left to spend on other things. If the father did not change jobs and the children had more than half a mile to go to school, at least S$20.00 would be needed for transportation each month (a rather conservative estimate). If each child were given, or allowed to retain (many children work), ten cents per day spending money, this would take an additional S$18.00. Thus, S$24.50 per month—or less than a dollar a day—would be left in the kitty for the wife's expenses, clothing, household goods, entertainment, ceremonies, contingencies, and all other expenses.

Clearly, a third of these 36 families could not afford to move into HDB flats. For another proportion, life in these flats would cause considerable economic and social strain. It might have been relevant to find out whether others—beyond these 36 families—might be facing similar problems, in order to determine what measures might be taken to minimize these strains resulting from physical, but not human, engineering. No such investigation was conducted.

PLANNING FOR INDUSTRY:
INADEQUATE INVESTIGATION

The principal purpose behind the Kallang Basin Reclamation Project was to produce an industrial estate. Yet in the course of budgeting, refining, and implementing the project no attention was given either to the effects of the project upon small marginal industries already in the Basin, or the suitability of the Basin for industry which might move into the project area.

Unfortunately, planned industrial estates do not offer an adequate solution to the problem of resettling cottage industries and workshops. Cottage industry is more than a business; it is a way of life. A small manufacturer's ability to stay in business is often dependent on his operating within structures that are only semipermanent and amid surroundings that are only semiorderly. The cost of building rent and upkeep can be cut to practically nothing. The workers can put up living structures around the premises—or can easily obtain part-time assistance for odd jobs from relatives and neighbors. It is possible to work all night if one wishes, and to hire workers for long hours. (Un)sanitary disposal can be effected informally. It is easy to avoid detection of products which circumvent copyright or labeling laws. Oil lamps can be used to save electricity. One can arrange to borrow transport from friends at odd hours to carry in supplies and carry out products. Living and working areas can be combined. Bulky objects can be spread around on the ground. The profit margin for the proprietor is small, but gross income can help to feed a number of individuals. Competition from such homemade goods can help hold down the cost of living.

Industrial estates are not well suited to this sort of cottage industry. The need to pay rent, electricity and water bills, to dispose of refuse in a sanitary way, to meet health inspections, to abide by labor and labeling laws, and to use regularized procedures for transport can raise production costs enough to make it difficult to compete with those who have the advantages deriving from large-scale production.

Nor is it easy for established cottage industries to relocate. Since 1962 the cost of land has shot up, and since the major emphasis on public housing, it has been difficult to find inexpensive private sites.

In addition, relocation means new problems for workers. For instance, the sawmills in Kallang Basin employed 435 workers; if they were to move twenty miles to Kranji (to be mentioned momentarily), the sawmills would have to provide transport for the workers, or the workers would have to move to the sawmills. Those workers who held more than one job might have to cease doing so as a result. In less extreme cases, where the distance separating the worker from the estate is a mile or so, the cost of transportation to and from work may increase.

The idea of setting aside an uncontrolled resettlement area was tried with ill success at Tanjong Rhu during the 1950's, when the Nicoll Highway was under construction. Resettlement cases—mostly coke dealers and small boat builders—were provided neither with structures and planned amenities, nor with layout restrictions. The result was chaotic.[15] Extra roads had to be built. The land was extended twice. The bay had to be dredged. The project, initially estimated at S$108,000, eventually cost S$700,000, yet ended up containing as many squatters as it did industries, inaccessible to public services, and at an inefficient location for the industries to operate.

At the beginning of the Kallang Basin project, some thought was given to reserving a portion of Kallang Basin for such a free-for-all resettlement area. The final decision was against sponsoring such a project. The following excerpt from a report in HDB files gives some indication of the considerations involved:

far from allowing "shanty" structures, every effort should be made to clear them away from the existing site. Resettlement of industrial cases is wishful thinking. If the industry is a successful one it will of its own accord look for new premises to expand; if it is only marginal or below average in capability and is resettled in the new industrial area it is not likely to prosper but will be occupying valuable land which could be better utilized. In such cases it would be more merciful to pay compensation rather than prolong an inefficient industry.

As resettlement of other areas continued, however, the problem began to grow. In Toa Payoh alone the resettlement officers noted forty-two "minor factory owners" on their forms. In Kallang Basin they reported forty-nine.

Efforts were made to disturb as few industries as possible. An early decision was made to leave intact the large Lee rubber processing plant (see Map 4) with its 1,000 employees. Businesses adjoining streets on the outer edges of the Basin were retained. Some small rattan manufacturers were only marginally in the way and were left intact. The largest ice factory on the island lay squarely in the path of the bulldozers, but it was allowed to continue. Beyond this, most of the existing factories lying in the path of reclamation were removed. The sawmills were the most noticeable of these; it was felt that their continued presence would

[15] Asokam Damu, "Problems of Resettlement in Singapore, as Illustrated by the Tanjong Rhu Resettlement Scheme" (Honors thesis, Department of Geography, University of Singapore, 1962/63).

cause undue congestion. A special resettlement site was provided for them at Kranji, in Woodlands (see Map 1); as of January 1970 only three of them had moved to this site.

Other manufacturers being removed by reclamation were entitled to apply to the HDB or Economic Development Board for resettlement sites. As of March 16, 1966, only ten industries had done so (three engineering firms, an engine and machine repair shop, a manufacturer of polythene plastic, a balachan factory, a tire retreading shop, a boatbuilder, a paint manufacturer, and a timber merchant).

On June 29, 1965—more than a year after reclamation had commenced—the HDB and the Economic Development Board entered into their first liaison over these industrial resettlement problems by holding a meeting to discuss them. At this and a subsequent meeting they discussed the notion of setting aside forty acres east of Bendemeer Road for industrial resettlement, and of surveying the industries which might be affected by resettlement.

Nothing ever came of this resettlement scheme. But the proposal to conduct a survey of affected enterprises soon received some invigoration. On September 29, 1965, the Permanent Secretary of National Development wrote to the Chief Executive Officer of the HDB to inform him that the Government had approved the Board's application to acquire more land in Kallang Basin.[16] He suggested, however, that a committee should be set up to study the physical conditions and economic viability of each factory being displaced by reclamation and urban development schemes. The committee should be chaired by a representative from the Ministry of Law. The Secretary should be the Lands Manager or an Administrative Officer of the HDB. It should include a representative from the Economic Development Board and from the Ministry of National Development.

The short history of this committee illustrates how little was known about or could be done for those who were displaced.

On June 27, 1966, the Committee to Study the Physical Condition and Economic Viability of Each Factory in Kallang Basin met in the office of the Commissioner of Lands, who was chairman of the committee. At this meeting the HDB Lands Manager presented the list of the ten industries which had applied for resettlement sites within Kallang Basin as of March 16, 1966. There was considerable discussion about

[16] See Chapter IV. On May 27, 1965, the Chief Architect of the HDB had written to the Permanent Secretary of National Development indicating that factory land below the high tide line must be acquired.

the desirability of allowing a large sago (tapioca) factory, temporarily halted by Confrontation with Indonesia (which supplies sago), to retain its site. It was decided that there should be a survey of all the factories within Kallang Basin. The number of employees, capital, exports, and other data about each industry in the area should be recorded. At the second meeting of the committee, held on August 24, 1966,

it was agreed that the Light Industries Services Unit (EDB) representative should conduct a survey to determine the number of factories presently operating in Kallang Basin, and subsequently submit a recommendation to the Committee on the type of industry to be accommodated within the industrial area together with a note recommending whether the area presently occupied by such industries required any adjustment. The Committee considered that certain factories outside the Basin may have to be accommodated within the industrial area now being prepared in the Basin.[17]

On September 5, 1966, the Light Industries Services Unit presented its survey. It had contacted all industries within the Basin, both on land currently scheduled for acquisition and on land not yet so scheduled, and had recorded the name of the company, nature of manufacture (e.g., "timber furniture," "tannery," "bolts, and nuts," "motor workshop," "making of concrete bars"), estimated number of laborers, and a one-to-nine-word general comment about the business. It found 103 factories employing 2,828 persons (excluding the rubber processing plant). Considering the fact that by mid-1966 over 1,000 families had been displaced from Kallang Basin, it is likely that a number of cottage and family industries had already been evicted by the time of this survey.

The minutes of the next three meetings of the committee may be summarized as follows:

September 14, 1966. It was decided that it would be difficult to do a more comprehensive survey of existing industries until there was a factory layout for future factories. It was decided to allow the sago factory to remain if it could resume production after Confrontation. A representative from Urban Renewal should be invited to the next meeting, since they probably had information on the kinds of industries going into Kallang Basin Estates.[18]

---

[17] The mimeographed minutes of these meetings, from which this quote is extracted, can probably be obtained by writing the Light Industries Services Unit of the Economic Development Board.

[18] On September 20, 1966, the Office of the Permanent Secretary of National Development wrote to the Architect/Planner of Urban Renewal inviting him to attend the next meeting of the committee.

October 5, 1966. Two junior representatives from Urban Renewal presented the committee with the road plans, phasing of resettlement, and future zoning for the Basin.

October 12, 1966. The problem of the sago factory was discussed at length and it was decided to give it nine more months to prove its viability to the Economic Planning Unit. It was also decided that the ice factory and a rattan factory should be permitted to remain.

This committee, in short, accomplished nothing, except to review the cases of a handful of borderline industries. Still lacking any information about the problem, the HDB nonetheless decided to take action. In 1966 it constructed a seven-story flatted factory behind the Bendemeer Road Estate in Kallang Basin. The floor space was divided into areas of 500, 1,000, and 1,500 square feet, to be rented at subsidized rents of S$150–S$400 per month. The experiment was not a success. Occupants found it difficult to pay rents, spread their working materials around the halls, and created traffic congestion below. In 1968 the Board decided to sell this flatted factory to the Economic Development Board and to build factory structures for resettlement cases to the north of Geylang Road. By January 1970 seventy-six small industries resettled from a variety of urban redevelopment schemes occupied these structures. Hence it was clear that some portion of the removed industries were operating at some percentage of their former capacity. It is, of course, not clear what these percentages are.

BROAD PLANNING: UNASKED
AND UNANSWERED QUESTIONS

We have now looked at people who draw up budgets, resettle families and businesses, acquire land, reclaim swamps, and lay out industrial and housing estates. Yet who can take a broader view? Who can link these disparate bureaucratic activities with a guiding vision?

The Architect/Planner of Urban Renewal was, of course, given the assignment of providing a comprehensive development plan for Kallang Basin, including existing land, reclaimed land, and land adjoining the Renewal Precinct N1.

Yet one gets the distinct impression that there was no comprehensiveness about the planning of the area. Take the matter of choosing sites for the many public housing estates located in the vicinity of Kallang Basin (see Map 3). *Toa Payoh,* "the most fertile land on the island" and "an important factor in the Singapore food supply" was originally envisaged as a farming reserve. The thought of making it a housing estate came only when the Singapore Improvement Trust was under pressure to come up with a large tract of land for this purpose. *Guillemard Road Estate,* a former airport, was public land unencumbered by squatters. *St. Michael's Estate,* as a former wireless receiving station, was also public land unencumbered by squatters. The idea of placing public housing in *Kallang Basin* emerged as the HDB began reclamation. These were separate decisions, spread over time, based on expeditiousness, unrelated to one another.

Immediately to the south of Kallang Basin, the land along the shore line has been set aside as urban renewal area. This, too, is being planned in a piecemeal fashion. The entire urban renewal area has been divided into parcels, each to be planned separately. The first of these parcels to be planned—S1 and N1—were chosen largely on the basis that the State owned more land there than in the other parcels.[19] The plan for N1, adjoining Kallang Basin, called for increasing its density from 260 to 500 persons per acre—mixing together public housing, hotels, and other structures.

The area immediately surrounding Kallang Basin contained well over a third of the island's population in 1966 (see Map 3). These unrelated decisions will help to ensure that this condition continues. No one has asked or sought the answers to the questions as to how this cramped and reshuffled populace reacts to its physical condition.

Given this density and rate of building, the need for some comprehensive traffic planning would seem obvious. The Planning Department first suggested this in September 1960, in connection with the Bendemeer Road Industrial Estate. It was decided to proceed with the estate and to put off planning the comprehensive road system until later. It was later decided to proceed with the entire Toa Payoh, Kallang Basin, and N1 projects, while still deferring a decision on a comprehensive

[19] In the Central Area (roughly, the first three categories of built-up land on Map 2), 50 per cent of the land is freehold or 999 year lease; 25 per cent is owned by the state, and 25 per cent is held on leases that will revert to the city by the end of the century. Much of the state land is confined to N1 and S1, to the "Golden Mile," and to Fort Canning Hill (the former three being the initial phases of Urban Renewal). Lee Weng Yon, "Urban Renewal in Singapore," Republic of Singapore, State and City Planning, *Notes for Consultant Briefing at Node One in the Plan of Operations* (Singapore: GPO, 1967). S1 appears on Photo 2 (No. 7) and Map 3 (No. 6).

road plan. Especially lacking was any plan for linking this crowded section of the city together internally, or with the downtown and harbor areas.

Singapore is located near the equator, and gets frequent heavy rains that cause flooding. A human interest story in connection with the Kallang Basin project raises a question or two about the comprehensiveness of drainage planning as well.

Back in June 1961, while Kallang reclamation proposals were tenuous, the Senior Civil Engineer of the HDB and the Chief Engineer (Bridges and Drains) of the Public Works Department got together and agreed on a drainage plan for Kallang Basin. After the UN expert's report of July 1962 (Chapter IV) there was apparently further liaison between these two regarding the drainage plan.[20] The plan that they drew up involved an important decision: that access to the Basin should be by roads and not by waterways. Unlike most earlier proposals, this river plan provided neither for canals nor for space for extensive wharfage. Its details were apparently worked out without consultation with the Economic Development Board, Planning Department, or harbor authorities.

Presumably agreement was reached during these meetings. Two years later, on October 1, 1964, tenders were called for dredging the Kallang and Whompoe River channels in the Kallang Basin. Two days after this the Senior Executive Engineer of the Public Works Department wrote to the HDB's Senior Civil Engineer, saying that after reading the call for tenders in the newspaper he realized that his office had supplied drainage canal sizes which were too small; he sent revised drawings. On October 16—two days after tenders were closed—a reply came back. It said that since this information had been received after tenders had been called it was too late to make revisions. This ended the matter.

It is conceivable that the question of Kallang Basin drainage might be raised again in the future, however. The Kallang and Whompoe Rivers handle much of the drainage from central portions of the island—and not too efficiently. In the 1950's an engineer named Pelton suggested diverting much of the central drainage to the west. In a piecemeal fashion the government is doing this, while at the same time widening and

[20] On March 18, 1963, the Chief Engineer (Bridges and Drains) of the PWD commented that the drainage sections proposed by the UN expert's report seemed excessively large by his standards.

relining some of the channels headed toward the Kallang Basin.[21] One would hope that the coordination goes more smoothly this time.

As these projects reached completion the agencies knew that the land was clear and earth-filled, the housing estates were filling up—many with resettlement cases—and factories were occupying the new land and buildings provided for them. Little else was known. Many questions remained unasked and unanswered. One searches in vain for men with the broader vision, who are to infuse the organizational processes with dreams, so that they may be transcribed into the ebb and flow of life.

[21] See Wong Poh Poh, "The Changing Landscapes of Singapore Island," in Ooi and Chiang, op. cit., 37–40.

PART THREE

THE SOCIAL ENVIRONMENT OF PLANNING

CHAPTER VI

Land-Use Planning vs.
Politics in Singapore

> The Central Area amounts to 1,700 acres or 1.2 per cent of the total land area of the Republic. Within this area live one-quarter of the total population of Singapore. Within this area too, are the city slums. Because of its strategic location and therefore immense real estate value, all developments on this land will have an effect on Singapore and conversely developments outside the Central Area will also have direct bearing on it.
>
> Alan F. C. Choe [1]

The question of who controls which land, and how this land is to be developed, is a central one in politics. It is especially crucial in urban politics.

A person reading the first two parts of this book cannot escape one obvious conclusion: Land-use decisions by public agencies are changing the entire face of Singapore island and affecting Singapore's way of life.

These decisions do not emerge from a vacuum or in an entirely random manner. They are the outputs of a political process and an approach to decision-making. I have suggested that this approach to decision-making is politically astute, as well as fiscally sound and administratively convenient. It produces speedy results. But there is little hard evidence that it has long-term merits for solving basic human problems or will produce an overall land use pattern which fits together. Land-use decisions may be popular, and easy to finance and to administer. At the same time, they may serve to segregate social strata rather than unite them. They may isolate the best resources in the hands of a few people and destroy cultural traditions without replacing them with new ones. They may narrow the occupational choices of large numbers

---

[1] Alan F. C. Choe, "Urban Renewal," in Ooi Jin-Bee and Chiang Hai Ding, *Modern Singapore* (Singapore: University of Singapore, 1969), 164. Mr. Choe is Head (formerly, Architect/Planner) of the HDB's Urban Renewal Department. The area he refers to includes virtually all of the built-up areas on Map 2, plus most of the white areas out to Outram Road and Kallang Basin.

of people, degenerate people's diets, reduce the options for leisure time, create congestion and incessant noise, and in other ways adversely affect the tone and substance of life.

Part Three of this book argues that politically astute, fiscally sound, and administratively convenient activities are not necessarily beneficial to human beings. The interests of those who control resources, skills, and administrative and political capabilities often run counter to what is needed to cater to the needs of people. By enhancing the power of these individuals, massive urban development and industrialization programs may be weakening government's ability to serve human needs, rather than strengthening it as is commonly assumed. Only if means can be found to broaden the power of those who do *not* control resources, skills, and administrative and political capabilities, can programs be made to enhance the tone and substance of the lives of broad masses of the populace. And only with some fundamental changes in current patterns of industrialization and urban growth can one hope to broaden that power to any significant degree.

This chapter applies the above argument to human problems arising from land-use planning in Singapore. The two chapters that follow apply it to additional problems and other nations and cities. The last chapter seeks out some means to avoid these problems.

THE ESTABLISHED APPROACH
TO LAND USE

While the Singapore government has taken a project-by-project approach to land use, a pattern has emerged. The old city is being razed, section by section, to make way for new high-rise commercial structures, middle class apartment buildings, and hotels. Clustered around this are high-rise public housing estates. The remaining shore lines of the island are becoming occupied with industrial estates and military installations, plus a few scattered public housing estates. Meanwhile, the interior portions of the island are filling with middle class duplex housing developments, constructed by private builders. Hills are continuously leveled to fill swamps and shore lines.

This pattern assures large investors, industrialists, and traders of places and projects for investing their money. Many kinds of modern skills are brought into play. The bureaucracy has a great deal to do. The government can rearrange the populace (especially in areas with high concentrations of political opponents) and give tangible evidence that it is benefiting the public—without moving people far from the city or acquiring a lot of land.

To those who hold political power this appears to be an ideal way to reduce tensions stemming from race, language, and class. Areas where single races lived in isolation can be cleared and replaced with new multiracial housing. Multiracial bilingual schools can be set up where all children learn the English language as a common *lingua franca*. Since public housing is located close to private housing, both rich and poor can shop and attend school together. Much of the building directly or indirectly affects the poor—giving them a feel of having a share in the operations of the government. Industrialization will create new jobs. If all races can become modernized, they may care less about their racial differences.

Still, there is some evidence that this approach to land use may not be satisfying, as effectively as it should, many wants and needs of people.

Singapore's greatest difficulties concern unemployment and economic growth. Professor Harry T. Oshima [2] calculates that from 1956 to 1965 Singapore was able to induce a growth rate in formal reported employment of only 1.5 per cent (6,000–10,000 jobs a year) at a time when the labor force was increasing at a rate of 2.2 per cent a year.[3]

The 1966 Sample Household Survey found that in the 1967–1971 period there would be 60,000 persons reaching working age (fifteen years old) each year as opposed to 50,000 in the previous five-year period.[4] This would raise the growth rate in the labor force to 3.5 per cent or 4.3 per cent. Oshima had estimated that 308,000 new jobs would have to be created between 1967 and 1977 to compensate for this—not

---

[2] Harry T. Oshima, "Growth and Unemployment in Singapore," *The Malayan Economic Review*, 12 (October 1967), 32–58.

[3] The 1966 Sample Survey (see footnote 4) estimated 443,475 "economically active" males (31,534 currently unemployed) and 133,180 "economically active" females (21,096 currently unemployed), out of a total population of 1,929,733, only 56.5 per cent of which is over fifteen. Considerable underemployment is also indicated. Ooi Jin-Bee indicates that 63,000 were registered at the Employment Exchange in December 1968. Ooi Jin-Bee, "Singapore: The Balance Sheet," in Ooi Jin-Bee and Chiang Hai Ding, *op cit.*, 6.

[4] Republic of Singapore, Ministry of National Development and Economic Research Centre, University of Singapore, *Singapore Sample Household Survey, 1966, Report No. 1, Tables Relating to Population and Housing,* (Singapore: GPO), 87.

to mention at least 42,000 more to compensate for British withdrawal.[5] He also estimated that the annual economic growth rate would have to rise from the 6 to 8 per cent experienced between 1956 and 1966, to 17.2 per cent.

Singapore's pattern of land use may not be contributing to the solution of this problem.

Twenty-two per cent of gross capital formation in Singapore, Oshima points out, has been concentrated on dwellings. This has helped keep construction workers employed. However, Oshima argues that "to generate $1 of income, dwelling investments require in the neighborhood of seven times more investment than other forms of investment." The construction program may be contributing more to the cost of living—both by raising rent and transportation costs and by increasing the demand for consumer goods, which one is tempted to own when living in a sturdier structure—than it is to the wallet of the workman.

Professor Oshima reports that between 1963 and 1966 Singapore had around 12,300 firms engaged in some form of manufacture. About 300 of these had 30 or more employees, while 11,000 had fewer than five. Two-thirds of the employment in manufacturing was in the 12,000 firms with fewer than 30 employees. Maps 1 and 4 indicate the location of most workshops and factories. A comparison of these with Maps 3 and 5 reveals that many of the smaller firms stand on land slated for public housing, modern industrial estates, or urban renewal. I have indicated in Chapter V the difficulties of resuscitating most of these marginal industries once they are displaced by development projects. So in carrying out its redevelopment programs the government will also be demolishing an unknown portion of the gross national product and of available jobs. Between 1965 and 1967 the exports from nonpioneer industries suffered a decline from S$260 million to S$194 million.[6] One wonders the role which the redevelopment programs might have played in this decline.

The same applies to small retail establishments. Photo 5 illustrates the contrast in atmospheres between the urban renewal area and the for-

---

[5] In January 1968 (after Oshima's article) the government of Great Britain announced its decision to withdraw its armed forces from Singapore by 1971, thus taking away 10 per cent to 15 per cent of the gross national product and at least 42,000 jobs for Singaporeans (Ooi and Chiang, *op. cit.*) estimated to derive from the British presence.

[6] Far Eastern Economic Review, *1969 Yearbook,* Hong Kong.

mer city. Many of the buildings in North Precinct 1 contained retail businesses before urban renewal. These businesses may have been marginal, but they served the function of providing considerable employment and keeping down the prices on consumer goods. The new urban renewal areas, with their higher overhead costs and fewer ground-floor and small rental spaces, will probably be able to rehouse only a small percentage of these businesses.

I have already noted the disrupted livelihood of fishermen when fishing villages are destroyed in the wake of development projects.[7]

The tourism industry, too, may be affected. Compared to other stops on the Asian circuit, Singapore offers few spots of natural scenic beauty. Many of the more scenic hills have fallen victim to the bulldozer gathering earth-fill material. The old city is Singapore's principal point of interest. As it gives ground to high-rise structures, there will be less and less of it to see. New tourist attractions are being readied.[8] It may be difficult to make them unique enough to overcome the disability of a city that is not itself interesting.

Little is known about how the elimination of former farmlands—or backyard fruits, vegetables, and livestock—might affect the economy or family nutrition. Little is known about how the continued concentration of the growing population on the southern tip of the island might affect social overhead costs, or family budgets, or the individual's sense of group identity. Little is known about how much new business, or how many new jobs, the building program might generate—or how many jobs and businesses it will destroy.

There are signs that Singapore may create the 350,000 jobs it needs

[7] Chapter V, p. 118. In the case of the Bedok Reclamation Project (see Map 1) there was not even resettlement provided for fishing villages whose shore line was filled by the reclamation.

[8] Jurong Bird Park, opened in January 1971, contains 8,000 birds from around the world and an 80-foot man-made waterfall on 50 acres. Seven-hundred-acre Sentosa Island just off Singapore is being transformed into a resort area containing an 18-hole seaside golf course, a swimming lagoon, maritime museums (including a fort with the famous guns fixed toward the sea), an aquatic park with coral reefs and marineland shows, local handicraft centers and tourist shops, fishing villages, discotheques, underwater and treetop restaurants, tourist chalets and bungalows (to compete with the 68 tourist hotels and 13,000 hotel rooms already available on the island by 1972), and an amphitheater for cultural performances. Transport will be entirely by horse carriages—or by monorail, with a cable car connecting the island with Singapore. The scheme would seem to hold great promise for attracting tourists. See Nancy Duncan, "If It's Not Here, We'll Make It!", *Far Eastern Economic Review*, 73 (August 7, 1971), 37–38.

between 1967 and 1977 for new workers entering the job market. Between 1959 and 1966 the number of persons employed by the entire manufacturing sector grew from 25,600 to only 52,800.[9] By December 1968 this figure had jumped to 72,227.[10] The years 1969–1971 created spectacular expansion in new industry, as investment funds poured in from companies abroad. By March 31, 1969, the estimate of those employed in industry expanded to 100,420.[11] At the end of that year, with official figures yet unpublished, the Economic Research Unit was projecting that the figure for those employed in industry had reached 150,000.[12] In addition, a universal military training law has been put into effect, with over a quarter of the national budget now devoted to defense spending. Singapore has become the center for oil exploration in the oceans of Southeast Asia. This will probably produce a number of jobs for Singaporeans.[13] If this trend continues, new jobs will more than replace jobs destroyed and compensate for population growth. The

[9] Goh Chok Tong, "Industrial Growth, 1959–66," in Ooi and Chiang, *op. cit.*, 135, 139, 142.

[10] Republic of Singapore, *Monthly Digest of Statistics,* 8 (December 1969).

[11] *Ibid. Fortune,* August 15, 1969, reported 25,000 workers in new electronics firms alone.

[12] The two fastest-growing industrial estates in this period were Jurong and Kallang Basin. The Jurong Town Corporation estimated in December 1966 that the new structures in Kallang Basin contained factories employing 6,000 persons. Unofficial government estimates late in 1969 placed the number of workers at Jurong at 24,000 (vs. 9,200 in 1967). There is a strong desire on the part of bureaucracy to demonstrate rapid growth in industrial employment.

[13] The existence of oil in these oceans has been known for about twenty years, but the information remained a tightly kept secret. Small oil operations were begun in the 1960's off Indonesia and Borneo. In 1969, with increasing regional political stability, oilmen began to arrive in Singapore to start further explorations. At a meeting in Singapore in April 1970, David Rockefeller of Chase Manhattan Bank predicted oil company investment of US $35 billion in the region over the ensuing twelve years. Henry S. Hayward reported in the February 18, 1971, *Christian Science Monitor* the presence of some 6,000 to 7,000 Americans residing in Singapore at that time—many of them involved in the oil explorations. Many of the oil rigs used in drilling are made and/or fitted in Singapore. Early in 1971, Esso opened a large addition to its Singapore refinery. The May 22, 1970, issue of the German periodical *Weltwoche* quoted geologist Joachim Joesten, who has been exploring these oceans for fifteen years, as saying that the combined output from the Southeast Asian seas could reach 400 million barrels a day—more than is now produced in the entire Western world. The low sulfur content of this oil makes it doubly attractive. The continuing influx of personnel, material, and capital for this venture would seem to indicate at least some optimism by the oil companies. Singapore continues to build more hotels, some of which house this personnel.

percentage of the populace who are middle class will increase, and there may be room for wage increases for the worker.[14]

Were this growth combined with a land-use program that destroyed fewer initial sources of income and affected the cost of living less, these positive trends might be enhanced even further. Should there be a slow-down in industrial growth due to world economic conditions, a land-use program that combines industrialization with preservation of older sources of income might appear as a real necessity.

Class, language, and racial rifts may also be exacerbated by the land use program.

The sight of more people being crowded together into small flats built at high density, while middle class semidetached duplexes cover sprawling areas, may eventually grow distasteful to the poor, especially if social mobility is limited to only a few. (Almost three-quarters of a million people now live in public housing estates covering only 2.2 square miles.) [15] They may also come to miss, during periods of recession, the economic security which backyard fruits, vegetables, and livestock offered them. If the new industrial estates do not provide adequate employment to everyone, the loss of the old shack industries may be resented. Resentment may also arise as sites for the small merchants—especially the street peddlers—diminish. These resentments could become tinder for the political incendiary of the future.

There may also be fewer everyday contacts between the social classes than in the past. The old city found millionaire and pauper living side by side and sharing in cultural organizations, ceremonies, and family businesses. Rich and poor could get to know one another, talk to one another, and help one another out on a personal basis. This undoubtedly had a tempering effect on class antagonisms—and helped the wealthy keep their ears open and respond promptly and appropriately to criticism which flared up. This lever of social control will be missing

[14] The economic advance is, however, being counterbalanced by inflation. Hence higher wages and salaries may not provide a passport into the middle class or even purchase a great deal more than previous incomes. The price of duplexes, for instance, has risen markedly, along with private rents; the government has decided to sell HDB flats even to individuals earning S$1500 a month (vs. S$800 earlier; see Chapter V, footnote 10) to offset this trend. Food, clothing, and automotive costs have also been rising.

[15] In 1968, 1.7 million persons, or 85 per cent of the population, lived on 28 square miles of the 224-square-mile island. Almost three-quarters of a million people lived in public housing flats occupying 2.2 square miles. Ooi, *op. cit.*, 6. See also Map 3.

in the future. Millionaires do not frequent housing estates. Today's modern factory is far more impersonal than the old business in which the proprietor knew and worked among his employees. The social classes even in schools are becoming more segregated, as school buildings are constructed as integral parts of housing estates.

The language issue could also re-emerge in a new form. The public housing estates will contain high concentrations of Chinese-speakers, while the sprawling semidetached duplexes will primarily house English-speakers. Instead of increasing contact between English-speakers and non-English-speakers, the land-use program may be decreasing it. Furthermore, a child living in a public housing estate and studying in an English-stream school will not hear as much polished English spoken outside school as will the middle class child. Slower acquisition of English (not to mention the sheer noise level in housing estates, and the limited cultural stimuli for learning) could affect his performance in his schoolwork and decrease his chances of going on for higher studies. Those English-stream housing estate students who complete higher studies are likely to move on to associate primarily with those in a different social milieu. Those English-stream students who do not go to a university are more likely to identify and associate with fellow high school graduates in the housing estates—whether English- or Chinese-stream —than with university graduates. They may speak English at work, but may have little empathy with (and perhaps some jealousy of) their managers. Meanwhile, Tamil-, Malay-, and Chinese-speaking unskilled workers may find little reason to associate with any of these groups, or among themselves. Hence the danger of social and political polarization involving language continues.

Singapore is famous for its many stories of men who literally moved from rags to riches—trishaw peddler to millionaire. One wonders how many such stories there will be in the future, and whether the mobility ladder is actually improving.

Nor does proximity of races automatically build neighborliness. When you destroy an old ethnic neighborhood environment, and move individuals to mass-produced high-rise public housing blocks, they do not necessarily associate with their neighbors. They may not like their neighbors, and they may simply feel alienated and alone in the new surroundings. Young people are likely to seek out friends among peers. But these peers may well be members of their own race. If they choose to have fights with members of other races, they can do so away from the eyes and knowledge of their parents. When racial strife, or conflict between generations, erupts, it will be less easy to cool by negotiations with the leaders of various ethnic blocs. The antagonists will have vanished into thousands of separate cubby holes.

I am about to show that the urban redevelopment program is being revised so as to deal somewhat with dangers such as these, but I will argue that, in a fundamental sense, these dangers cannot be avoided so long as urban redevelopment continues.

AN ALTERNATIVE APPROACH TO LAND USE

Two major consultant analyses—the Lorange Report and the Abrams/Kobe/Koenigsberger Report—have advocated land uses for the island unlike those currently in process. Had their approach to planning been followed, Singapore would be a much different city than it is today. Whether it would be a *better* city the readers, or preferably, teams of researchers, need to judge for themselves. Yet, I maintain that this question is purely academic. The political structure could not support the professional planner's approach to urban development.

In February 1962, Erik E. Lorange, a United Nations consultant, arrived in Singapore. He conducted a six-month study of the potentials for urban renewal in Singapore. At the end of his stay he issued a report.[16]

The principal distinction between this report and the policy subsequently pursued lies in its recommendation that the old city (see Map 2) be rehabilitated rather than demolished. Instead of negatively viewing the old city as a slum, Lorange looked upon it more positively as the location of many improvable businesses and buildings. Some buildings needed demolishing. But (after some excess inhabitants moved to housing estates) most could be subjected to *code enforcement,* to induce the owners to widen shop frontages and make selective repairs on their buildings. He suggested that the N1 area (see Photo 5 and Map 5) would be a good place to start, since it was in a generally better state of repair than some of the other areas in the old city, much of its land was state owned, and there were many interesting small businesses located

[16] See Tan Jake-Hooi, "The Intentions of the Master Plan and Its Amendments; the Lorange Advice, Advice by the U.N. Experts' Mission, the Department Plan," in Republic of Singapore, State and City Planning, *Notes for Consultative Briefing at Node One in the Plan of Operations* (Singapore: GPO, 1967).

here. (It must have been with some chagrin that Mr. Lorange later learned of the wholesale demolition of the N1 district to make way for the first phase of "urban renewal"!) He advocated that those taller buildings needed for administration, civic, and cultural purposes be confined south of the Singapore River, in an enlarged central business district (see Map 2 and Photo 1). He called for some segregation of vehicles from pedestrians, and for multistory car parks. He also emphasized the need for a regional land-use plan for the whole of Singapore Island and Southern Johore, including an integrated traffic plan.

Such a plan was soon forthcoming. In June 1963 a second United Nations consultant group arrived. It consisted of three eminent authorities on city planning: Charles Abrams of Columbia University, Otto Koenigsberger of the Architectural Association in London, and Susumu Kobe of Japan. In November 1963 they issued their report.[17]

Their plan had three parameters: a guiding concept, proposals for action programs, and a recommendation for performance standards.

The guiding concept foresaw *a ring of settlements*—self-contained except for employment—around the island. These would be connected by a fast pan-island circular freeway, ferry services, and a monorail.

Implementation would be carried out in a series of action programs. Each settlement would be planned as a unit under an action program, with all aspects of planning for the settlement being carried out in tandem. All public and private agencies involved in designing the particular settlement could get together to formulate the action program— fixing objectives and agreeing on timing and division of responsibilities in implementation.

To give coherence to the detailed planning of these disparate action programs, the report suggested that performance standards for privacy, safety, comfort, lighting, ventilation, protection from noise, housing design, and ease of transport be established. All public and private builders would be required to adhere to these performance standards. They would prevent social and economic segregation; ensure proximity of houses to the sea, open country, shops, schools, and places of work; and promote other such social and economic objectives.

The team was most emphatic that urban renewal should not mean the

[17] *Growth and Urban Renewal in Singapore* (New York: 1963). Report prepared for the Government of Singapore by Charles Abrams, Susumu Kobe, and Otto Koenigsberger, appointed under the United Nations Technical Assistance Department of Economic and Social Affairs.

wholesale demolition of structures. They spoke of conservation, rehabilitation, and rebuilding, and stressed that urban renewal should form part of an overall plan for the island. They also suggested lowering certain rent controls and property taxes to encourage improvements on private property.

Many specific recommendations contained in the report have subsequently been adopted. Nonetheless, the principal suggestion—that of *scattering self-contained communities around the island while leaving the general features of the original city intact*—has until recently been ignored. Hence it is of interest to explore the report's rationale for this suggestion.

The basic ideas are summed up in this paragraph on page 13:

A Guiding Concept is needed to ensure that many separately planned Action Programmes grow into a coherent pattern. The Guiding Concept we have recommended for Singapore emerges from the Performance Standards and principles we have recommended for future planning. The shape of the island, the climactic advantages of life close to the sea shore, the grouping of houses into settlements of diverse character and size, the need to reserve the center of the island for other essential urban needs, and the utilization of the sea for cheap mass transit lead to the concept of ring or necklace settlements around the perimeter of the island.

The team suggested that all new settlements be located within a mile of the sea or of open country. The center of the island should be left for water collection, intensive agriculture and horticulture, recreation in hills and forests, and fast cross-island traffic. Hills should not be removed. Level high ground would be ideal for building low-cost, high-rise buildings and would provide inexpensive drainage. Sloping high ground allows attractive solutions for higher-cost housing. Reclaimed marshland would be ideal for factories and businesses, which could afford the extra cost and need access to the water.

Social segregation, they urged, should be avoided. Each new settlement should offer employment opportunities for all—rich, middle class, and poor—in industries, trade, administration, professions, and services.

Still, many people would have to commute to the center of the city. Hence the highest priority should be given to an urban transport system. This would consist in part of a limited-access freeway around the island, with access points at least one and one half miles apart. The freeway would run on the landward side of the new settlements. Some overpasses downtown would help speed traffic to the parking areas. In addition, coastal settlements would be served by waterbuses, preferably hydrofoil, which would carry two hundred passengers and their cycles and scooters. A monorail system would also connect some of the most populous centers. Transfer tickets, synchronized timetables, and a carefully planned route network might further speed up commuting.

The report commented that "it is evident that urban renewal cannot cure the malaise of overcrowding unless it is made possible even for low income earners to live further afield and reach the Central Business District cheaply and quickly." It pointed to the "futility of any attempt to solve urban renewal problems in isolation from the settlement, employment, traffic and transport problems of the whole island."

Within this context, the United Nations mission "rejected the idea of wholesale demolition of large quarters" of the old city.

This decision was motivated primarily by the desire to minimize the social upheaval and the suffering that would result from the dislocation of large numbers of people and business undertakings. It is based also on the recognition of the value and attraction of many of the existing shop houses and the way of living, working, and trading that produced this particularly Singapore type of architecture.

"Every big city," they said, "needs escape hatches from sameness and order, and areas like Chinatown can emerge into important examples if they are treated with something more subtle than the steam shovel."

If this or some similar approach to land use were not taken, the mission had a pessimistic warning. If the city simply continued to grow outward from the center, by 1984 it would become a "concrete jungle," or "a jumble of little semi-detached houses in their own gardens, interspersed by groups of HDB flats and separated from each other and the rest of the world by an intricate network of traffic jams." "We must beware of the bulldozer 'addicts' who are straining to flatten out every hill, fill in every valley, and cover the resulting flat desert with a dull network of roads, factory sheds, and regimented blocks of houses."

These suggestions have been frequently criticized by Singapore administrators, who argue that Singapore is too small an island for such extravagant use of land and that the nation is too poor for such expensive planning.

Such criticisms do not stand up under critical examination.

Singapore's projected population for the year 2000 is 4,750,000. There is room for this many people.

Suppose—as an extremely unlikely case—that all the 4,072 families resettled from Toa Payoh (Map 5) had been offered resettlement plots identical in size to those they had occupied and farmed in Toa Payoh (or had simply been left to farm Toa Payoh). Suppose further that all the land outside the cordon surrounding the city on Map 3 were occupied at this same intensity (4,000 families, or approximately 25,000 persons, per square mile), and the area inside the cordon stayed at approximately the same density as before. There would still be room for 4,500,000 persons on the island, along with considerable agriculture and industry.

In fact, if every family on the island were allotted a 30 x 50 foot lot to build a single-story dwelling—complete with chickens, trees, and garden—10 million persons could still be accommodated within 150 of Singapore's 224 square miles—including streets.[18]

Yet the residential densities envisaged by the United Nations mission were nowhere near as low as these.

With regard to cost, the mission's report argued that "the savings that are possible through careful timing will outweigh many times the higher overheads caused by the strengthening of the research, planning, and design establishments necessary for the programme of action." Planners generally argue that carefully coordinated planning saves money. There is no reason to believe that this would not be the case in Singapore. Nor were the structures in the new settlements envisaged as being more elaborate than those currently being constructed.

Another objection to the mission's proposed land use concerned time. New settlements of this type must be carefully staged. Land must be acquired. Until the transport network was ready and some businesses established, people could not be expected to move to outlying homes. Highway construction takes longer than building construction. The housing shortage would fester while all this elaborate planning progressed.

This is probably not a valid argument either. The mission suggested that the first New Town be established at Jurong, where the new industrial estate was already under construction. They suggested that two passenger transport companies—one for road and one for sea—be established immediately to handle traffic until the pan-island freeway was complete and until jobs were created at Jurong itself. Work could begin immediately on streets, sewers, parks, stores, public housing, and 5,000

[18] See Hans Blumenfeld, "The Modern Metropolis," *Scientific American*, 213 (September 1965), 70, for this calculation.

units a year of private housing. An emphasis would be made on bringing in people from several class levels. The report suggested a target population for Jurong of 200,000 in 10 to 15 years.

Instead of this, the government chose to concentrate all of its efforts at Jurong upon land clearance and the creation of industrial water, sewerage, and buildings. It built little housing there, arguing that it was difficult to attract people to live this far from the city.

It is questionable that construction of the new town at Jurong would have taken longer or cost more than construction of the housing estates that were built closer to the center of the city. It would, however, have demanded that the government devote a portion of resources and skills to the transportation problem at a time when it wished to focus on the politically popular housing program. Such construction would have demanded close coordination and synchronization of several administrative agencies. It would have required public relations to persuade people to make a move so far from their original homes. And the mission's suggestions about scattering population along the periphery of the island would have involved extensive land purchases, which would have either been expensive or highly upsetting to landowners.

This political orientation is reflected by the selective manner in which the government adopted the mission's proposals with regard to administration.

The mission emphasized that its proposals would require careful synchronization. First, data would be needed, then layout planning, land acquisition, roads and public facilities, and building design. Public and private developers would have to work together on all this so that the finished developments could receive funds from both sources, yet reflect an overall guiding concept. The action programs "should be comprehensive in so far as they should deal with all aspects of urban life. They should include plans for employment, shelter, communications, traffic, education, welfare, capital formation, stimulation of savings, community development, and public relations."

To achieve this synchronization of diverse functions the report recommended that Singapore hire a planning coordinator. He would be an experienced physical planner and would be connected to the Ministry of Finance, where he would work closely with the economic and budgetary planners of that ministry in their assessment of the development and land-use plans of all government departments and in the coordination of public and private development investment. Without such a coordinator, the report emphasized, "the Government of Singapore would be plagued by a multitude of un-coordinated projects competing not only for funds, but also space on the island." Since there was probably not a man of sufficient experience in Singapore to fill such a post, it was suggested that the first planning coordinator be brought in from abroad.

The report suggested that individual projects themselves be coordinated by action teams. For instance, a "New Town Corporation" would be responsible for the comprehensive planning and correct timing of all operations at Jurong. This corporation might ask the United Nations for a team of experts to do the initial designing.

Many other action teams might center around the Housing and Development Board, which contained people with a wide variety of skills. The HDB should become a "development authority," with functions of overall planning, programming, designing, budgeting, executing and managing projects, controlling private development, traffic planning, creating public transport, managing estates, recording, cost accounting, conducting research, and supplying feedback.

This is reflected in the mission's recommendation that an urban renewal section be added to the HDB. The mission also recommended a traffic section with several full-time traffic engineers and computerized testing facilities. It was suggested that other departments within the HDB receive additional staff—especially architect-planners, engineer-planners, land surveyors, soil and drainage specialists, valuers, land and resettlement officers, housing managers, public relations officers, cost accountants, and financial planners.

The mission was concerned that there should be close cooperation between the HDB and the Chief Planner, It proposed that the Chief Planner be given enough staff for three separate divisions: one devoted to long-range planning, a second devoted to traffic planning, and a third for planning control of both public and private development. His offices should be transferred to the HDB to facilitate day-to-day cooperation and enable him to give more assistance to the action programs and the urban renewal teams of the Board.

The government partially responded to these suggestions: (1) It decided not to create a planning coordinator or to add a physical planner to the Ministry of Finance. (2) It created a "New Town Corporation" for Jurong, but turned actual planning over to the HDB and to the Economic Development Board—thus preventing the development of anything like an action team for this project. The Jurong Town Corporation was later established to manage Jurong and other industrial estates. This action took place in June 1968—after these estates were designed and close to completion. (3) The Urban Renewal Section of the HDB was created immediately. It lacked, however, the "rent administrator" (to operate a modified system of rent controls) and the "social welfare and research section" recommended in the report. This was symptomatic of diversions from the mission's overall approach to urban renewal. (4) No action teams were created to deal with individual portions of the island in a comprehensive manner. (5) A traffic section of the type recommended has yet to be created. (6) Some additional specialists with the titles mentioned were added to the HDB.[19] (7) The Chief Planner's Office was brought under the purview of the Ministry of National Development. But the principal point of the mission's recommendations in this regard—increasing the HDB's liaison with the Chief Planner—was ignored, and he was not given the new long-range planning, traffic planning, and planning control divisions.

In adopting these reforms, the government carefully refrained from adopting those proposals that would have necessitated increased interagency coordination, as the next section indicates. Hence it failed to create a basis for planning the entire island as an urban complex.

[19] In the latter part of 1967, Barbara Tyrwhitt, an urban planner and a long-time Doxiadis associate, came to Singapore from Harvard University for one month to submit a report on the expansion of the curriculum at the Singapore Polytechnic. She recommended that people in the community with varying talents related to urban planning be brought in to teach special courses at the Polytechnic. In addition, some students might go to Harvard for six months or a year on special scholarships. At around the same time, a special program at the University of Wisconsin began sending professors to the Polytechnic on one-year appointments. With this strengthening of the curriculum, students who took certain combinations of these courses became entitled to receive various urban planning titles along with their undergraduate diplomas from this technical institute. This procedure permits the various bureaucratic organizations to fill their specialist slots with these graduates, rather than seek individuals with more advanced training. Thus, while the new programs will undoubtedly improve the quality of education at the Polytechnic, they may subtly tend to hold back specialization in the bureaucracy. If there is no one available with the title of architect-planner from a local institution, an agency may feel impelled to seek someone with both an undergraduate degree and an advanced degree in planning. If someone can be found whose undergraduate degree already carries the appellation of architect-planner, the agency may not seek further than this.

WHY POLITICS IS UNFRIENDLY
TO ALTERNATIVE APPROACHES

In August 1967, Singapore opened the door for a fresh approach to planning. During that month a United Nations participation and assistance project was inaugurated to reassess Singapore's planning process. The four-year project was headed by an employee of the United Nations, and a private Australian firm was commissioned to provide most of the staff. Eight consultants would remain in Singapore throughout the four-year period; another eight or ten men would come in for short assignments. To accommodate the project, Singapore set up a new organization, called State and City Planning. This had the Planning Department as its nucleus and was headed by the Chief Planner (see Chart 1).

Five months later, when Britain announced its decision to withdraw its troops by 1971, the Bases Economic Conversion Commission was also established. This commission was headed by a prominent member of the civil service, and charged with deciding the eventual use of the 12,000 acres of British army land on the island.

The United Nations participation and assistance project engaged in many useful activities. It conducted an extensive traffic survey and drew up many maps for eventual land use of the island—similar in style to those in the Abrams/Koenigsberger/Kobe Report. It initiated discussions between members of different bureaucratic agencies who had common interests. Some officers were loaned to specific State and City Planning projects, in order to pick up experience from foreign experts with counterpart skills. Many statistics and facts were gathered and assembled. Road schemes for the island were considered for the future. A detailed proposal for a mass rapid transit system was presented to the Ministry of Finance for approval, but has not been acted upon. Revised guidelines for zoning and building activities were created.

The overall planning process has been affected very little. Economic planning remains separate, in the Ministry of Finance, as before. State and City Planning remains separate from the HDB and from Urban Renewal. The procedures for controlling development and approving new projects of the public sector are similar to those in the past.

Yet there are some subtle changes. Certain portions of land on the island have achieved a new status. State and City Planning became a member of an action subcommittee of the Interdepartmental Co-ordinating Committee of the Bases Economic Conversion Commission. Together, the members of this subcommittee are planning for the future of the bases being vacated by the British (see Map 1), except for the base land on the west end of the island that has been set aside for military purposes. There seems to be a good deal of interaction among these agencies in planning for the use of this land. The same competitive urges that motivated the various agencies before Kallang Basin was finally assigned to the HDB are probably still at work. At least this time the insulation that separated the agencies has been broken to a greater degree.

One hopeful tangible result of the new interaction will be the Telok Blangah area (Map 1). State and City Planning drew up plans to convert this attractive hilly land by the sea into an area of residences and recreational facilities. The tops of hills will largely be used for recreation. Hillsides will be used for residences. The HDB will build blocks of flats up to thirty-six stories high with an emphasis on the three- and four-room improved-type flats.[20] Blocks will be placed on hillsides in positions to afford them a view of the sea. It would appear that State and City Planning prevailed in their view that the number of flats to be built in the area should be around 25,000—lower than the number anticipated by the HDB. The Prime Minister has referred to an era of "gracious living"—giving the plan a seal of approval as a new programmatic departure. There is some talk of creating an urban corridor to link Jurong with the city.

The 1970–1975 plans of the HDB show changes in emphasis— perhaps partly engendered by thought processes emerging from State and City Planning. The Board will construct around 100,000 units of public housing between 1970 and 1975—its most ambitious targets to date. The amount of floor space in flats will be increased. There will be more emphasis than in the past on building flats for sale, in addition to those for rent. Ground-floor flats will be eliminated, so as to provide additional playing space for children and room for shops and cottage industries. There will be at least one playground for every 2,000 to 4,-000 flats; an experiment is being conducted with building swimming pools on HDB estates. All blocks of flats will contain two elevators. While additional units will be constructed in Queenstown and Toa Payoh, the Board will also begin another satellite town further away on

[20] For a discussion of the HDB 1970–1975 program see *Straits Times*, December 17, 1969.

the land leveled to produce the Bedok Reclamation Project (see Map 1). On the northern edge of the island at Woodlands, work will begin on an additional housing estate. Extensive development there, however, will probably have to wait until some decision is made about road plans.

Also at Woodlands, the Jurong Town Corporation is planning a new industrial estate. The British naval facilities being abandoned at Sembawang, Changi, Seletar, and Tengah are being converted into repair and shipbuilding stations for civilian vessels. The Lockheed and Gruman companies have set up aircraft repair and maintenance facilities on the RAF base at Seletar, and may do the same at Changi.

These departures will help move Singapore's planning emphases away from the extreme centralization around the city area. They do not accomplish all the objectives of Abrams, Koenigsberger, and Kobe, however. Telok Blangah's housing will largely cater to the lower middle class, who will thus be separated both from lower class and middle class housing. Jurong will still fail to receive large amounts of housing— making it necessary for most of its workers to continue commuting. The same applies to Woodlands. Bedok will become another public housing estate—not a planned city with various types of public and private housing mixed together. Because a comprehensive plan for roads and mass transit has not been decided upon, it will remain difficult for all these areas to grow.

The central city areas (the built-up areas on Map 2) are still the focal points for change. The HDB estimates that it will resettle 60,000 central city inhabitants between 1970 and 1975.[21] Many additional HDB flats will be constructed in the central area. Luxury structures are blossoming there—the S$50 million building to house the Development Bank of Singapore, large luxury hotels, the Central Provident Fund Building. A number of separate urban renewal projects are under construction. The Raffles International Centre comprises several square blocks in the central area designed by a private development firm. The "Golden Mile" along the shore line to the south of Kallang Basin has been divided into separate parcels for sale to different private developers of hotels, shopping centers, and offices. Kallang Park is being developed into a luxury amusement site with a stadium, convention center, marina, ice rink, and other attractions. At other scattered central area

[21] *Ibid.*

locations lots have been sold for development of office buildings, shopping centers, cinemas, private flats, hotels, car parks, and restaurants. In between, some small businesses and historical buildings will be permitted to remain intact. Meanwhile, harbor improvements are in progress along the perimeters of this area.

Piecemeal planning of the city area—where the great majority of the population live—will not be easy to eliminate. The United Nations mission's warning about "a jumble of little semi-detached houses in their own gardens, interspersed by groups of Housing Board flats and separated from each other and the rest of the world by an intricate network of traffic jams" still remains relevant. So long as urban renewal is phase-by-phase, it will be difficult to design an overall road network for downtown. With island-wide plans still uncertain, it will be difficult to design mass transit with assurance that it will serve areas where it is most needed. Increased interaction might induce the HDB to lower the densities of its housing estates or change design details. Yet central city planning involves industrial planners, harbor planners, road planners, public housing planners, private builders, financiers, and urban renewal planners. These remain separated in different agencies and organizations. Unless frequently interacting action teams are created to bring them all together, there remains a strong possibility that many projects will proceed before information is gathered regarding their overall consequences for the area and its inhabitants.

Should one agency not like something being done in the city by another agency, it can argue its case before the ministers, as in the past. Many such suggestions would necessitate population shifts, or increased land purchases, or slowed implementation of projects, or higher costs for individual projects, or extensive coordination among agencies, or expensive information gathering. If the government were to try to follow up on the plan of the United Nations mission, the chances are great that it would repeatedly need to pursue one or another of these inconvenient courses. Projects in outlying areas often require considerable coordination. If no committee or agency is given the authority to decide on such conflicts—possible inconveniences notwithstanding—it is likely that projects will be tampered with as little as possible. When a government can complete desired projects without such inconveniences, it is tempted to do so.

The present methods of allocating authority have served the government well. They have helped it to speedily build public housing, industries, public works, and many other amenities. It is unusual for power structures to rearrange relationships which suit their purposes simply on the theory that the rearrangement *might* better serve popular needs.

When a government has something in mind that it wishes to accomplish, it is likely that it will try to achieve its end in the simplest manner possible. This is especially true when the simplest manner also happens to be the most popular manner politically.

Even if Government ministers should choose, for instance, to give State and City Planning more power to coordinate, there is another stumbling block. The government does not have full say on the matter. It must also heed the needs of those who command investment funds, industry, and entrepôt trade—or risk a depression. These individuals may be expected to judge a program more in terms of its effect on their businesses than its effect on individual lives. Businessmen are usually cost-conscious and do not like heavy expenditures for intangible and difficult-to-assess benefits. They prefer flexibility in planning future commitments, so that they do not need to commit themselves too far ahead. They can be expected to prefer leaving the bulk of the land for industries and middle class housing. Businessmen generally avoid involving themselves in complex projects that demand extensive interaction with government. In researching and planning a project, they are more interested in generating maximum profit than in considering how the project affects the neighbors—especially if the neighbors happen to be smaller competitors. Proposals such as the guiding concept of the Abrams/Kobe/Koenigsberger report may conflict with some of these priorities.

Yet, why should the government heed the wishes of those who command investment, industry, and entrepôt trade? True, it is they who ultimately foot the bill for urban renewal and industrial estates, and even for the rent paid by public housing tenants, and it is their business operations which determine the prosperity of the nation. All this notwithstanding, there are Governments that inhibit manufacturers and traders and others that aid them only sporadically and in the face of considerable opposition. In Singapore, however, it would appear that no Government—left, right, or center—could survive politically if it seemed to be inhibiting trade and manufacturing.

A fundamental fact about Singapore is its dependence upon trade and industry. The vast majority of the populace is directly or indirectly dependent upon trade, industry, and urban services for their livelihood (see Table 1). Nearly everyone is involved in a monetary economy. Commercially profitable development is virtually a universally desired aspiration.

Table 1. Estimates of economically active population of Singapore, 1957 and 1966

Industry group	Employed, 1957 * (10 years and over)		Employed, 1966 † (12 years and over)	
	Persons	%	Persons	%
Agriculture, forestry, hunting, and fishing	31,500	7.0	22,700	4.8
Mining and quarrying	1,600	0.4	2,000	0.4
Manufacturing	68,000	15.1	106,300	19.6
Construction	22,000	4.9	30,100	5.0
Electricity, gas, water, and sanitary services	5,600	1.2	6,600	1.2
Commerce	115,000	25.5	116,800	21.5
Transport, storage, and communications	48,800	10.8	62,100	11.5
Services	156,000	34.6	184,400	34.0
Activities not adequately described or not stated	2,100	0.5	10,700	2.0
Total employed	450,600	100.0	541,700	100.0
Total unemployed	29,600		43,400	
Total economically active	480,200		585,100	

* Estimated from Singapore, Statistics Department, *Report on the Census of Population, 1957* (Singapore: GPO, 1964).

† Figures from 1966 National Registration appeared in a news release by the Minister of Finance.

Prime Minister Lee Kuan Yew—echoing Calvin Coolidge—told a Washington, D.C., audience [22] that "the business of Singapore is business." The statement is even more true of Singapore in the 1960's than it was of America in the 1920's; only a small percentage of Singapore's population is engaged in agriculture, and these farmers are not always friendly to the interests of traders and manufacturers. When they move to town, or compete for governmental resources, they may create problems for trade and manufacture. Because of its relative isolation from any extensive hinterland—its only connection with the mainland is a half-mile causeway across the Straits of Johore—Singapore has avoided

[22] *Straits Times,* October 19, 1967.

problems faced by virtually every city of comparable size: assimilation of rural immigrants, shanty towns, unchecked urbàn sprawl, and a sharing of resources with the rural sector.

Influx from Malaysia probably does not exceed 25,000 a year, and many of these immigrants come from other cities.[23] By issuing identity cards and work permits in 1966 and establishing strict passport and visa regulations in 1967, the newly independent government has brought even greater control over immigration of unskilled labor.[24] Because of this control, Singapore is affected far less severely than most cities of the developing world by squatter colonies.[25] The problems of

[23] United Nations, Department of Economic and Social Affairs, *Future Population Estimates,* Report III, The Population of Southeast Asia 1950–80 (1958), 35, estimates the flow of immigrants from Malaya to be around 12,000. Prime Minister Lee Kuan Yew estimated, from changes in identity card addresses, that 10,000 young men came to Singapore during 1964 looking for jobs; of these, 3,500 were Malays. *The Battle for a Malaysian Malaysia* (Singapore: Singapore Ministry of Culture, 1965), 37. J. C. Caldwell, "Urban Growth in Malaya: Trends and Implications," *Population Review* (Madras), January 1963, 47–48, reports that a 1958 analysis of surrendered Federation of Malaya identity cards indicates that half of the immigrants in the sample came from the State of Johore. This analysis also found that Singapore's immigrants included more Indians and fewer Malays than was true of immigrants to cities in the Federation of Malaya. A small number of Indians also come from India each year, nearly always with the aid of relatives in Singapore. There is some reason to believe that these Indians come mainly from other urban areas. This pattern contrasts sharply with that of many other urban areas; see footnote 25.

[24] On February 17, 1967, the Prime Minister announced that unskilled noncitizens holding work permits would gradually be told to find work outside the Republic. He estimated that there were approximately 60,000 persons in this category. In retaliation, the Malaysian government announced a similar move, involving approximately an equal number of Singaporeans. The result was probably a slowdown in Singapore's attempt to implement this policy.

[25] The 1955 *Report of the Singapore Master Plan* (Singapore: GPO) estimated that there were 246,000 city and 150,000 rural squatters on the island—that is, unauthorized occupants of land who built themselves temporary shelter. By 1966 there were far fewer squatters. [In 1966, Singapore had an estimated 331,901 dwelling units; of these, about 50,972 were "deteriorating" or "dilapidated" atap- and zinc-roof living units, and there were 84,359 units of public housing (Economic Research Centre, *op. cit.* 228). Family sizes in the "deteriorating" or "dilapidated" structures were not appreciably different from those in other dwellings. If all of those living in "deteriorating" or "dilapidated" structures were squatters, this would place the island's maximum squatter population at about 300,000 (or 15 per cent of total population). Actually, most of these occupants probably pay rent, and hence are not squatters, so the total squatter population is considerably lower than 300,000.] The fact that the vast majority of those resettled by the HDB have proved to be Singapore citizens shows that even those who were

constructing public housing are thus reduced.[26] Likewise, Singapore's politicians and planners avoid what is the chief problem of planning in most nations: the integration of the city with its hinterland. Singapore's urban planning can take place without regard for the influence this planning has upon the rural sector, and with immunity from the values of the rural sector.[27]

From the time Lee Kuan Yew entered public life he has pounded

---

squatters were not rural immigrants, but had probably been living in Singapore for some time. They had simply been victims of the severe housing shortage. A study of zinc and atap dwellers in Kallang Basin (Ian Buchanan, "Squatter Resettlement in Singapore," 1967) found that a high percentage of the families under study had come to Singapore before the war.

Thus the number of squatters in Singapore is decreasing. In contrast, squatters are estimated to be increasing four times as fast as the rest of the population in metropolitan Manila. In 1971 they numbered around 700,000—over 20 per cent of the population. Paula Milone, "The Disaster Cities," *Far Eastern Economic Review*, 43 (October 23, 1971), 58. Metropolitan Manila had nearly 283,000 squatters in 1963 (20 per cent of the population), and is expected to have over 800,000 by 1980. In Peru, the number of squatters grew from 45,000 in 1940 to 958,000 in 1960. Charles Abrams, "The Uses of Land in Cities," *Scientific American*, September 1965, 151–152. In 1963, 50 per cent of the population of some Philippine provincial cities, and 45 per cent of Lima's 1965 population, were estimated to be squatters. The same is true of 40 per cent of Caracas, Venezuela's 1964 population, 50 per cent of Ankara, Turkey's 1960 population, and 40 per cent of Recife, Brazil's 1965 population. Some cities are experiencing a 12 per cent per annum increase in squatters. Morris Juppenlatz, *Cities in Transformation: The Urban Squatter Problem in the Developing World* (St. Lucia: University of Queensland, 1970), 14–15. Djakarta, Indonesia, grew from 450,000 just before World War II to about 4.5 million in 1971—largely due to rural-urban migration; many of these new inhabitants are squatters. Milone, *op. cit.*, 59.

[26] Between 1960 and January 1, 1965, Singapore's HDB resettled around 6,000 families (State of Singapore, Housing and Development Board, *Homes for the People* [Singapore: GPO, 1965]). Many, if not most, of these were not squatters. During 1964 alone, Hong Kong cleared 46,659 squatters (Government of Hong Kong, *Report of the Year 1964* [Hong Kong: GPO]). Hong Kong's figures are in terms of individuals rather than families. The figures probably mean that Hong Kong cleared as many families in one year as Singapore did in five. Annual turnover of tenants and evictions for nonpayment of rent for the Singapore HDB is under 2 per cent of total tenants. In contrast, one of the chief problems faced by the Calcutta Improvement Trust is instability of tenancy caused by the great seasonal rural-urban migrations experienced by that city. When public housing flats were constructed in Caracas they attracted an unwelcome influx of immigrants from the rural areas, who simply intensified the city's housing problem, removed stability of tenancy from the flats, and caused virtual "social anarchy" within the public housing area. *Journal of Housing* (Chicago), October 1959, 311–314.

[27] See Chapter VIII for further discussion of this problem. Singapore's artificial isolation from the countryside makes it something of a special case.

away on the theme that Singapore must increase its trade and manufacturing. In fact this has been one of the few matters on which he has remained thoroughly consistent. His critics from the left have not challenged him on this. When the Chinese middle school agitation began,
there was agreement on all sides that the curriculum should be
modernized; [28] the main point of complaint was that Chinese-speakers
were not obtaining jobs quickly enough or on an equal basis. The left
wing of the PAP, and later the Barisan Sosialis, advocated higher
wages, yet supported a continuance of private enterprise and heavy government expenditures to support private trade and manufacturing. Lim
Chin Siong, the Barisan leader, himself wrote:

The central requirement today is capital for the most rapid possible industrialization. If private capital is able to fulfill this requirement it should be
welcomed. But should it fail to do so, as is the case today in Malaya, then
state participation in areas of industrialization should be immediately effected.[29]

During the 1963 campaign the Barisan issued a press release stating
that, though it believed in a planned economy in the long run, "for the
present and for some time to come" Singapore would have to work
"within the limits of a free enterprise economy." [30]

[28] In a rural kampong with religious schools the curriculum would, in contrast,
have been the point of greatest contention. The new subjects are viewed as a
threat to the old. The Singapore Chinese teachers' unions objected to eliminating
the classical curriculum or laying off Chinese-stream teachers, but they agreed on
the need for adding modern subjects.

[29] This quotation is from a comprehensive policy statement of the Singapore
Association of Trade Unions. It appeared in the official Barisan Sosialis organ,
The Plebeian (October 15, 1962). It was written principally by Lim Chin Siong.

[30] F. L. Starner, "The Singapore Election of 1963," in K. J. Ratnam and R. S.
Milne, *The Malayan Parliamentary Election of 1964* (Singapore: University of
Malaya Press, 1967), 346. In contrast, both the Barisan and Lee Kuan Yew have
shown a willingness to attack private enterprise in Malaya. The following utter-
ance in a May 26, 1965, speech by Barisan Sosialis Party Chairman Dr. Lee
Siew Choh (*Plebeian Express,* June 15, 1965) is one he has frequently repeated:
"The real oppressors (are) the British and other foreign monopoly capitalists, the
foreign and local landlords, the estate and mine owners, the foreign banks, the
foreign agency houses." His only other policy suggestion with economic implications in this speech is: "We must help raise the livelihood of, and give special aid
to, the poor Malay farmers and fishermen." Note that the only *local* capitalists he
attacks are the landlords and the estate and mine owners. Estates and mines exist
only in Malaya. At the same time as Dr. Lee Siew Choh's speech, Prime Minister
Lee Kuan Yew was himself emphasizing a similar theme in his "Malaysian Malaysia" campaign. For instance, on November 20, 1964, he told an audience (see

Lee Kuan Yew focused his campaign on an issue that might seem obscure to an outsider: the notion that Singapore needed a common market with Malaya so that her trade and industry could survive. He found wide popular support on this issue.[31]

In many societies, farmers, religionists, traditionalists, intellectuals, and working people would find appealing counterarguments to respond to these suggestions and policies. In the Singapore context, they are virtually unassailable. Without some combination of these emphases there is little hope of the island's surviving economically as an entrepreneurial society, and the people know it.

Given this agreement on premises, it is easy to argue a step further. Small traders and manufacturers cannot survive in the competitive international market. Hence a healthy commercial situation implies healthy big businesses. Healthy big businesses require a healthy public infrastructure designed to serve them. By a subtle mental process, the poor man finds himself a supporter of the interests of the rich—deferring to the leadership of big businessmen and of the bureaucrats who carry out public projects with them.

The one group that shares least in the Singapore economic system centering around industrialization and trade is the Malays. They come from a rural culture. Until they can share in the rewards—and thus the values—of industrialization, or until their cultural leaders develop a stake in industrialization, the Malays will probably not be so prone to accept the inherent inequalities involved in industrialization. With the Singapore Malay, class and racial heritage reinforce one another in promoting a political cleavage from the mainstream of society. Those Malays who are most alienated long for a return to the rural society. Yet

---

Some Problems in Malaysia [Singapore: Ministry of Culture], 29, 32): "Well, look, basically you cannot do it on the basis of private enterprise. The leadership of the Malay mass base is linked up with Chinese and Indian private enterprise at the top, so there is a contradiction which cannot be resolved. . . . Our job is to help the Malay intellectual leadership to put their finger on the real causes of economic backwardness—the social and economic systems that prevent this rural people from keeping abreast of development." He said that the final Malay leadership that emerges "must either be socialist, or if it is not socialist, it will be communist." These points are made by the leader of the left-wing Labour Front and Party Rakyat in Malaya, Lim Kean Siew, in virtually every speech.

[31] See pp. 31–32. Were large percentages of the populace engaged in mining and primary production, this issue would hardly have received an enthusiastic response (it has never received an enthusiastic response in Malaya). Primary producers have little to gain from eliminating tariffs on manufactured goods.

that society, too accepts inequality—between the peasant and the land-owning sultans [32] whom the poorer peasants tend to respect and admire. Malays, too, lend support to the interests of wealthy people.

In both rural and urban societies, the majority of the inhabitants have learned to accept a power elite as part of life. When rural people move into urban jobs, they gradually (and painfully) change their allegiances to economic systems, and to the concomitant political elites of each. They demand political favors for themselves in a more aggressive manner than before. But they do not generally demand the sorts of changes that would give the poor real political power or a strong basis for having their most fundamental needs adequately catered to. Both rural and urban poor are usually satisfied with a share in some of the fruits of the particular economic system in which they are involved (e.g., land and more mosques and drainage ditches and wells in the case of the rural dweller, or wages and houses and schools in the case of the urban). And they support that economic system because it gives them these fruits, regardless of the quality of the fruit. Insofar as their insecure position causes personal tension, they take it out on slightly differing classes or ethnic groups, or foreigners, rather than on the elite or the economic system itself. Meanwhile the government finds it easier to manage those tensions by coercion, rather than by planning in a manner which would serve to reduce the tensions.

For the short time that Singapore was part of Malaysia, the government found itself sharing power with a rural-oriented elite. The existence of a balance of power between a rural and urban elite is no assurance that the needs of the poor will be catered to. To the contrary, it is likely to reduce efficiency and coordination and harm economic stability. The rivalry of two economic elites can result in the decay of both

[32] Before the nineteenth century, Malaya was dominated by Muslim sultans. After the British arrived, their policy of indirect rule allowed the sultans to retain control over large stretches of that land which was not devoted to British mines and plantations. After independence, the sultans took on figurehead roles. Malaysia has a unique system of revolving kingship—the sultans take turns at holding this office. The sultans have nonetheless retained some large portions of the land, which they make available for mining and plantations in return for shares in profits. They still maintain huge palaces, fleets of custom-made Rolls Royces and Lincoln Continentals, large stables of Arabian horses, and the like. Their power is bolstered by the continuing support of the peasants for the Muslim faith, and its mosques, *imams,* and royalty. Lee Kuan Yew frequently criticizes the "feudalist system" that supports this situation. The sultans are the linkage to which he refers in footnote 30.

their economic systems. Planning coordination—probably meager in the first place—may be hampered even further in the face of tension. By exacerbating communal rivalries, such a power balance may reinforce the tendency of the poor to rally around the wealthy elites of their own particular race and economic system.

Today that rivalry is over. Singapore's government is free to follow the wish of its citizens that trade and manufacturing be promoted. It is free to offer whatever concessions are needed to attract trade and investment. So long as this is the case, it seems inevitable that problems of the unemployed, low wages, personal anomie, decreasing backyard crops, traffic congestion, potential future slum characteristics in housing estates, and segregation of social classes will receive less attention than the promotion of rapid construction, industrialization, and increase in sales and tourism. Speedy bureaucratic implementation of programs will seem more essential than careful coordination to ensure that the rapid changes do not disrupt the lives of individuals. As urbanization progresses, both the industrialization and the disintegration of personal environments have an opportunity to increase at a faster pace. The leadership is strengthened and unified at the same time that the society is Balkanized into rival factions.

It is often argued that industrialization must entail temporary neglect of some of the needs of the poor; but perhaps that neglect is inherently permanent. As prosperity grows, so, perhaps, will the disruptions in the life of the poor that prevent them from sharing in the prosperity. For the poor man to achieve economic status, he must either demand that industrialization programs become more sensitive to his needs, or resist industrialization. He is unlikely to do either. He is asked instead to have fewer children and buy a television set and miniscooter.

Prime Minister Lee has been exhorting his people to hold down the size of their families, so as to be able to plan for television sets, washing machines, and miniscooters. On the surface, this exhortation to acquire such soft goods contrasts somewhat with his exhortation to be vigorous, to build community and a new culture, to climb the ladder in school, and to save and persevere. Yet the two focuses seem consistent. People are being asked to accept the life that industrialization has created for them, and hope for the best. Citizens are still called upon to be disciplined—in keeping their streets and flats clean, in queuing up for the bus, in learning technical skills, and in working in the factory. There was a time when they were asked to carry on this discipline after work—to attend organizational meetings, and work on ways in which their life could be improved. Now—though these are the critical formative years for molding the environment of Singapore—they are invited to relax and partake in the "gracious living" of miniscooters, television, and spectator sports. They are being asked to set their personal goals low—on blue collar jobs, rather than on white collar or family entrepreneurial pursuits.

Vituperative speeches that used to be directed at British imperialists, Communists, and Malay chauvanists are now directed at hippies—the counterculture that most questions the values of industrialization. The Republic has even gone so far as to ban long hair and acid rock records. There seems to be a genuine fear that a fundamental questioning of industrialized values might set in before the industries and housing estates and hotels are permanently set in concrete and steel.

Lim Shee Ping—a Barisan Sosialis Executive Committee member— wrote in the Barisan official organ, *The Plebeian,* on November 20, 1962, shortly before his arrest and subsequent detention:

We in the Barisan Sosialis believe that industrialization there must be, that private capital must be allowed to perform their legitimate role for as long as it wishes provided it will not entrench itself in a position to chart the course of our political, social, cultural, and economic progress. One thing that we will never do is to subjugate the national need of the country's reconstruction to the rule of free market forces and to those who do not care two hoots for the needs of the people except for the profits that can be made from them. In the final analysis, our people can only profit most effectively from the fruits of industrialization if the economy of the whole country can be placed on a planning basis in the strictly socialist sense.

Industrialization without control by industry; the fruits of industrialization combined with planning that will meet the needs of the people. I fear that Mr. Lim could as well have been asking for the moon— regardless of who won the election.

CHAPTER VII

Singapore and Other Urban Areas

> Urban renewal must . . . be a joint partnership between private entrepreneurs and the Government to attain the overall objectives of creating a balanced society whereby everyone will not only have improved living but also better employment opportunities.
>
> Alan F. C. Choe [1]

The inadequacies in Singapore's urban development programs do not appear exotic to those familiar with development programs in other urban areas. Bureaucratic agencies working on their own projects with little regard for how they relate to other projects, inadequate information about how projects affect the social and economic condition of the public, and a dearth of long-range planning are common problems everywhere. Nor is it unusual for the middle and upper classes to have suburbs largely to themselves, while poorer citizens live at higher densities nearer the heart of the city. While poorer citizens throughout the world have in recent years been receiving an increasing number of programmatic concessions from government, few of them have achieved the power to ensure that the programs are pieced together in a manner that resolves their most fundamental problems (not the least of which is the fact that they continue to be poor).

CITIZEN PARTICIPATION
AND THE MIDDLE CLASSES

There are those who advocate metropolitan government (dissolving the jurisdictional lines that usually separate suburb from central city) as a means of resolving such inadequacies. They argue that if entire metro-

---

[1] Alan F. C. Choe, "Urban Renewal," in Ooi Jin-Bee & Chiang Hai Ding (eds.), *Modern Singapore* (Singapore: University of Singapore, 1969), 165. Mr. Choe is Head (formerly Architect/Planner) of the HDB's Urban Renewal Department.

politan areas share common taxes, utilities, and problems, there can be more coordination in planning and greater efficiency in dealing with human problems. It should be noted that Singapore has one powerful government with complete sovereignty over its entire territory and over land-use decisions, taxation, and budgeting. This is obviously not in itself the solution.

Nor will eradication of housing shortages for the poor, valuable as this is, erase these problems. Singapore is adding 20,000 units of low-cost housing to her supply each year; the entire United States produces only 30,000 units annually.[2] Aside from Hong Kong (whose public housing units are generally smaller and more crowded than Singapore's), China, Israel, Kuwait, and perhaps Puerto Rico and Cuba, other nations of Asia,[3] Africa, and Latin America are generally far behind Singapore in providing housing for the poor. In Europe, West Germany is unusual in that, spurred by its heavy wartime losses, it has

[2] The 1960 Census found one-eighth of Americans housed in structures it classed as dilapidated. Conference on Economic Progress, *Poverty & Deprivation in the United States* (Washington, D.C., April, 1962), ch. 10. The 1966 White House Conference on Civil Rights estimated that 2 million new units—500,000 of these designed for low income families—were needed each year. The AFL-CIO has suggested 2,500,000 new units a year. The 1968 Housing Act set a goal of 20 million homes—5 million of them for the poor—over a ten-year period. The National Association of Housing and Redevelopment Officials has supported this goal; HEW Secretary George Romney endorsed it in April 1969. The most careful scholarly study on the subject is William G. Grigsby, *Housing Markets and Public Policy* (Philadelphia: University of Pennsylvania Press, 1963), in which he calculates future needs in housing for the poor and suggests that housing subsidies to the poor and basic changes in the urban renewal programs might greatly diminish the serious problem of supplying these needs. Nothing has been done with these suggestions. He expresses his increasing pessimism over this in "Housing and Slum Clearance: Elusive Goals," *Annals of the American Academy of Political and Social Science* 352 (March 1964), 101–118.

[3] India, with probably the worst housing shortages in Asia, has built almost no public housing. Only Bombay, Calcutta, and Madras have had public housing programs of any size. Madras, with perhaps the most impressive program, had built only 10,372 public housing units as of 1966, with only 4,658 of these for relocation of slum dwellers. See Alfred P. Van Huyck, "The Housing Threshold for Lowest-Income Groups: The Case of India," in John D. Herbert and Alfred P. Van Huyck (eds.), *Urban Planning in the Developing Countries* (New York: Praeger, 1968), 102. More recently there have been proposals for bustee (squatter colony) improvement programs that would allow for rebuilding of mud huts under rental terms more favorable than those currently experienced by many in the slums and bustees. Only a few pilot projects have been begun, and there are practically no results yet visible.

maintained vigorous output in both low and middle income housing,[4] and it still has a housing shortage. Despite active building, Eastern Europe and the Soviet Union still experience housing shortages.[5] Singapore is thus among the few nations in the world that has overcome housing shortages; yet she too experiences problems in coordination and meeting other human needs.

The planned new towns of Europe that delight the eye seem to have circumvented some of these coordination problems. They have done so only because they were built on virgin land several miles from the center of the old cities, or on bombing rubble. With the rare exception of Dublin, slum clearance projects have not constituted a prominent feature in postwar European development.[6] Much of the construction that has taken place in European cities has been as devoid of an overall plan as that in Singapore. And in the Soviet Union the urban planner seems to have as little power as elsewhere. One writer comments:

Soviet factories are often placed on river banks in the middle of cities, for convenient transportation and waste disposal. There they pollute the air and water and may find themselves boxed in when they want to expand. These

[4] Paul F. Wendt, *Housing Policy—the Search for Solutions: A Comparison of the United Kingdom, Sweden, West Germany, and the United States since World War II* (Berkeley: University of California Press, 1962), 11–144, 230–274, for a report on West German housing. For more references on housing policies and programs around the world, see the Bibliography.

[5] See Philippe J. Bernard, *Planning in the Soviet Union* (Oxford: Pergamon Press, 1966), 129, 193. On pages 272–273: "Furthermore, the increase in urban housing (22% from the end of 1958 to the end of 1961, or almost 7% per annum) is counteracted in the USSR by an increase of 3.5% per annum in urban population. . . . It is, of course, evident that there is a greater degree of inequality in the distribution of housing in Western countries than there is in the USSR. . . . Be that as it may, the difference in the amount of housing available in the USSR as compared with other countries is such that the families of Soviet workers are clearly worse off in this respect than their counterparts elsewhere and will obviously continue to be so for some time to come." I recently inspected new public housing projects in Moscow, Leningrad, and Prague and found them generally sturdy, well laid out, convenient to transportation, and very extensive. It took some effort to find these projects in the Soviet Union, since they are not on regular Intourist itineraries for some reason. I am amused at the continuing Western tendency—even among those who have visited the Soviet Union—to assume that all Soviet public housing looks like the badly constructed and designed housing of the Stalinist era. About two million apartments are constructed each year in the Soviet Union.

[6] See the Bibliography for references on urban renewal programs around the world.

same factories are supposed to use part of their "enterprise funds" . . . to build and maintain streets and other community facilities. But they often prefer to build 'company towns' for their workers only.[7]

Hence exhortations to follow the examples of Europe and the Soviet bloc may have little meaning as well.

It has also been suggested that the existence of interest groups and free speech will help make urban redevelopment compatible with citizen needs. In America there is much free speech, and the rhetoric of interest group politics is constantly heard. Singapore has less free speech, and its few democratic institutions are more for show than use. Yet in neither place does there seem to be much citizen participation in urban redevelopment. In the case studies on urban redevelopment [8] there are some instances in which middle class neighborhood groups staved off attempts to renew certain areas or effected changes in urban renewal proposals.[9] Although it is generally the poor who are displaced by urban redevelopment projects, the case studies to date have not contained a single instance in which a lower class neighborhood group won a major redevelopment battle against either a middle class group, or the redevelopers, or institutions, or bureaucrats, or property owners, or

[7] Robert J. Osborn, "How the Russians Plan Their Cities," in Sylvia Fleis Fava (ed.), *Urbanism in World Perspective: A Reader* (New York: Crowell, 1968), 559–560. Osborn indicates that Gosstoi, the central urban planning agency, has inadequate control over industry. Other centralized agencies are charged with siting factories; there are interagency rivalries. See also Bernard, *op. cit.*, 172–219. One's eye is met by a profusion of badly juxtaposed structures in major Russian cities.

[8] The case studies on urban redevelopment that had appeared at the time I did this research (1970) are listed in the Bibliography. Unfortunately, I was unable to locate similar case studies of urban redevelopment projects outside the United States.

[9] In Chicago (Meyerson and Banfield; see footnote 8) middle class groups won out over the planners concerning the siting of public housing. In New York's West Village (Davies) Jane Jacob's groups won their battle to keep urban redevelopment out of their area. In Rockaway (Davies) the Chamber of Commerce succeeded in getting the bulk of the renewal project moved from a white area into a black area. On the West Side (Davies) a coalition of middle class individuals led by two men—one a priest and the other a politician with a strong following among New York Puerto Ricans—effected a change in the redevelopment plan from 400 low-income, 2,400 middle income, and 5,000 high income units to 2,500 low-income, 4,900 middle income, and 2,000 high income units. The opponents of the metal houses (Dahl) won out over the wealthy owner; but the potential occupants of the metal houses won nothing.

businessmen, or others involved in the urban redevelopment process.[10] Nor have I found such an instance in Singapore.

Thus it would seem to me that these inadequacies in coordination and meeting popular needs will not be overcome by attaining a certain level of economic development, or by gathering socio-economic information, or by developing sophisticated planning techniques, or by integrating government units, or by strengthening democratic processes. Nor will they be countervailed by increasing the number or volume of urban development programs. The key to making programs conform to needs would instead seem to be participation in the planning processes by those who are most affected by urban development.

Middle class groups are showing some signs of becoming more involved in these planning processes. They have succeeded in gaining concessions because they command some resources, skills, and administrative capabilities. However, the poorest segments of the populace seem to have little chance of becoming more involved or of bringing such capabilities to bear on planning. Hence they will continue to be left out when the most critical decisions are made determining how programs affect their lives. Since there are incompatibilities between the interests of middle class people and the needs of those who are poorer, this situation may not be a great improvement over the era when urban development took place without citizen participation. If governments cannot find means to bring poorer citizens more directly into these policy processes, the inadequacies in urban development are likely to continue.

A comparison of urban development programs in Singapore and Boston offers an illustration of this argument.

[10] In Rockaway (see Davies), Scarborough's lower income black groups lost both their battle to keep urban redevelopment out of their neighborhood and their later battle to get more assistance in relocation problems. In Chicago (Rossi and Dentler) both the attempt by lower class residents to organize for themselves and the Catholic Church's attempt to speak for them failed. The West Side case (Davies) represents a partial win by a coalition with a city-wide base. The compromise effected still failed to provide homes for 2,500 resettled families and ignored the interests of the small merchants and of important lower class factions in the FDR–Woodrow Wilson Democratic Club. In Washington Park (Keyes), Otto Snowden forestalled opposition from lower class citizens about to be bulldozed by what proved to be false promises of low-rent relocation housing within the neighborhood (p. 183). In Newark (Kaplan) opposition by inhabitants of the North Ward to clearance of their neighborhood failed. Lisa Redfield Peattie, *The View from the Barrio* (Ann Arbor: University of Michigan Press, 1968), Ch. 7, describes the complete failure of some barrio dwellers to effect compromise on a sewer pipe being discharged into their village in Guyana, Venezuela.

REDEVELOPMENT IN SINGAPORE AND BOSTON

The clearance of the West End in Boston is among the best known of American urban redevelopment projects, thanks to some first-class writing which has been done on the subject.[11] Boston's newer redevelopment projects under the supervision of perhaps the world's most famous urban redeveloper, Edward Logue, are not yet so well known.[12] Together these projects help point up some basic problems. The parallels with Singapore would seem to indicate that these problems are not the problems of American redevelopment alone and that some of them may be inherent in urban redevelopment itself.

Early in the 1960's, Boston razed 48 acres of the 72-acre West End —a mixed-income Italian residential district near the central business district. The original structures were replaced with middle and high income apartment buildings,[13] a shopping center, and an extension of the Massachusetts General Hospital. This was intended to benefit the central business district by removing blight from its fringes and by replacing it with high income shoppers and taxpayers.

The inhabitants of the neighborhood paid for this benefit in a number of ways. Their former neighborhood, which Herbert Gans [14] shows to have been quite cohesive, was broken up. Sixty per cent of the inhabitants had incomes low enough to make them eligible for public housing. Many did not choose to move into public housing, however. Chester Hartman shows that 41 per cent of the West Enders already lived in good housing in this so-called slum; after the move 73 per cent relocated in good housing (something which would not have been the case had they been black). Concomitantly, the median rents for all those dis-

[11] Herbert Gans, *The Urban Villagers* (New York: Free Press, 1962); Gans, *People and Plans, Essays on Urban Problems and Solutions* (New York: Basic Books, 1968), 208–230, 260–265; Chester Hartman, "The Housing of Relocated Families," *Journal of the American Institute of Planners,* 30 (November 1964); Jane Jacobs, *The Life and Death of Great American Cities* (New York: Random House, 1961), 8–12.

[12] Langley Carleton Keyes, Jr., *The Rehabilitation Planning Game: A Study in the Diversity of Neighborhood* (Cambridge: M.I.T. Press, 1969).

[13] Hartman, *op. cit.,* reports that 126,000 dwelling units had been demolished as of March 1961, and about 28,000 new ones built. The median monthly rental of all those erected during 1960 came to $158, and in 1962, to $192.

[14] *The Urban Villagers, op. cit.*

placed rose from $41.00 per month to $71.00 per month. Many land-lords and small businesses lost their income as a result of the move. The landlords found that the money they received for their buildings was not enough to buy new ones. Many of the businessmen were unable to find new locations in a city already oversupplied with small stores.

Besides this, Gans found that a great many of the inhabitants liked their neighborhood as it was. They had developed friends and a way of life there which they did not care to change. Marc Fried,[15] a clinical psychologist who studied the West Enders after relocation, reported that 46 per cent of the women and 38 per cent of the men "give evidence of a fairly severe grief reaction or worse" in response to questions about leaving their tight-knit community. Twenty-six per cent of the women remained sad or depressed two years later. A number of older people died during the transition period, and their families attributed their deaths to the trauma of moving. The move scattered the West Enders into various parts of the city.

There was virtually no neighborhood involvement in the project plan-ning, which took eight years. The little information that was released, Gans reports, could not be deciphered by most of the West Enders. When the redevelopment officers got around to setting up relocation of-fices, posting notices that buildings were being acquired under eminent domain and the like, they remained officious and vague, causing confu-sion and concern among the residents. The resulting hostilities and frus-trations among the West Enders—which Gans documents—were greeted with surprise by the officials, who could not understand why the residents were not willing to cooperate in a project which was for their own benefit.

One reason for this may have been the lack of social planning. No sociologists were connected with the redevelopment agency. Social wel-fare agencies were in no way involved in relocation. Gans asserts:

American redevelopment planning so far has proceeded on the assumption that relocation is secondary to redevelopment. Thus, great pains are taken with planning for clearance and reuse of the site, but plans for the present occupants of the site are treated as by-products of the redevelopment pro-posal. For example, the local and federal redevelopment agencies had de-tailed maps of the West End's street and utility system, but they did not

---

[15] Marc Fried, "Grieving for a Lost Home," in Leonard J. Duhl (ed.), *The Urban Condition* (New York: Basic Books, 1963), 151–171.

seem to know the simple fact that a number of owners living in the area depended on the rents they collected for their income.[16]

All this parallels actions discussed in earlier chapters of this book. The Singapore government decided where urban redevelopment projects were to take place. An unknown number already lived in adequate housing. The moves caused many to pay increased rents and in other ways raised their cost of living. Many landlords and small businesses probably lost their income as a result of the move. The psychological traumas involved have not been looked into, but probably existed. There was little neighborhood involvement until the resettlement officers began to post notices concerning termination of residence. Considerable latent hostility was evident. The redevelopment authorities had detailed plans for clearance and reuse of the sites, but knew little about the problems of the people being cleared. They gave those being relocated some financial assistance and helped them find a new place—but nothing more.

In 1965 some of my students and I conducted a survey in three neighborhoods of Singapore.[17] One of these, Hong Lim, is in the heart of Chinatown and is generally recognized to be one of the most crowded and deteriorated sections of the city.[18] Another is one of the original neighborhoods of the Queenstown housing estate—buildings two to six stories in height, built farther apart and at much lower densities than the later public housing projects. It is one of the more attractive public housing estates. We conducted lengthy interviews, using a stratified random sample which proved to reflect fairly accurately the demographic features of the respective neighborhoods, and we were quite careful about our survey technique. There were 48 interviews in Hong Lim, and 40 in Queenstown.

One of the questions we asked is, "Do you like your place of residence very much, a fair amount, not very much, or not at all?" The results reinforce Gans' findings. Twenty-five of the 48 in Hong Lim re-

<hr>

[16] Gans, *People and Plans*, 220.

[17] Robert E. Gamer, "Political Socialization in Three Working Class Neighborhoods of Singapore" (mimeo, 1965), 66 pp.

[18] Barrington Kaye, *Upper Nankin Street, Singapore: A Sociological Study of Households Living in a Densely Populated Area* (Singapore: University of Malaya Press, 1960) described wretched living conditions on one of the streets included in our sample. The conditions on this street are now better because the public housing program has provided a haven for some of the surplus population in this and other inner city neighborhoods.

sponded that they liked their place of residence "very much." (When asked elsewhere in the questionnaire to explain why, 8 gave answers which coded as "I have lived here a long time," 3 stated that it was their place of business, 4 liked the low rent, and 7 liked the nearness to school, market or work.) Only 4 indicated a desire to live in a Housing Board flat.[19] In the Queenstown sample, 21 of the 40 said they liked their place of residence "very much." (Nine felt that the gangster element was less in evidence than before, 2 said they were used to the place, 1 mentioned low rent, 1 liked having his own house, and 4 found themselves near work, market, or school.)

Despite the fact that we compared one of the worst neighborhoods in the old city with one of the best public housing estates, the same percentage in the "slum" as in the housing estate expressed great satisfaction with their home. Some wanted to move from the "slum," but many wanted to stay.

We found other responses of interest too. Thirty-three per cent of the heads of household in Hong Lim reported family incomes so low that they could not afford to move to an HDB flat. Also, as income increased in Hong Lim, so did job satisfaction. In Queenstown the reverse was true; job satisfaction decreased as income increased. This may indicate that residence in HDB flats speeds the desire for mobility, without necessarily satisfying it. Thus residence in the public housing flat may contribute to social frustration and dissatisfaction.

The Singapore Government does not like many of the reasons given by the residents of Hong Lim for wanting to stay. It considers their old way of life backward and disruptive of national unity. Be that as it may, there is still some sign that urban redevelopment of a neighborhood like Hong Lim might work hardships on, and increase the frustrations of, the inhabitants. This data supports many less systematically gathered communications to the effect that today urban redevelopment and public housing in Singapore, as in America, is not necessarily in response to solid demands of the poor.

One difference between Singapore and Boston is the extent of Singapore's public housing program. Boston tried a public housing program. Then its middle class decided that these units were slums in themselves, lowering the value of the property around them. So it ceased to build public housing projects. Today American redevelopment projects gener-

[19] Twenty of the 48 in the total Hong Lim sample indicated a desire to live in an HDB flat.

ally tear down more lower income housing than they replace. The inhabitants of redevelopment areas are resettled into older housing in formerly middle class neighborhoods—thus speeding their deterioration. Or, in the case of some ethnic minorities, the densities of older neighborhoods increase as resettlement cases move in. Singapore's approach contrasts with this. Great quantities of public housing are furnished to take care of resettlement.

The difference between Singapore, with its massive public housing program, and Boston, with its relative inattention to public housing, might be less than it seems at first glance, however.

American cities tend to have a fairly large stock of deteriorating houses, which enter the housing market when their inhabitants move to the suburbs. As Map 2 indicates, Singapore's housing supply was located in a far more compact area than was the case in any American city of comparable population.[20] The move to the suburbs and public housing is not freeing a stock of housing; it is simply lowering the density of occupancy in the shophouses. Rent control was, until recently, in effect in much of the original city, as well as laws which protect tenants from eviction. It is rare for space in any of these shophouses to become available for rent, except for a few buildings downtown where small cubicles or undersized rooms may be rented for high prices.

If a household of low or moderate income is displaced by an urban redevelopment project, it is unlikely to be able to find space in a shophouse. Purchase of a new suburban home would be beyond its means. The family has the choice of squatting or moving into public housing. Land for squatting is becoming scarce, and many move to public housing.

[20] The response of every Singapore administrator to whom I showed this map was identical: "Why don't you show bungalows and wooden structures? The map is deceptive this way." Our map, which was carefully designed by a cartographer using the best extant historical and current map sources, shows only areas covered more or less contiguously by permanent buildings. This category does not include the large bungalows built originally to house the British and laid out on spacious lawns. These bungalows do not constitute housing stock suitable to house resettlement cases; they are the more or less permanent domain of the middle and upper classes. Very few of them have furnished sites for public redevelopment projects, though they are easy to tear down and they cover (together with their lawns) a good deal of territory. In fact, they would be much easier to tear down than those areas where the clearance projects are taking place: the built-up area on this map, squatter-populated land, and farmland. Had someone had a "deceptive" map earlier, one wonders whether history would have been any different. (I think not.)

As in Boston and many American cities, the downtown area is being redeveloped for use by large and middle-sized businesses, and for middle and upper class apartments. Much of the rest of the middle class is moving to the suburbs. In between—in an area as circumscribed as possible—is space for the poor man. The difference is that in America he lives in the former houses of the middle class, while in Singapore he lives in public housing. Each situation has its advantages and drawbacks.

An added irony: The Homes for the People program, in which some special blocs of HDB flats are sold to their occupants, is designed to bring lower middle class people into the housing estates; this program is being expanded in the 1970's. So while the upper middle class move away from the poor, or move the poor away, the lower middle class are left to adjoin the poor. This tale, too, has a familiar ring.

A 1964 HDB publication sounds like an American redevelopment plan brochure, with its middle class rationale and its superficiality about the needs of the "slum" dweller:

What is Urban Renewal and why the need for it in Singapore? In Singapore, Urban Renewal means no less than the gradual demolition of virtually the whole 1,500 acres of the old city and its replacement by an integrated modern city centre worthy of Singapore's future role as the "New York of Malaysia."

The problem is that much of the city centre—the area bounded by Cantonment/Outram Roads south of the Singapore River, and Kallang Basin to the north—consists of dilapidated slum property. . . . Most of the buildings consist of run-down, two-and-three-story shop houses, dating from the second half of the 19th century. Built originally to house a single merchant and his family, whose descendents have long since moved out to the residential suburbs, these properties have degenerated into squalid slums . . . without proper sanitation or any other modern amenities, and often housing ten times as many people as they were ever intended to accommodate . . . the highest incidence of crime and gangsterism is in these central area slums.

Apart from the slums in the city centre, there is the problem of traffic congestion . . . the narrow streets . . . are hopelessly choked with motor traffic . . . while parking facilities are grossly inadequate . . . the whole road system will have to be boldly and drastically redeveloped.[21]

[21] State of Singapore, Housing and Development Board, *50,000 Up*, 84–88.

The emphasis is on removing blight and building a road system to handle the incoming traffic. It is stated that the entire 1,500 acres is a slum, although even casual observation revealed considerable differences in the age and quality of various buildings and neighborhoods. Many buildings currently in disrepair could be repaired. There is the implication that the only way to relieve overcrowding in a building is to tear down the building.[22] There is the astonishing implication that all the merchants have moved away; yet nearly every shophouse contains a business of some sort, and often the family lives upstairs. It seems to be assumed that the demolition of this area would somehow diminish crime and gangsterism.[23] It is taken for granted that life will be better for the inhabitants of these 1,500 acres after they move to an HDB flat, although clearly very little was known about their activities in this slum and how these activities can be transferred. The publication assumed that urban renewal would be good for business.

Total demolition may be good for big business which can take over some of the trade formerly handled by the marginal firms that are forced out of business. On the other hand, the demise of these small businesses might reduce the buying power of the community by cutting out former trade channels and imbalancing the distribution of wealth. The money earned by the big businessman may not circulate in the community as many times as that earned by the small. Total demolition may help big business by giving the city a slick look to catch the eye of the international market. Yet slick looks might be attained in many ways that do not involve wholesale demolition of the entire old city. And the bland new buildings of the urban renewal project may look less interesting to the international market than the unique and colorful buildings of the old.

The whole program had not been thought out very clearly.

Boston's West End project operated on a philosophy similar to that

[22] There are many one-room HDB flats containing eight to ten people. See pp. 116–117.

[23] Interestingly, within Singapore's urban renewal area, the blocks containing the highest concentrations of gangsterism, overcrowding, sanitation problems, deterioration, and traffic congestion are within the areas phased for later action, rather than those where initial demolition took place. New housing estates like Bukit Ho Swee and Toa Payoh are experiencing severe difficulties with gangsters; see R. A. Cloward and L. E. Ohlin, *Delinquency and Opportunity* (Glencoe: Free Press, 1960), 209–211 for a possible explanation.

expressed in the HDB publication. When the project was complete, Boston businessmen did some rethinking. They noted that they had removed a neighborhood of people who did all their shopping, except food buying, downtown, and replaced them with people who had already shopped downtown anyway. To top it off, newcomers were attracted by a new shopping center within the renewal project. The businessmen noted that by taking such an active interest in moving the upper middle class downtown they had put pressure on the middle income housing market, and created a danger of spreading urban blight. The plan for the central business district—the "New Boston"—was complete, with the gargantuan new government and office buildings already rising. If they had any further interest in urban renewal, it was for purposes of stabilizing the neighborhood environments in the rest of the city. So for their next round of urban renewal they decided to try a new approach: citizen participation in planning.

All too often, citizen participation means the creation of neighborhood committees to rubber stamp the plans which the redevelopment authority has drawn up. It is a search for allies in the neighborhood who can be used to combat others in the neighborhood who do not like the new development plan. When Edward Logue took over Boston's urban renewal program in 1961,[24] he aimed for citizen participation that would serve this purpose. Yet he also wanted participation that would deal as much as possible with the needs of those in the neighborhoods while at the same time moderately increase the percentages of the middle class. He wished to keep mass demolition to a minimum and concentrate on rehabilitation and spot clearance. For relocation, he hoped to rely upon existing housing stock more than on public housing.

To get started, he sought existing neighborhood committees which could sponsor the citizenship participation. He found such groups in the South End, Charlestown, and Washington Park. The fact that two of these areas were located near to the downtown area, and that one was on the border line between poorer inner city and wealthier outer city neighborhoods probably did not harm his chances of having these de-

---

[24] This discussion of the South Side, Charlestown, and Washington Park is based upon the case study by Langley Carleton Keyes, *op. cit.* Stephan Thernstrom, *Poverty, Planning, and Politics in the New Boston: The Origins of the ABCD* (New York: Basic Books, 1969), discusses the political interactions that led to this particular approach to citizen participation.

clared urban renewal areas. Two of them contained serious decay, but none was a site of the city's worst hard core poverty.

In South End he found a mixed group of people which Keyes describes as the Skid Row community, the Night People, the Lodging House owners and occupants, the Public Housing People, the Urban Villagers (pockets of third-generation ethnic groups), and the Newcomers (middle class professional people). These people were relatively free from group antagonisms toward one another and committed to the neighborhood as it was.

After considerable interaction between the redevelopment officers and a gamut of local groups, a plan was agreed upon that called for the relocation of less than 20 per cent of the populace (1,652 households) and, overall, rather minor modifications in the neighborhood. More substandard buildings were left standing than the redevelopment agency would have wished. Demolition mainly affected liquor stores and rooming-house tenants. A number of new rental housing units (subsidized under article 221 d3 of the federal housing legislation) renting from $75 per month upward would absorb part of these, as would 300 new units of public housing, 500 new apartments for the elderly, and nonprofit rehabilitation housing and a rent supplement program. Still, a fair number of the poorer citizens—especially from Skid Row—would be left to try to fend for themselves elsewhere in the city. Efforts were made here—as in the other two projects—at combining social planning with the physical planning, so as to look to broader human needs than housing. They came to nothing.

In Charlestown, a homogeneous lower middle class Italian community, the results were similar. Few houses were to be demolished, while a number would be rehabilitated. There would be no public housing except for the elderly. The outcome seemed generally satisfactory to everyone.

In Washington Park, a group of upper middle class blacks and whites were organized to remove the influx of lower income blacks from their neighborhood. The lower income black took little part in the planning process. In the end 35 per cent of the structures were demolished (vs. the neighborhood groups' desire for 60 per cent and the rehabilitation officers' desire for 25 per cent) and 6,500 rehabilitated. Except for 200 units of housing for the elderly, all the replacements were to be middle class housing. This pushed 1,582 lower income households out of the neighborhood. While 75 per cent of the families were eligible for public

housing, many had families too large for the small units available elsewhere in the community. A later attempt by Logue to create 30 large-
family public housing units in the neighborhood was heatedly and deci-
sively rejected.

Overall the three plans were less disruptive to the poor than would
have been total demolition. Yet they displaced many poorer people
under conditions which tended to raise their cost of living without a
commensurate rise in income. The poor benefited little from citizen participation, and in Washington Park may have lost more from its presence than they would have without it.

Logue could take this approach to planning only as long as he was
freed from pressures by big developers to rebuild these areas or from
political pressures that would have forced him to give less discretion to
neighborhood opinion of these groups otherwise without political
power. This approach to planning could succeed only because it did not
happen to step on the perceived interests of anyone with power. Stated
another way: the biggest contenders had opted out of this round, because the general direction things were taking was satisfactory. Had the
areas been closer to downtown, or had those downtown cared more ag-
gressively about totally rebuilding the city, they could probably have
had their own way.

I find it hard to imagine that Singapore would move this far toward
citizen participation. The social structure is strong enough to support
such activities. If the fear of Communist involvement could be removed,
the political structure would probably be adaptable to it as well. The
economic and bureaucratic structures might not be so adaptable.

The fact that Urban Renewal is shifting its position since the *50,000
Up* article quoted a few pages back—which called for total demolition
of the downtown area—is evident from this 1969 article by the Head of
Urban Renewal:

Contrary to misinformed belief, urban renewal does not mean just the pulling down of slum sections and rebuilding on the cleared area. There are actually three indispensable elements of urban renewal: conservation, rehabilitation, and rebuilding. . . .

Initially there will be a high percentage of public re-development. But as
the renewal process moves towards the Central Business District around the
Singapore River there will be a greater emphasis on conservation and rehabilitation rather than reconstruction, and also greater participation by private enterprise. It is envisaged that the Government will, to an increasing

extent, merely provide the overall planning, co-ordination, and infrastructure for the private sector, which could then undertake renewal of its own initiative. This has the advantage of not involving the Government in the complex task of acquisition and resettlement.[25]

Singapore, too, seems to be on the road toward citizen participation —by the upper and middle classes.

The present problem that urban renewal faces in Singapore is that of bringing private investors into the action. The government is concerned to stimulate a tremendous burst of investment activity in order to create employment for the large number of people entering the job market (see pp. 134–137). If urban and industrial estates are to succeed, the government must attract private investors to fill up the portions of renewal areas not occupied by public housing. To do this it has had to bring private investors in on planning more than in the past.

The government must compromise with these investors in order for its program to succeed. Should it wish to pursue rehabilitation it will also need to negotiate with present owners of buildings; the effects of this would probably be to drive out many present poorer occupants. It need not compromise with the ordinary residents of the inner city.

POLITICAL CAPABILITIES AND THE POOR

The governments of Boston and Singapore have the political capabilities to create programs that give benefits to the poor. They do not necessarily have the capabilities to give benefits to the poor when doing so would run afoul of the interests of those who control resources, skills, and administrative capabilities.

There is no fixed power structure where one group wins on every issue. Sometimes the big contractors win, and sometimes they lose. The same is true of mayors, or aldermen, or prime ministers, or middle class neighborhood committees, or administrators, or big investors. That is because all these people are among those who share political power. Yet the poorer citizen has no resources, skills, or administrative capabilities that give him a share of power. The programmatic concessions he has won have usually been attained during times of political crisis. He has not won the power to see that the programs are pieced together in a manner that meets his most fundamental needs.

[25] Alan F. C. Choe, *op. cit.*, 164–168.

CHAPTER VIII

Singapore and Other Developing Nations

Ours is a highly urbanized and complex money economy. If there is any recession, any trade fall-off, any adverse balance of payments, we must all remember that there is no going back to the land and living off the land.

Lee Kuan Yew, *The Mirror,*
October 10, 1966

Singapore is a modern city. It is also a developing nation. Some people consider this paradoxical. They feel that developing nations have fewer preconditions for planning, more corruption, lower politicization, and less firmly established political systems than modern ones. Singapore has many preconditions, a highly politicized populace, high political stability, and low corruption. Hence it must be modern—not developing.

In retort, one might argue that the United States is developing—not modern. Under the Soil Bank program in the United States, big landowners receive large subsidies for leaving their land fallow while tenants on many of their farms go hungry; yet legislators repeatedly defeat proposed legislation that would bring relief to these tenants. This subsidy is a "legitimate" receipt of payment from a "legitimate" program. Its presence, nevertheless, connotes a corrupted political system. This is the same corruption displayed when wealthy Indian politicians and judges refuse to make monetary and land reforms that might improve the distribution of income there. These major corruptions that prevent political systems from answering human needs should receive far more attention than the question of whether civil servants receive money under the table (a practice not universally present in "developing" nations, and not unknown in "modern" political systems either). They are present in virtually every nation. Hence, if corruption is a characteristic of underdevelopment, the United States shares in this characteristic.

On the other hand, much international capital has flowed to create dams, law schools, roads, water filtration plants, factories, institutes and universities, scholarships, and other resources around the world. India, Indonesia, Ghana, Venezuela, and Egypt, and others have developed many aspects of their infrastructures and have a manpower pool containing advanced skills and administrative capabilities (though severe poverty persists despite all this). So they are, at least to some degree, modern.

Many developing nations experience periodic revolutions; many others do not. In either case, they often have a high degree of continuity in the way their political systems behave. Blinded by exotic nuances in the forms of operation in political systems around the world, those of us who have been brought up on textbooks comparing simply Britain, Germany, the Soviet Union, and the United States often fail to recognize political stability when we see it dressed in non-Western garb, or political instability when we see it in our own system.[1]

Our assessment of differences between developing and modern nations is, in short, often superficial. Yet one very real difference does exist. The middle class is much smaller in developing nations than in developed ones—especially in rural regions.

INDUSTRIALIZATION
AND THE MIDDLE CLASSES

There have been many plans propounded for increasing the size of the middle classes in developing nations. Nearly all of them call for increased modernization in some way. Some call for a modernization of the economic infrastructure. Others call for upgrading the efficiency of the army or administration.[2] Some want increased democracy, or more authoritarianism. Nearly every nation is upgrading education. There are those who feel that the spread of consumer goods is a healthy indication of advance. Economists are concerned with increasing gross national product, inducing savings, diversifying trading bases, and promoting investment. New industries are usually sought and welcomed, for they seem to contribute to all these processes.

[1] For lengthier discussion of this subject see Robert E. Gamer, "Southeast Asia's Political Systems: An Overview," *Journal of Southeast Asian History,* 8 (March 1967), 139–185.

[2] The best of this genre: Samuel P. Huntington, "Political Development and Political Decay," *World Politics* (April 1965), 393–427.

Faith that such plans will succeed in creating a large middle class in developing nations is perhaps implicitly rooted in the notion that they appeared to produce a large middle class in the developed nations. The appearance is deceptive. The United States offers an example. The middle classes did not emerge in America because of industrialization; their roots go back to the vast land grants programs that preceded and accompanied industrialization. America already had a landholding and town-dwelling middle class when it began its industrial revolution in earnest in the 1840's. When industry grew, middle class individuals could demand a price for their participation. They occupied much of the cultivated land, and they constituted the only readily available consumers for manufactured goods. The small businessman became an important part of the economy, and a wide variety of skills was called for. The union movement was resisted by industrialists, but skilled workers did have other employment options available, and they were also potential consumers and had achieved a degree of political efficacy —especially in urban politics. And, by the time the rest of the world joined the industrial revolution, many of the most valuable resources were already in the control of United States and European investors. They had a head start, and the colonial and corporate expansion abroad offered still additional opportunities for Americans to join the ranks of the middle class.

In Africa, Asia, and Latin America, there was practically no middle class at the inception of modernization. Most people were subsistence farmers, hunters, and fishermen. They could offer little resistance to the colonialists and businessmen. When a class of kings or nobles was present, these individuals often made deals with the foreigners, allowing them to take land from the populace without giving them resources in return.[3] The foreigners could take the resources away and make them into products to sell to consumers in the nations where industrialization was already more advanced.

Furthermore, rural America at the start of the industrial revolution had a money economy, formal ownership of land, elected officials, and

[3] When there was a king or class of nobles, the industrializers usually made treaties or agreements with these individuals, giving them a share in profits from the new economic ventures. In turn, they were left to rule over their former territories and to become major landholders. This arrangement served as a buffer between the industrializer and the peasant. In time, as the sons of the kings and nobles receive modern educations and accumulate modern gadgets, they themselves may contribute to the breakdown of the values of the old society.

trade links with other parts of the country.[4] Industrialists worked within this existing system. In Africa, Asia, and Latin America, although rural areas often lay outside the money economy, people generally had developed fairly sophisticated political systems.[5] When the businessmen and industrialists arrived there, they often destroyed the old political systems, which would have been difficult to adapt to the modern economy.

For instance, families would formerly build themselves dwellings, using materials and skills immediately at hand. Should a dispute arise concerning the location of a dwelling, or a robbery, or an inheritance, the community had convenient procedures worked out for settling the argument. Often these matters could be decided directly, and completely, by the kinship leader; should he fail, there were specialized community bodies—composed of friends and neighbors—for this purpose. Water came from individual wells or watering holes, and fuel was collected in the forests or fields. Individuals could dispose of waste where they chose.

Then came plantations, mines, absentee landlord economies, cities, and rapid population growth. People were shifted about, and their lands were sold to the highest bidders. The old social structures disintegrated. To build or rent a house, or buy fuel, the displaced peasant now needs money. To get a land deed or to settle a dispute or apprehend robbers or obtain water or dispose of waste he has to rely on the assistance of the formal government and administration, which are composed of people he does not know. Whereas these functions were inevitably performed under the older political systems, it is now often difficult for the displaced peasant to obtain either the money or the government services to ensure their performance. Most of these people own no resources to begin with. They have no titles, and are not required as immediate consumers. And for its most advanced skills, industry can generally rely on its workers in the more advanced nations. Hence the displaced peasant has no claim on the money and services he needs to adjust to modern life.

In short, industrialization does not necessarily produce a broad middle class; for such a class to emerge under industrialization, land and

---

[4] For a good bibliography on self-sufficiency in rural United States see T. Lynn Smith, *The Process of Rural Development in Latin America* (Gainesville: University of Florida, 1967), chapter 6.

[5] For books and articles discussing how modernization breaks down village life and makes it depend on urban elites see the Bibliography.

skills and other resources must already be spread among a large number of people. The main difference between nations that industrialized early and those industrializing late is that the former were able to distribute the fruits of industrializing to a fair percentage of the already-resource-bearing populace, and then proceed to exploit the resources of the rest of the world so as to keep that distribution intact at home. Those without any resources in the first place may have little to gain from this process; the system can maintain itself without adding large numbers of people to the ranks of those initial middle classes. As the per capita wealth of the middle classes increases, they can purchase and consume more goods just among themselves (thus increasing their per capita wealth even more), without admitting many more people to their ranks. The vast majority of the world's populace is poor; there is some reason to expect that this is the way things will remain unless they can devise means to *demand* rewards from the system.

Nations must develop the will and capacity to right the imbalances caused by this revolution in modernization,[6] to allow those whose former social systems have been upset to absorb the transformations in their lives. They must develop this will and capacity fast enough to right the imbalances of their urban sectors,[7] yet cautiously enough that they do not destroy the self-sufficiency of their rural sectors.

The attempt to solve this problem by accelerating industrialization may not work. Industrialization may increase the size of the middle classes somewhat, and the wealth of the upper classes. Yet it may at the same time create interdependence between the middle and upper classes and give them a vested interest in programs that maintain the poverty of the lower classes. If this is true, then the whole question of using urban redevelopment and industrialization needs re-examination. In this Chapter, I question whether the vigorous pursuit of urban modernization is in the best interests of Singapore and other developing nations.

---

[6] I borrow this phraseology from the writings of Manfred Halpern. See Manfred Halpern, "The Revolution of Modernization in National and International Society," in Carl J. Friedrich (ed.), *Revolution—Nomos VIII* (New York: Atherton, 1966).

[7] The peripheral slums of Latin America contain 35 million people, and continue to grow. See Francis Violich and Juan B. Astica, *Community Development and the Urban Planning Process in Latin America* (Los Angeles: University of California, 1967) and Morris Juppenlatz, *Cities in Transformation: The Urban Squatter Problem of the Developing World* (St. Lucia: University of Queensland, 1970) on the sorts of urgent problems that confront cities in the developing world. Also see Chapter VI, footnote 25.

When programs fail to deal with popular needs we often assume there is something lacking in the details of administration. The pursuit of urban development and industrialization may in itself be the culprit.

The position of the middle classes in the developing world is more tenuous than the position of the middle classes in North America and most of Europe. Not only is their size smaller in relation to their total population; they are also relatively far from the sources of industrial power and do not carry much weight when the big decisions that affect the world economy are made. The more farsighted among them might recognize these as reasons why they would have an interest in markedly increasing the size of their own ranks. Yet even if they should develop the *will* to do so, they probably are not in a *position* to do so. The very processes that gave them middle class status may be their Achilles' heel.

Although, as an entrepreneurial outpost and an urban center Singapore probably developed a larger middle class than most developing nations, her middle class is smaller and less prosperous than those in most of Western Europe and the United States. Though she is unusually cut off from the rural sector, her stability and prosperity are ultimately linked to the rural areas that surround her. This will be especially true in the event of a world recession. The course her urban development is taking may subtly help to weaken the self-sufficiency of those surrounding areas, and in so doing hamper Singapore's ability to solve her own problems. The following comparison of Singapore and Malaysia with Cuba—which has taken a different approach to urban development—explores this argument.

URBAN DEVELOPMENT: SINGAPORE VS. HAVANA

Singapore is basing her prosperity on mines, plantations, and industries. The mines and plantations provide the raw material for the industries, for consumer goods, and for trade. Singapore's businessmen have an interest in keeping the costs of raw materials low. They have more than sufficient unskilled labor, without immigration from rural areas, and are under no pressure to invest in rural development ventures other than those that supply their raw materials. Singapore's people are being moved to housing that must generate revenue for years to come; any return to rural areas by large numbers of people would harm her ability to amortize these structures. Hence Singapore is not helping considerably to eradicate rural poverty or to absorb surplus rural population.

The Malaysian government has been working more extensively on aiding the rural poor. It has been building wells, drains, roads, schools, and mosques in rural areas, has distributed some state land to farmers as small holdings (though the percentage of rural people affected by this program is small), and is assisting in rice production and setting up craft workshops. Yet Malaysia, too, bases her prosperity on mines, plantations, and industries. To generate profits, she needs to keep the costs of raw materials and labor low and to hire only that labor which is needed in production. The rural standard of living remains low, and many are unemployed or underemployed.

It is commonly remarked that the population explosion is the most serious crisis facing the modern world. Perhaps, instead, the crisis lies in the direction that development programs are taking. Most development programs focus on increasing production of industrial goods, metals, oil, sugar, natural rubber, pineapples, bananas, oil palm, cotton, cocoa, coffee, tea, meat, and other such plantation goods. These commodities are used for satisfying the consumer cravings of a minority of the world's populace: the upper and middle classes. Or they are consumed by military machines and industrial establishments, which, in turn, also produce primarily for the middle and upper classes. The lower classes have little to gain from this involuted process (even in the form of decent wages on the plantations). Despite this, the developing nations are trying to improve the lives of their people by becoming wrapped up in the process of producing these very items. Economic growth means the middle and upper classes producing for the middle and upper classes, while borrowing some labor from the lower classes.

This production includes some residue in the form of housing, medical attention, welfare, basic foodstuffs, new clothing, transistor radios, small wage increases (for the small percentage who are on wages), and other benefits for the broader populace. Yet it also creates a group of people with a vested interest in preventing anything from standing in the way of increased profits from production of these items. Only a limited number of people are involved in producing and consuming these items. The remainder can be ignored.

Nations like Malaysia and Singapore might have to think twice about some projects that might actually improve the economic status of poorer rural dwellers. Investment funds are readily available from the governments of wealthier nations, international agencies, corporations, and banks to develop large land holdings in the countryside. They are also readily available for armies that might be expected to protect such development projects. They are not so readily available for projects that might enhance the position of the rural poor or markedly raise the cost of urban labor.

For instance, an electrical power dam will aid industrialization, increase productivity, and generate further investment income if it is made to serve paying consumers in mines, plantations, and cities. It will serve none of these purposes if it is used to provide irrigation and electricity for small farmers who cannot pay. And income from large plantations (which is enhanced by low wages) can be quickly reinvested. Increased productivity for small farms may take heavy investment, yet never be translated into anything more than an improved diet for those on the farm. It may at the same time increase the cost of labor and provide farmers with a means to charge middlemen more for the commodities they raise.

That is what the population explosion means. Population crisis, viewed from this perspective, means that an increasing number of poor people (larger than the number needed to man the plantations, industries, and armies) want a share in the action, and the economic system is not geared to giving it to them. This is by no means proof that population is growing at a rate beyond that which the earth's resources and technology can support in comfort.

Those who control investment processes are not the only ones who resist the changes that are needed to right the imbalances caused by the revolution of modernization. There is also likely to be resistance to rural development among those who are still absorbed in intact preindustrial social systems. They are not likely to relish the major changes in their way of life that real increases in rural productivity and adjustment to a monetary economy would entail. Or at least they are suspicious of the modernization that is serving to replace former self-sufficiency with helplessness and social disintegration.

The hostility to innovation that results from the rural dweller's sense of helplessness makes it easier for those who control resources, skills, and administrative and political capabilities to rationalize their natural proclivities toward emphasizing development based upon industrialization, mining, and plantations: The peasant does not want to be modernized, so start modernization elsewhere. But the increasing disintegration of rural life, the spreading squatters' colonies, the growing numbers of unemployed and underemployed, make one wonder where this approach will lead.[8] These are blamed on the population explosion, rather than on the system. They presumably involve a stage in the industrial revolution that will eventually be passed through if population can somehow be held down. The innovators argue that education will create new jobs along with new job skills. They suggest that hard work will overcome the problem.

Industrialization in America and the more advanced nations began with a middle class already established and has depended upon continuing exploitation of the resources and people of the world's hinterlands. Even so, poverty persists in America. It may be that industrialization in the developing nations will also continue to exploit the people in the hinterland, and those who have crept from the hinterland to the shadowy edges of the city.

Cuba has made efforts to circumvent these problems. Only time will tell how successful she might be. But the directions she has taken give some idea of the sorts of emphases needed if the situation is to improve.

Singapore/Malaya and Cuba have a lot in common. Both have approximately the same shape, size, latitude, climate, topography, and flora. Both have populations around 10 million. During the past two hundred years large plantations, owned by foreigners in conjunction with local interests, have come to dominate the developed portions of their hinterlands. More recently, mining was begun—also by foreign corporations in conjunction with local capital. Much of the indigenous population has been left to small holdings, with a moderate number of medium-sized farms. The nations are racially heterogeneous, exhibiting considerable racial tension. The trading, investing, and white collar classes have gravitated into cities—Singapore and Havana being the largest in the two cases. Here industries have sprung up in recent years. It is in the cities that most civil servants have been recruited. The majority of the populace lives on a near subsistence economy, or on a very low income. Many have become dissatisfied with life on the farm in the

---

[8] For similar arguments see Peter C. W. Gutkind, "The Poor in Urban Africa: A Prologue to Modernization, Conflict and the Unfinished Revolution" in W. Bloomberg and H. Schmandt, *Power, Poverty and Urban Policy* (Beverly Hills: Sage Publishing, 1968) and Lisa Redfield Peattie, *The View from the Barrio* (Ann Arbor: University of Michigan Press, 1968). William Mangin, "Poverty and Politics of Latin America," in Bloomberg and Schmandt, *op. cit.*, offers a more optimistic perspective.

face of the possibilities of urban existence and have moved to the city —although this problem is probably less severe in Singapore and Malaya than in many other places.

When Castro first came to power he took a more traditional approach to development; like the leaders of Malaysia and Singapore, he emphasized the development of plantations, industry, mining, and trading. These policies led to the same problems: despite increased welfare and educational programs for the poor, rural poverty persisted. There was little for the unemployed on the outskirts of the city to do. Factories could not absorb many of them.

In 1964, Castro changed his course.[9] The emphasis on industry, mining, and trading manufactured goods decreased. The emphasis on plantations continued, but with a difference: Rather than emphasizing the production of sugar cane, the focus was upon increasing production of crops that would appeal to a broader range of consumers. Livestock and milk output was encouraged. Thousands of citrus trees were planted, along with winter vegetables, fibers, and precious woods. Experiments were conducted in harvesting tropical fruits and in planting rice, coffee, gandul beans, and other crops.

To aid these efforts, men and resources were mobilized to produce and distribute fertilizer; construct rural roads and electrical installations; improve agricultural technology and technique; and develop rural housing, education, and welfare.

About 30 per cent of Cuban land, according to Castro, remained in small and some middle-sized holdings. In regions where the agricultural program is well off the ground, these farmers receive free seed, fertilizer, use of tractors, and technical assistance, in exchange for raising particular crops. They also pay no rent and receive free medical attention and free education.

The large plantations, which occupy most of the usable land, now belong to the government. Production here is organized on a large scale. Profits not needed for foreign exchange are supposed to be used to extend various welfare and educational benefits to the workers and to finance additional rural development projects.

If the farmer is aided in producing crops that he can both eat and sell on the market, and if he is allowed to retain some of the profits, his economic and social position is likely to be stabilized and his well-being

[9] See Bibliography.

improved. A program based on agriculture rather than industry directly aids many people rather than just a few; it can be quickly promulgated before the level of technology is high and without heavy dependence on imports. Yet this approach could probably not have been attempted had there not first been a political and economic revolution.

First of all, in order to be placed in a position where he can experiment with new crops the farmer needs to be assured of a market for these crops. Marketing mechanisms (trucking, middlemen) and mills are nearly always in the control of capitalists, whose operations are designed to handle only certain kinds of high-profit crops. Gandul beans generate less profit than sugar cane. If the middlemen do not wish to see low-profit crops develop, they can refuse to market them or pay a price so low as to make them worthless for anything other than personal consumption. It is difficult to circumvent these marketing operations. Those who control them generally have considerable political influence.

Second, the small holder needs fertilizer, technical assistance, seed, and sometimes irrigation. He usually cannot afford to pay for them. Creditors supply these items for him, and in so doing keep the farmer perpetually indebted to them.

Third, if the farmer does not own his own land he is likely to derive little from it other than mere subsistence. The surplus must largely go to pay the landlord and creditors.

And fourth, much of the foreign exchange that supports the city's (e.g., Havana's) standard of living derives from selling basic agricultural products abroad. There is apt to be little support among the urban middle class for programs that might reduce such exports or divert the profits back to the countryside.

To compound the difficulty, the marketer, creditor, and landlord often have close ties. Frequently they are the same people. Furthermore, they tend to live in the city and invest profits in urban enterprises. Fertilizer factories are a favorite investment. To assure their favored position, they become active in politics. They are likely to resist heavy government spending on rural projects that do not serve to increase their profits.

In order to cut through this maze it is necessary for the government to gain some control over market mechanisms, to eliminate the farmer's need for creditors, and to give the farmer some control over his own land. To do so is to attack the most fundamental interests that rule developing nations today. In addition, since most of these interests have ties with foreign corporations, such reforms usually mean tangling with the United States as well.

A program of this kind also means hitting at the favored position of the city. In developing nations, cities are the most comfortable places to live. They offer the best jobs. If the peasant is to be persuaded to remain on the farm rather than migrate to the squatter colonies around cities, the future prospects on the farm must be made to appear more dramatic than in the city. The magnetic field must be reversed so that the pull is toward the countryside. To aid farmers, the engineer and teacher and doctor and administrator will have to move to rural areas —seldom an attractive prospect for the urban middle class. Money spent to aid subsistence farmers will contribute little to the gross national product. At the same time, it will consume resources which might have been spent on urban development.

Castro has attempted to foment such a reverse trend toward rural areas. The biggest employment opportunities for educated young people entering the job market are in the countryside—not in the city. They can work as engineers in the roadbuilding or dam projects. They can serve as managers of the agricultural production centers (the former plantations taken over by the state). Or they can work as doctors and nurses and teachers in the many welfare facilities being established in rural areas. The new construction on low-income housing is going on in smaller cities rather than in Havana.

Meanwhile Havana is experiencing economic stagnation. Wages are frozen, food is rationed, import of automobiles and luxury goods is banned and housing grows older. This is partly due to the inefficient use of funds during the early years of the Castro regime. The exodus of private investment funds and the United States boycott also have taken their toll. One might argue that the latter were inevitable, given the land reform, takeover of marketing and credit, and crackdowns on business profits; perhaps they were not. But it does seem likely that a nation with limited financial resources that markedly increases social expenditures in the countryside and shifts its emphasis from export commodities to consumables would have to cut back on urban development and middle class salaries.

The economic opportunities offered the middle classes under such rural development programs can never be as great as those they might receive from industrialization of the city. Yet the economic horizon offered the poor peasants under such a program is infinitely wider.

Thousands of individuals—mostly middle class—have left the island. Their departures have relieved the regime of the need to use severe coercion on its citizens. Many other educated Cubans seem to be supporting the attempt, at least to be giving it a try for a time. There seems to be evidence of enthusiastic support even among many who have so far gained little except a new sense of pride and anticipation of betterment from the regime.

It seems unlikely that the international corporations, major investors, and large landowners could have been persuaded to turn to these new policies by anything other than force. They were not likely to accept voluntary expropriation of land, businesses, and middleman and credit operations. Nor were they likely to voluntarily kill the goose that lays the golden egg by themselves promoting the sorts of rural reforms that would do away with the profits of landlords, middlemen, and creditors, and reduce the profits of mines and plantations.

Faced with heavy foreign indebtedness, Castro has had to plow back many of his gandul beans to make way for more marketable sugar cane. He has few profits to retain from the sugar cane for rural development. The pursuit may be more than he can manage. He is working with many liabilities—some of his own making—which might prevent success. Yet it seems significant that a nation has been able to go even so far as to develop and begin to pursue goals that call for agricultural development at the expense of big landowners, industrialization, and the urban middle classes. And one wonders whether a city like Singapore could retain its exceptional prosperity if it were surrounded by a countryside in the process of reforms such as Castro has instituted—whether the rural reforms could be accomplished without causing the landowners, industrialists, and middle classes to suffer. Are Havana's deprivations an accident of history, or an inherent part of rural development?

Shortly after it was announced over the Singapore radio on the morning of August 10, 1965, that Singapore had separated from Malaysia, I heard the sound of firecrackers coming from populous downtown areas. Though I was over three miles away, the staccato was loud and lasted for some minutes. I feared that rioting had greeted the surprise announcement. The noise proved, however, to be that of celebration. Later that day when the Prime Minister appeared on television to discuss Singapore's ejection he was in tears. He said that one of his dreams had been shattered. In speeches during ensuing days, however, he complained about the development funds that Singapore had contributed to the federal government of Malaysia and referred to them as wasted expenditures. There must have been some satisfaction that Singapore would be freed from catering to the wishes of rural areas. I have often wondered how Singapore might have reacted had it been asked to make real sacrifices to aid the rural folk.

POLITICAL CAPABILITIES AND THE POOR

Political capabilities in today's world are weighted in the direction of urban modernization. This is so because a high percentage of those who control the resources and skills needed by governments if they are to rule successfully have a vested interest in urban modernization. Their interest is primarily in the modernization of the large business enterprise. Their lack of interest in the marginal business, the small farmer, and the bottom wage earner or unemployed individual may prove a fatal flaw in modernization and in political power based upon modernization. Two horses (one considerably stronger than the other) are pulling the rope in opposite directions. What is needed for rural development (and aiding the urban poor) may slow urban development. And vice versa. The world of factories and mines and plantations may be working at cross-purposes with the world where the majority of the earth's people live. As cities like Singapore and Kuala Lumpur progress in modernization, the possibility diminishes that their governments would ever desire to backtrack and take the road of Havana. So the gap widens as industrialization progresses.

Unless resources, skills, and administrative capabilities are in the hands of a relatively few people, government may be *unable* to solve the problems that the revolution of modernization is creating in preindustrial rural hinterlands. With these resources, skills, and administrative capabilities in the hands of a relative few, it may be *unwilling* to solve them. Governments are easily committed to modernization that gives health, education, and housing benefits to the poor; governments are not easily committed to programs that give social and economic betterment to the poor when this means opposing those who keep them in power. What is profitable to the resource bearers is politically expedient.

The time may come, however, when a new dimension is added to political expediency. Great masses of people have never found themselves in a position to effect programs that conflict with the interests of resource bearers. Nor have they shown an interest in amassing sufficient power to overthrow resource bearers. So it has never appeared necessary to enact programs that are not profitable to at least some of the major resource bearers. Less advantaged citizens have usually been willing to go along with whatever compromises the middle and upper classes reach among themselves. Should they cease doing so, they might force governments to choose between the interests of the major resource bearers and the interests of large numbers of people.

A day might come when Singapore would regret that it has reduced the number of marginal businesses, diminished the number of small farmers, and moved the zinc- and atap-dwellers to Housing Board flats. Once men have been absorbed into urban culture, it is hard for them to return to rural culture. If worldwide economic recession makes it difficult for Singapore's urban culture to offer job security to all its people, they may wish that they could fall back on the partial security that semirural existence can provide. They might begin to look past racial and cultural differences to see an advantage in rural living: urban development does not provide a minimal income for everyone; a developed rural economy can at least provide sustenance. Government might then begin to feel tension about the active pursuit of urban development programs. Yet, even that is not likely to divert its development funds into rural development. Those resources that its investers do not transfer abroad are more likely to go into urban public works programs to bolster a sagging economy. Unless the unemployed and underemployed could attain real means of political power, the government would still not find it politically necessary to make marked shifts in policy toward a more self-sufficient rural economy.

CHAPTER IX

Environment, Community, and Economic Growth

What's the use of learning a trade you can't enter? What good is a nice house if the payments are so high you have to skimp on groceries? What good is a group, if there's no one who cares?

Most individuals living in today's world are experiencing some degree of change in their jobs, education, places of abode, and/or peer groups. Unless means can be effected to change the four aspects in a synchronized manner, personal insecurity can result. Innovations are not in themselves uplifting unless a balance is achieved in the manner in which they affect the individual. If they put his expectations out of line with his potentials, or his rent out of line with his income, they may serve to decrease the stability of his overall environment.

Yet it is inherent in bureaucracy and economic institutions that they deal with the various aspects of environment piece by piece, rather than in an integrated manner. An economic institution determines a man's rent. A bureaucratic establishment sees to his education. Another economic institution has control over his pay check. A set of social and economic forces determine who his neighbors will be. Other separate bureaucratic and economic groupings determine the transportation network that will surround him, how his garbage will be collected, whether the tree or vacant house next door can be removed, what price he will receive for his produce, and where he can obtain his water and buy his groceries and even bury his dead. Whether these functions cumulatively improve or degenerate his environment is left largely to chance.

We do not often measure economic growth in terms of how much stability it lends to the environments of how many people; we usually measure it in terms of how many dollars are generated by the owners and operators of plantations, marketing operations, mines, construction firms, and factories selling things to one another.

We do not often measure the success of welfare operations in terms of the balance they bring among the home, job, educational, and social situations of the poor; rather we focus on dollars spent or units of things constructed or distributed.

We do not think of an efficient bureaucracy as one that has carefully coordinated with other groups whose interests their projects affect; we more often think of bureaucratic efficiency in terms of number of units produced.

We tend to assess political processes in terms of the width of political participation, or the amount of free speech, or the degree of political or economic stability, or the size of the middle class, or the number of development projects they generate; we do not often think of them in terms of how evenly and effectively they distribute the power to look after personal needs.

We analyze government goals in terms of how they affect political cleavages; we tend to take it for granted that programs that contribute to lowering political tensions are at the same time successful in catering to human needs.

Perhaps one reason for this is that suburbanites often have the resources and skills needed to follow up on political compromises so as to assure that they are adapted to their own personal needs. When the dead tree crops up next door, they get it removed. If they want a school, they get it built. If they are frightened of certain kinds of neighbors, they keep them out. If the local college rejects junior, they find him another.

They cannot empathize with situations where such needs remain perpetually unattended to because those having the needs do not command the resources and skills necessary to assure that programs will be adapted to those needs. In such situations political latency may simply affirm a sense of impotence over satisfaction of needs. Political activism may produce programs for removing trees or building schools or opening up colleges. But those involved in the activism may not command the follow-up skills and resources needed to ensure that *their* trees are removed, that the schools serve their particular needs, and that the college programs are adapted to the peculiar requirements of their children.

In the suburb, when something in the environment gets out of line, means can often be found to get it back into line. In an inner city or a rural small holding, the political capabilities to perform this feat are often unavailable.

The poor will never achieve the power needed to live in big houses and dine regularly on fatted calves. They might at least attain access to enough political power to permit some of the imbalances which creep into their environments to be removed. Without such power, there is little likelihood that any Comprehensive Planner will do it for them. Lacking the resources and skills of the middle classes, they probably need to explore new and different paths toward attaining such political capability.

Some experiments have been set up with an intention to give such power to the poor. We shall examine three of these programs, to see what hope they may hold.

THE MODEL CITIES PROGRAM
IN THE UNITED STATES

In the wake of racial rioting, the United States Congress passed the 1966 Demonstration Cities and Metropolitan Development Act. As a result of this legislation, Model Cities Programs have been organized in cities throughout the United States.

Under this program, Model Cities Field Offices are set up in each participating city, with a director and a planning staff. These are responsible to the mayor, and their activities are federally financed. An area, or areas—generally in the inner city and generally containing a disproportionate number of people of lower socioeconomic standing—is chosen for the project. This area is divided up into separate neighborhoods. Public meetings are held to alert the citizens and existing organizations to the program; as an outgrowth of these meetings, neighborhood planning groups are elected within each neighborhood.

The purpose of the program is to allow these neighborhoods to make a concerted and coordinated attack on their housing, health, municipal services, recreation, transportation, education, welfare, social service, crime, law enforcement, economic development, and employment problems. Each neighborhood planning group is to spot its own problems and recommend solutions. With the aid of the Model Cities Field Office they draw up a proposal incorporating programs in all these areas of concern. This is submitted for approval by the city and by Washington. The Model Cities Field Office and the neighborhood planning groups then act as coordinators with the local and federal bureaucratic apparatuses which must implement the programs.

One of the above-mentioned areas of concern is housing. The approach of the Kansas City, Missouri, Model Cities Program to this problem will give an indication of how the program works.

The neighborhood planning groups identified [1] such grievances as inability to make home improvements, overcrowding, abandoned or boarded structures, high insurance rates and cancellations, lack of proper housing code enforcement, inadequate knowledge of tenant rights, lack of home ownership opportunities in and out of the Model City neighborhoods, and discrimination in rental and sales of housing.

To deal with these grievances, the Model Cities Program set forth a set of goals: Over the next five years it intended to initiate a program to rehabilitate 1,820 moderately run-down housing units in the Model Neighborhoods, build 750 units of public housing for the elderly and construct 2,850 units of other kinds of housing, assist 405 families in achieving home ownership, add 19 additional inspectors for concentrated code enforcement, remove 1,000 dilapidated or abandoned structures and rehabilitate 1,300 others, and update minimum housing standards and building codes and zoning regulations. It also intended to set up a Housing Development Corporation and Information Center to secure home insurance for Model Neighborhood residents at reasonable rates, advise tenants of their rights, and encourage the philosophy of open housing.

In the other program areas (such as transportation and welfare) goals were drawn up in a similar manner.

A number of agencies would be involved in administering the housing programs. Model Cities itself was to have some money available for home improvement loans for 120 units of housing and for some relocation assistance; the rest of the loans would come from agencies of the federal Housing and Urban Development Department. This would involve one new program of code enforcement loans, administered by HUD. Under this plan, after the Buildings and Inspection Section of the city Public Works Department and the Housing Section of the city Health Department make their inspections under the concentrated code enforcement, loans would be made available to some homeowners for stipulated improvements. Loans for rehabilitating condemned structures would come through the Federal Housing Authority (which underwrites the loans of private lending agencies). New public housing would be

[1] Model Cities Department, City of Kansas City, Missouri, *Model Cities Comprehensive Demonstration Program,* Parts I and II (Kansas City: Model Cities, June 1, 1969).

built by the Kansas City Housing Authority, under the Operation Turnkey and Housing for the Elderly programs. Other new construction would be arranged through various loan programs underwritten by the FHA and undertaken by private developers. Part of the Model Neighborhoods lie within the boundaries of an Urban Renewal area; this means Urban Renewal must decide on its own course of action within this section. The home ownership assistance would come from private lending institutions.

The goals in other program areas involve many additional agencies. The task of coordinating all these agencies will be difficult. The mechanisms for doing so remain uncertain.

Most of the housing programs are based on loans—not grants. Whether the loans make economic sense to homeowners and builders will depend to a large degree on how the program affects individual blocks. If the block seems to continue to deteriorate, it will not make sense for a homeowner to assume the additional financial burden of a rehabilitation loan on a house whose property value is declining. Private builders will want to know where the public housing is to be located, its quality, and the prospects for removal of dilapidated buildings in the blocks where they propose to build.

In addition to difficulties in coordinating all the agencies involved, there were several omissions in the proposed program that will make it difficult to tackle the problems of any individual block or neighborhood comprehensively. For one thing, at the time the proposals were presented, the housing code applied only to multiple family units. It covered such things as plumbing, wiring, abandoned automobiles, trash, and the rigidity of the frame of the structure. It did not allow for the condemnation of a building that is simply dilapidated in appearance, or even of a structurally sound building that is vacant and standing open. The procedures for condemning a building were long, expensive, and complex; the proposed Model Cities budget did not include extra funds for such court procedures. Even after condemnation and demolition, an owner could not be forced to give up his lot for nearly five years. State legislation later shortened and simplified these procedures somewhat, but there is little strengthening of budgets for those purposes or broadening of the code.

The FHA sets top limits on the prices that private institutions can pay for dilapidated structures to be rehabilitated under their loans. Many such structures belong to investors who do not care to sell for these prices. Hence it is inevitable that a number of structures will not be rehabilitated or demolished under these procedures, and that many others that are rehabilitated will remain in generally dilapidated condition.

Furthermore, most of the loan programs for new housing construction require a lot fifty feet wide, so that in most cases two adjoining houses must be acquired and demolished. A builder's odds of finding many such adjoining houses on favorable sites are not good.

Little can be done within the portion of the Model Neighborhoods overlapped by the urban renewal area until Urban Renewal makes up its mind what its overall objectives are for its area. The Program had no jurisdiction over a proposed post office truck center and a freeway designed to run through the Model Neighborhoods, although these roused considerable controversy.

Until it is possible to demonstrate some overall pattern of progress, it will probably be difficult to talk insurance companies into making major adjustments in their rates, extent of coverage, and cancellation policies, which currently inhibit the rehabilitation and new building (which are the prerequisites for demonstrating such a pattern).

The proposed figures probably fall short of those needed. A 1965 survey [2] found 25,782 dwelling units within the Model Neighborhoods, 41.4 per cent of which were classified as deteriorating or deteriorated. Much of the program is designed to be implemented between 1972 and 1975. At this time (1971), there are probably many more structures in deteriorating or deteriorated condition. In the face of this, the proposed program (fewer than 4,500 demolitions and rehabilitations) if fully completed would constitute little more than a holding action.

Insofar as the program is successfully administered, it is bound to raise the housing costs of inner city residents. If income rises commensurately this would be no problem, but there is little reason for such assurance.

The program is designed to operate within the existing power structure. It is designed largely to coordinate programs already developed by those in power. It has not made suggestions opposed to the interests of the investor, the mayor, the congressman, or the middle class. Because it has not done so, it has weakened its own potential for dealing comprehensively with the problems it is trying to solve.

[2] *Ibid.*

Already the Kansas City, Missouri, Model Cities Program exhibits signs of tension within itself. At the time of setting up the neighborhood planning groups, several organizations were competing over who should control them. Compromises were effected so that different points of view could be represented. Still, a number of individuals and groups active in the various neighborhoods never became involved.

The program has a board, consisting of two members of the City Council, three nominees of major community-wide organizations, six nominees from community organizations serving primarily within the Model Cities area, and the mayor. The board has also created technical resource committees on crime, economic development, education, employment, health, housing, recreation, transportation, and welfare. These contain experts and prominent individuals from the community, and a minority of Model Neighborhood residents. Specific project proposals must be approved through the board and the relevant technical resource committee.

One of the first specific proposals—for converting an aging apartment building into housing for the poor—roused a controversy.[3] Some Model Neighborhood residents on the board charged that the project was being approved without adequate consultation with residents of the neighborhood. They questioned that the procedures being used reflected the views of the residents involved.

The ultimate sanction available to these dissidents would have been to harrass any attempts at rehabilitating the structure. Short of this they might have arranged for some public meetings with interested citizens regarding the proposed usage for the apartments. Since several organizations had differing views on the matter, it would have been difficult to arrive at any clear consensus from such meetings. Had a consensus

---

[3] The apartment building, located on the edge of the Model Cities area, is directly across the street from the elegant American Legion headquarters and a fashionable Greek Orthodox Church. Most of the occupants were white, though much of the surrounding neighborhood is black. The owner, an investor in slum property, was unpopular with many political activists. There are other apartments that some in the neighborhood preferred to see turned to this purpose: given the limited resources budgeted under Model Cities for such housing the question of priorities was important. The prime mover behind the proposal was a Catholic hospital in the neighborhood that had organized a community organization to sponsor neighborhood improvements. The group was unpopular with some Protestant clergy. See Robert Dumachel, "Urban Planning Revitalizes Itself through Hospital-Neighborhood Cooperation," *Hospitals* (November 1, 1969), 59–64, for a discussion by the organizers.

emerged that ran counter to the interests of the bureaucratic agencies or investors necessarily involved, it could not have been acted upon. The dissidents did persuade the neighborhood planning group to vote down this proposal. The Model Cities board vetoed the decision of the neighborhood planning group. After the federal government fell short on funding, the hospital-sponsored community group decided to by-pass the Model Cities program and fund this project directly through the FHA's 221 d3 program. They gave the owner of the building a price he probably considered more than sufficient, and rehabilitated the structure themselves. This project is one of the few tangible signs of housing progress in that neighborhood. It is not a product of the Model Cities Program, and it will probably not greatly affect the housing situation of people in the lowest income brackets.

The Model Cities Program has attempted a comprehensive approach toward restoring balance to the environments of individuals of lower socioeconomic strata. But it has a long way to go.

CITIZENS' CONSULTATIVE COMMITTEES
IN SINGAPORE

After the racial rioting of 1964, the Singapore government set up multiracial goodwill committees throughout the island. Their immediate purpose was to organize night patrols that could seek out and report additional disturbances; their long-range purpose was to eliminate the underlying causes of the strife.

Soon the night patrols by neighborhood volunteers were subsumed into a program called the Vigilante Corps, and Citizens' Consultative Committees were created to cater to substantive needs of the various neighborhoods.

There is one Citizens' Consultative Committee for each of the fifty-two districts of the Parliament. Members are selected by the Member of Parliament, and the list is cleared with the Prime Minister. While few, if any, of high income are involved, membership consists primarily of established citizens in the neighborhoods. Although People's Action Party members are a minority on each committee, individuals whom the government considers hostile are seldom committeemen.

The committees meet regularly, with their Member of Parliament present. They review projects which are of interest to residents of the area: additional street lights, storm drains, paving of roads, repair and construction of bridges, extension of electrical power or water or sewerage. The committees' jurisdiction seldom extends beyond such projects. They sometimes engage in the sort of liaison described on pages 79–82.

Ancillary to the Citizens' Consultative Committees is the Urban and Rural Services Committee. This consists of the parliamentary secretaries of the Minister of National Development, the Deputy Prime Minister, and the Minister of Social Affairs, together with the members of the Parliament. This group is responsible for creating the working budgets of the Citizens' Consultative Committees and for coordinating with bureaucracy for the implementation of the projects.

Priority seems to be frequently given to projects in areas which have exhibited a favorable attitude toward the Government. Once projects are approved their implementation has usually proceeded quite swiftly. Community organizations and interest groups other than the Citizens' Consultative Committees themselves have little involvement in this decision-making process. In general, people prominent in other organizations have not been appointed to the Consultative Committees.

THE RURAL DEVELOPMENT PROGRAM
IN MALAYSIA

The Rural Development Program in Malaysia has some common features.[4] Shortly after coming to power in 1959, the Alliance Government set up a Ministry of National Development. This Ministry created a state development officer in each state, who became executive secretary of the state Rural Development Committee (chaired by the chief minister of the state). Heads of all technical departments were on this committee. Similar committees were set up at the district level. Local committees were formed at the village level, consisting of local technical officers and village leaders.

Generally, committee members, chosen by the district officer, were government supporters.

The actual procedure used for eliciting proposals from the people varied greatly among the approximately seventy districts of the nation. In

---

[4] Gayl D. Ness, *Bureaucracy and Rural Development in Malaysia* (Berkeley: University of California Press, 1967); Marvin L. Rogers, "Politicization and Political Development in a Rural Malay Community" (mimeo).

some cases the committees organized village meetings and went in force to explain the program and get suggestions for projects. In other cases the village leaders were called to a general meeting at the district office and asked to solicit suggestions from the people. In other cases the suggestions were drawn up in the district office by the committee members.[5]

Proposals submitted were for roads, bridges, schools, minor irrigation, wells, health centers, adult education, agricultural extension, electricity, playing fields, weekly markets, mosques, and prayer halls. To insure implementation, the Deputy Prime Minister (now Prime Minister), Tun Razak, traveled throughout the nation from district to district. There he met with the committees, personally prodding them to produce and sometimes making decisions that technical officers had been hesitant to make. It was known that he had power to remove or transfer political and administrative officers and to give or take away funds. This made his confrontation quite effective. An operations room was established in Kuala Lumpur to keep track of the projects that had been completed. Areas that withhold political support have found it difficult to obtain funds for their projects; in other areas, projects of all the types mentioned are developed and under development.[6] The most noticeable improvements are the mosques, schools, roads, wells, meeting halls, and electricity.

An effective approach to improving rural productivity and standard of living would probably require intensive efforts to teach the farmer new farming techniques, to encourage him to farm large tracts of land that lie fallow, to provide him with free fertilizer and seeds, and to free him from the grip of the creditor and marketing middleman. The program does not provide for this. It provides instead a scattering of benefits for which the small farmer is often grateful to government, but which may be peripheral to raising his standard of living.

The same may be true of the Singapore Citizens' Consultative Committees. They can bring speedy action, because they concern matters over which government bureaucracy has control, and because they are a vehicle through which government officials at the highest level can prod

---

[5] Ness, *op. cit.*, 148.

[6] The Rural and Industrial Development Authority and the Federal Land Development Authority—that form rural cooperatives, give loans for small business, and turn federal land into resettlement projects for small farmers—are administered separately and autonomously from this process.

bureaucracy into performing as planned. Both programs provide services that improve certain aspects of the individual's environment. But
they do not deal with the individual's most central needs. To give control of marketing to Rural Development Committees, or control over public housing policy to Citizens' Consultative Committees, would be un-
thinkable. Those who have political capabilities have strong reason to
want these powers to reside where they currently reside.

The local committees have only the powers it is deemed suitable to
give them.

THE FUTURE OF INTEREST
GROUP POLITICS

The Singapore Citizens' Consultative Committees and Malaysia's
Rural Development Committees make decisions about projects that it is
entirely within the power of Government and bureaucracy to complete;
the American Model Cities projects for the most part require the participation of private owners and investors as well. In Singapore, the Government can for all practical purposes determine its final budgetary
priorities on its projects and the laws under which it operates; in the
United States, city councils, state legislatures, and the Congress have a
hand in these activities. This overlapping makes it doubly difficult for
the Model Cities Program to cater to the expressed needs of the local
groups. It also offers extra channels of access for interest groups outside
the neighborhoods to influence the neighborhood programs.

In all three instances the principal decisions about planning—the location, type, and amount of housing; the sectors to be demolished; the
quality of community services; the sorts of available education and employment; the distribution of resources—are made and administered by
those outside the area being affected. Furthermore, there is little coordination among those who make these decisions. The decisions conform
to the needs of the institutions involved in the implementation; there are
few mechanisms to ensure that they also conform to the most serious
needs of those they affect. The competitive party system of the United
States does not seem to ameliorate these facts of political life; it may
exacerbate them.

If any of these three programs offers more community control, it is
Malaysia's Rural Development Program. Were it a program designed to
rapidly change the Malay's way of life, that would be less the case. In-

stead, that program is well designed to preserve the integrity of Malay social life. It provides mosques and meetinghouses, wells for community use, and schools that teach about Muslim tradition—often with only a modicum of modern subjects. It has instituted few projects that drastically conflict with the traditional way of life. The fact that it negotiates the program with local leaders prevents the more modernized bureaucrats from instituting programs in a manner that would create such conflict. The Government that desires to retain political power is well advised to negotiate with these leaders. The community leaders of the Malay kampongs have control over most aspects of the economic and social life of their inhabitants. This is normal in preindustrial societies where a monetary economy remains weakly established and land remains under local control, and where education and communications are minimal. Undiverted by moral, cultural, or political relativism, the inhabitants tend to do what these leaders say and owe little allegiance to anyone else. If given the power to do so, the leaders will keep out influences that conflict with this monolithic community spirit.

The situation in a modern city is quite different. There, no individual or institution is likely to exert comparable influence over all aspects of the individual's life. For food, housing, jobs, transportation, consumer goods, ideas, and other necessities, one must turn to a variety of groups who constitute separate power centers—each controlling only a portion of the individual's life. No one body can speak or act with authority on all matters pertaining to the needs of the individual. At most, Government acts as a coordinator of these various activities—not the supreme commander.

Individuals, responding to this fragmentation, have formed interest groups. These groups deal with only a part of the individual's total needs and concerns. To deal with his landlord he participates in one interest group; to deal with his employer, in another; with his education another; and so forth. The interest groups then develop their own organizational identity, which in turn forms another set of layers between the individual and those who control his life. The various interest groups to which an individual belongs may actually quarrel among one another. This fragmentation of the individual's effort is in a way beneficial to government, because it keeps him from devising means to improve his whole environment without the aid of government, and so increases his dependence on the ruling powers.

Unfortunately, government leaders may be unable to exert enough control over their various partners in control to improve the individual's total environment. Physical planners frequently present schemes for building this environment. The planned community—Le Corbusier's plan for Rio de Janiero, Frank Lloyd Wright's Broadacres, the Soviet plan for Baku—is one such approach. Unfortunately, governments have never found it possible to persuade those who control the various aspects of human environment to coordinate their efforts sufficiently for such total schemes. Only in suburbs—relatively specialized portions of the total metropolitan environment—has it been possible to apply some comprehensive scope of this sort (though the disjointing influences of the free market creep in here, too). Urban renewal is another approach to planning total environment. Yet when urban renewal has succeeded in being most comprehensive—with total demolition—it has often been the least responsive to the needs of those it affects. When it has been conducted piecemeal, it is easily diverted to serve piecemeal interests of interest groups, bureaucrats, and investors. The ideal type of bureaucratic coordination presented in the Introduction and in the Abrams/Kobe/Koenigsberger report is also an attempt to induce coordination that takes into consideration the needs of the overall environment of the individual. Chapter VI indicates the limits of this path.

What is lacking is the power of the city dweller to express his political interests in the manner of the rural kampong dweller. The kampong (while often failing to adapt to change), is capable of expressing what it needs to maintain its integrity; the neighborhood can, it often seems, only express its conflicting interests. Since the decline of the city bosses [7]—and of the kongsi organizations—the power brokers have shown little inclination to deal with the elites of the inner city. Some fragments of community remain. The Boston West Enders had something of an integral community that they failed to defend; they lost it. The citizens of Charlestown managed to preserve theirs. But even the small sense of community that ethnic neighborhoods, machine politics, and the politics of independence movements afforded has largely been lost in the modern city—especially among the poor. Crime, ethnic animosities, and moving about by renters whittle away further at remnants of community consciousness among the poor. Their only power is to

---

[7] For an enticing discussion of the harm caused by the breakdown of urban machine politics: Theodore Lowi, *The End of Liberalism* (New York: Norton, 1969); also Robert K. Merton, *Social Theory and Social Structure* (Glencoe: Free Press, 1957), 193–194.

create waves of rebellion, followed by reforms that only vaguely benefit them and that are often capped by repression and reaction.

Planners or politicians cannot create a City Beautiful whose beauty is reflected in the lives of its inhabitants unless the democratic process is broadened to include the majority. To accomplish this, there must be communities other than the financial community, the bureaucratic community, and the political community.

We already have much information about people as faceless portions of conglomerated interests. We know something about the income of labor and the price index of the consumer and the number of units of housing constructed for those who can pay certain rents and how many people have migrated. We have information about how businessmen will be affected by corporate income taxes and why the sportsman must keep his gun and what teachers think should happen to the schools. But the knowledge available to government about the accumulated package of needs of individual citizens as they lead their daily lives is meager. Until individuals can find a means to press this knowledge upon the government, the programs designed by government will miss the mark of substantially answering human needs. Until individuals can band themselves back into communities they will probably fail to express their needs effectively—or even to know what they all are. Through the individual's envigorated sense that he has something in common with his neighbors, he and his neighbors may come together to develop the power to protect their common interests and their individual identities.

I do not refer to anything like Saul Alinksy's ad-hoc organization-of-organizations project-action approach, though I consider it a useful experiment.[8] The existence of organizations with varying interests within an alliance fighting battles over specific issues is likely to lead to the same kinds of compromises between organizational and human needs that take place in traditional interest-group politics. As in so many other approaches, interest groups intercede their interests between those of the citizen and the government. Most individuals in the community remain uninvolved. Without some *initial* sense of community,

---

[8] See Hans B. C. Spiegel (ed.), *Citizen Participation in Urban Development*, Vol. 1 (Washington: Center for Community Affairs, 1968); Warner Bloomberg, Jr., and Florence W. Rosenstock, "Who Can Activate the Poor? One Assessment of 'Maximum Feasible Participation,'" in Warner Bloomberg, Jr., and Henry J. Schmandt, *Power, Poverty, and Urban Policy* (Beverly Hills: Sage Publications, 1968).

there is little in this approach to assure that the citizen will get his way when his interests interfere with those of the involved interest groups.

The Office of Economic Opportunity approach of creating self-help organizations to carry out specific tasks or intercede with specific agencies (e.g., tenant associations) again breaks down the life of the individual into its separate interests—allowing him to fight for only one interest at a time, in isolation from his other problems. It is easy for such organizations to be co-opted by the agencies that they are designed to put pressure upon, or that have produced them in the first place.

The creation of new leadership—whether through political or radical groups, or through government-sponsored leadership-training programs —also seems to fall short of what is required. Leaders tend to be drawn from among those slightly more advantaged than their peers and to develop organizational attachments and interests separate from those of their peers. They often seem to become an artificial strata, negotiation with whom substitutes for negotiation with the actual community. Their problems of creating followership and consensus can easily become paramount over the problem of solving the real needs of the community.

The problem is more than that of creating coordination and communication between the citizens and the various governmental agencies. It is the problem of creating communities with enough power to get their way during such coordination and communication. And to get their way in a manner that will cater to the needs of those who live in them.

Organizational attempts to provoke citizen participation may help to arouse increased community awareness, while at the same time sharpening the edges of intracommunity conflict. Liaison and leadership and protest are undoubtedly important; they are not enough. Cultural and racial factors can also be emphasized in an effort to build a sense of cohesion, although these appeals can easily backfire: There is apt to be conflict over the question of who best represents the cultural or racial tradition, and hence who is to lead it. Leadership conflicts can easily prevent such an alliance from accomplishing programmatic objectives.

A myriad of small actions involving a myriad of agencies must be performed within each acre of ground on which people live. Unless some sense of basically apolitical neighborliness can develop within such acreage, it seems unlikely that community power will ever emerge to direct this performance. Until such states of community power are achieved among all socioeconomic strata it is unlikely that government will achieve the willingness and political capabilities necessary to cat^r to the needs of the poor. The formation of such neighborliness [9] probably depends in large part upon the character of environmental change in local neighborhoods. But this in turn depends upon broader political and economic trends.

Planning—physical, economic, and social—is done because it is useful to politicians, bureaucrats, and/or investors. A stage needs to be attained at which the highest concern of planning becomes the goal of preserving the physical, economic, and social integrity of the communities in which men live.

Politicians vie to put before the people plans of action for new roads, new jobs, new towns, new affluence. They have a grab bag with something for everyone. A day may come when there can instead be a continuing contest between right and left over who can best give the people what they need, rather than what seems politically and economically most convenient at the time.

Bureaucracy is keyed to dealing with only pieces of human life, and responding to interests that govern and represent only portions of man's existence. We may be better served if functional specialization retreats somewhat so that the bureaucratic organization can be fitted to dealing with groups of individuals as embodying groups of needs.

Industrialization has brought in its wake much economic suffering and social decay. Yet, while scholars have developed some critical perspective toward the statement that what is good for General Motors is good for America, they have come to accept more uncritically the notion that industrialization is good for solving human problems, or that what is good politics is therefore good remedy for human needs. Given the chance to speak from a forum where they would be noticed, the people might raise doubts about these contentions. The time may be at hand when we must subordinate technology to man, our cities to our countryside, productivity to social equilibrium, and the growth of the middle class to the well-being of the poor.

We have too often tended to view attempts at social cohesion as an obstacle to economic change, rather than as a political force that may at times be helping to keep economic change compatible with personal integrity.

Technology has broken down the social structures, and hence the

---

[9] For works that provide thoughts on this subject see the last section of the Bibliography.

sense of community, of large numbers of people. Whereas they once could look after most of their felt needs, they now have little power to do so. If they are to regain such power, they must develop some control over technology. If they are to develop any control over technology, technology must be adapted so as to allow them some return to community.

It is a riddle. But it is perhaps the riddle on whose solution the success of our future urban development depends.

APPENDIXES, BIBLIOGRAPHY, AND INDEX

The Organization of Ministries and Agencies

Chart 1 on page 50 shows Singapore's ministries and bureaucratic agencies as of January 1968 [1] (also see Appendix II).

Each minister is provided with his own office and office staff. Each ministry has one or more permanent secretaries and one or more parliamentary secretaries, depending upon the number of divisions it contains. Some ministries have ministers of state as well. The government and statutory boards together employ some 62,000 persons.[2]

Most of these ministries and their subdivisions evolved gradually over the years. Before World War II the Straits Settlements of Penang, Malacca, and Singapore had a common colonial administration and governor. In 1946, Singapore became an independent colony. From 1946 to 1955, Singapore's Executive Council and Legislative Council, both of which remained under control of the Governor's appointees, made laws and policy. Public administration was the responsibility of the Colonial Secretary's Office, which contained four branches: (a) the Administrative Branch; (b) the Legislative Council Branch; (c) the Financial Branch; and (d) the Defence and Internal Security Branch.

The Administrative Branch had six principal assistant secretaries; the portfolios for all operational agencies of the administration (aside from financial and defense agencies) were divided among these six men. The Administrative Branch also had an Establishment Section with four assistant secretaries, who were collectively responsible for staffing, office and building

---

[1] In April 1968 a Ministry of Science and Technology was added. It was taken over by Dr. Toh Chin Chye, who at that time gave up his post as Deputy Prime Minister to become Vice-Chancellor of the University of Singapore. The post of Deputy Prime Minister was then discontinued.

[2] Loh See Hong, "Labour and Unemployment," Republic of Singapore, State and City Planning, *Notes for Consultant Briefing at Node One in the Plan of Operation* (Singapore: 1967). In 1958 the government and statutory boards together employed some 48,000 persons. Colony of Singapore, *Singapore Annual Report, 1958* (Singapore: GPO).

maintenance, and other establishment problems of all operational agencies. An Organization Section helped demarcate areas of responsibility.

The Financial Branch and the Defence and Internal Security Branch were charged with the agencies and functions which their names imply, and the Legislative Council Branch was responsible for liaison between the Legislative Council and the administrative establishment.

In 1955 the Rendel Constitution created elected ministers for the first time; it also took the administrative apparatus out of the hands of the Colonial Secretary and placed it in the hands of these new ministers.[3] The Constitution specified the following portfolios for the six new elected ministers:

1. Commerce, Industry, Shipping, Agriculture, and Fisheries
2. Labour, Immigration, and Social Welfare
3. Education
4. Housing, Lands, Administration of Adjacent Islands, Town and Country Planning, and Local Government
5. Civil Aviation, Communications, and Public Works
6. Health

In short, the functions formerly handled by the Administrative Branch of the Colonial Secretary's Office were now to be brought under the purview of the six new elected ministers.[4] The Colonial Secretary's title was changed to Chief Secretary.[5] The Chief Secretary (an appointee of the Governor) retained ministerial rank, but his administrative tasks were reduced to handling external affairs, internal security (including police and prisons), defense, public relations, broadcasting, and appointments in the civil service.[6]

[3] The Rendel Constitution provided that each ministry should contain a civil servant's post "comparable to . . . Permanent Undersecretary of State in the United Kingdom." Colony of Singapore, *Report of the Constitutional Commission* (Singapore: GPO, 1954), 18. After 1959 the PAP continued this post, with the title of Permanent Secretary. The changeover of personnel was a gradual one. In 1968 two of the permanent secretaries under the Rendel Constitution still retained permanent secretary posts—in the Ministry of Interior and Defence and in the Ministry of National Development. The Rendel Constitution also suggested that some, but not all, of the ministries might be provided with a parliamentary undersecretary and/or a junior minister. This provision soon became a bone of contention between the Governor and David Marshall; the latter wanted more junior ministerships and the former did not wish to create them. Eventually under the Lim Yew Hock Government the number was increased. The PAP Government also continued these posts, under the titles of Parliamentary Secretaries and Ministers of State.

[4] This division of portfolios roughly corresponded to the division of responsibility among the six assistant secretaries of the former Administrative Branch.

[5] Like the Colonial Secretary, the Chief Secretary was an employee of the British Foreign Office, appointed by the Governor.

[6] In addition, he kept charge of religious affairs, film censorship, the Botanic Gardens, statistics, ceremonial duties, national registration, elections, marriage

Two new ministerial-level posts were created for appointment by the Governor from the British Foreign Office: Financial Secretary [7] and Attorney General.

From 1955 to 1959 the portfolios of the elected ministers were divided as follows, so far as administrative departments were concerned:

1. The Minister of Commerce and Industry was handling the Departments of Agriculture, Veterinary Services, Fisheries, Fisheries Research, Co-operative Development, Registration of Companies, Registration of Trade Marks, and Registration of Business Names, and was charged with policy on trade, commerce, industry, and production. An Industrial Promotion Board was established in 1957 to develop industry, and the Colonial Development Corporation established a branch in Singapore (Singapore Factory Developments, Ltd.) to help finance industrial development. These also became his responsibility, as did the promotion of tourism.

2. The Minister of Labour, Immigration and Social Welfare handled the responsibilities implied in his title, as well as relations with the Central Provident Fund Board.

3. The Minister of Education was responsible for primary and secondary education, the National Library and Museum, and relations with the institutions of higher learning.

4. The Minister for Local Government, Lands, and Housing was in charge of relations with the City Council,[8] and Singapore Improvement Trust, and of Lands Surveys. The City Council operated the Electricity Department, the Gas Department, the Water Department, and the Sewerage Department.

5. The Minister for Communications and Works was in charge of the Public Works Department, Civil Aviation, postal services and telecommunications, meteorological services, and of relations with the Railway Board. The Public Works Department built roads, drains, school buildings, and hospitals. A Highway Coordination Committee, on which the Singapore Improvement Trust and other relevant bodies were represented, planned roads.

6. The Minister of Health was in charge of medical services and public health. Then the People's Action Party came to power on June 3, 1959; for the first time there were no appointed ministers and no constitutional limita-

---

registration, registration of births and deaths, archives, and the Establishment and Organization Branches. See State of Singapore, *Singapore Annual Report, 1959,* 250–251.

[7] Charged with financial, revenue, banking, insurance, exchange control, and currency policy, customs, income tax, estate duty, stamp duty, and the Accountant-General's office.

[8] The Rendel Constitution replaced the former appointed City Council and Rural Board with an elected City and Island Council. This came to an end after the PAP took power in 1959.

tions on how the government was to be organized. The following paragraphs describe the evolution from the 1955–1959 setup into the organizational pattern presented in Chart 1 and Appendix II.

The Ministry of Local Government, Lands and Housing, and the Ministry of Commerce and Industry's responsibilities for fisheries and agriculture, were immediately assimilated into a new *Ministry of National Development*. In keeping with the recommendations of a White Paper in 1956 and of a Legislative Committee in 1958, the Singapore Improvement Trust was transformed on February 1, 1960, into the Housing and Development Board. The development control functions formerly vested in the SIT were given to the Chief Building Surveyor's Office. The 1956 White Paper and the 1958 Legislative Committee had intended that a Planning Department do all-island planning and advise local authorities on planning control; on February 1, 1960, a Planning Department was created. It was charged with approving layouts for building sites. The planning of roads, formerly carried out by the Highways Coordination Committee, was also vested in the Planning Department. Since its inception the Planning Department has operated alternately within the Prime Minister's Office and the Ministry of National Development. The HDB has been continuously attached to the Ministry of National Development. On January 1, 1960, the Departments of Agriculture, Fisheries, Fisheries Research, Veterinary Services, Co-operative Development, and Rural Development were merged into the Primary Production Department,[9] which also remained within the Ministry of National Development.

A *Ministry of Finance* was created to take over the Establishment and Organization Branches from the Chief Secretary and the duties of the Financial Secretary. The Industrial Promotion Board was also added to this portfolio; on August 1, 1961, it was reorganized into a statutory board, the Economic Development Board. A Political Studies Center, established in September 1959 with the purpose of giving short courses to civil servants to increase their political and national awareness, was placed within this ministry as well.

The *Prime Minister* brought the Planning Department, the Public Works Department, the Registrar of Titles, the Survey Department, the Commissioner of Lands, and the Harbour Board (established in 1913) into his portfolio, along with the City and Island Council. The latter council was subsequently discontinued, since the advent of internal self-government had made it somewhat redundant. The Water Department, Gas Department, and Electricity Department, which the City Council had operated, were combined on May 1, 1963, into a statutory board, the Public Utilities Board, and placed in the portfolio of the Minister of Law; this board was subse-

[9] A merger previously made more difficult because of the existence of the City and Island Council.

quently moved to the Ministry of National Development. The Sewerage Department was moved to the Public Works Department, which in turn became a part of the Ministry of National Development. Some of the more political functions formerly carried out by the City and Island Council (e.g., building rural roads, standpipes, and street lights) were taken over by the Urban and Rural Services Committee created within the Ministry of National Development. Until April 1, 1964, the Harbour Board had conducted port construction and operation of the wharves; on that day a statutory board, the Port of Singapore Authority, was created to take over these functions. It came under the jurisdiction of the Ministry of Law. In 1965 the Planning Department was moved to the Ministry of National Development. The Registrar of Titles, the Survey Department, and the Commissioner of Lands were moved to the Ministry of Law. Hence the Prime Minister's Office served as a caretaker ministry for these functions until a more suitable home could be found for them. Subsequently the Prime Minister's Office was freed from direct functional responsibilities, until 1968, when it became caretaker for the new Bases Economic Conversion Commission [10] set up to transfer to Singapore ownership the 12,000 acres of land and equipment formerly used by the British forces.

Initially in 1959 a Ministry of Labour and Law was established under a combined portfolio. In 1964 this ministry was split and a separate *Ministry of Law* was established. In 1965 the Ministry of Law and the Ministry of National Development combined into the *Ministry of Law and National Development,* but it kept two distinct divisions. As can be seen in Appendix II, the Ministry of Law handles the duties, in addition to those mentioned in the previous paragraph, that were formerly the direct responsibility of the Attorney General, as well as some of the duties of the Minister of Commerce and Industry.

In 1959 the *Ministry of Labour* and Law took responsibility for the functions mentioned in the previous paragraph, and for the Labour and Welfare Departments. The new permanent Industrial Arbitration Courts opened in 1960 came to operate under this ministry.[11] In 1964, however, the creation of the separate Ministry of Law removed the legal responsibilities of the ministry, including the Industrial Arbitration Courts. The creation shortly after that time of the combined Ministry of Culture and Social Affairs also removed the Welfare Department from this portfolio. By 1958 all community centers were being operated by the Department of Social Welfare. The reorganization of the community centers and youth programs into the People's Association, and the establishment of the Singapore Work Brigade, in

[10] See Chapter VI.

[11] The Industrial Arbitration Courts were probably the chief reason for initially forming this joint Ministry.

March 1960, was directed by the Minister of Finance. Subsequently these activities moved into the jurisdiction of the Ministry of Interior and Defence as the political emphasis turned from controlling the labor and student movements toward the establishment of a strong defense structure and national consciousness. As a result, the Ministry of Labour emerged with a reduced portfolio.

In 1959 the Broadcasting and Information Services and the National Library and Museum were incorporated into a *Ministry of Culture.* At the same time a *Ministry of Social Affairs* was placed in charge of marriages, religious affairs,[12] parks and gardens, legal aid, the fire brigade, hotel licensing, and rent conciliation. When full independence in 1965 gave the Singapore government control over prisons, the two ministries were combined into the *Ministry of Culture and Social Affairs,* which also took on responsibility for prisons and social welfare.

In 1959 a Minister of Home Affairs took over the former duties of the Colonial Chief Secretary not absorbed by the Ministry of Finance, plus the Department of Immigration. As Singapore subsequently became a part of Malaysia and later fully independent, this ministry was transformed into the *Ministry of Interior and Defence.*

The *Deputy Prime Minister* took over all the functions of the former Minister of Communications and Works, except for the Public Works Department, plus the Marine Division [13] of the Ministry of Commerce and Industry.

The *Ministry of Health* and *Ministry of Education* have undergone no major reorganization since their establishment in 1955.

The *Ministry of Foreign Affairs* was created after full independence came in August 1965.

It can be seen, then, that Singapore's bureaucracy manifests a high degree of structural differentiation and functional specialization. It contains many individual units performing relatively separate functions.

[12] A responsibility that has also at times shifted directly to the Prime Minister's office.

[13] Responsible for receipt of reports of ships' arrivals and the issue of port clearances, the Registry of Shipping, the engagement and discharge of seamen, the examination of masters and mates and for the various boards concerned with seamen.

A List of Ministries and
Their Subdivisions, January 1968

Aside from the heirarchy of their own ministries, most of these agencies have no formal liaison with other agencies, or with private groups, when it comes to policy making. Some of them do, however.

Those bodies starred with *one* asterisk (*) contain members from two or more government or semigovernment agencies, along with representatives from among the general public. Appendix III lists the members of these bodies.

Those bodies starred with a dagger (†) contain members from one or more government or semigovernment agencies, but no representatives from the general public. Appendix IV lists the members of these bodies, or indicates the functional links these bodies provide between agencies.

Those bodies starred with a section mark (§) provide a formal liaison channel between a ministry and some segment of the private citizenry. Appendix V indicates the sort of public participation involved.

Those bodies starred with two asterisks (**) are development boards or educational bodies. These educational bodies have private governing bodies without official government members but are under the jurisdiction of the Ministry of Education. The development boards are incorporated and/or partially self-sufficient financially and have governing bodies to approve their budgets and make major policy decisions. These governing bodies are discussed further in Appendix VI.

Naturally, the composition of individual bodies may change somewhat over time. This is how they stood in January 1968.

Prime Minister's Office
Bases Economic Conversion Department

Deputy Prime Minister's Office
Air Registration Board
Civil Aviation Department
Elections Department

Marine Department
≂ Board of Examiners
  Light Dues Board *
  Nautical Advisory Committee, Polytechnic †
  Seafarers' Welfare Board *
  Seamen's Lodging-Houses Licensing Authority *
  Seamen's Registry Board *
  Singapore Asian Seamen's Club *
  Singapore Sailors' Institute Committee *
Marine Surveys Department
Meteorological Services
Omnibus Services Licensing Authority †
Postal Services Department
Registrar of Vehicles Department
Singapore Airport Commercial Committee †
Singapore Telephone Board **
Telecommunications Department

Ministry of Finance

Treasury Division
Establishment Branch
Financial Administration Branch
  Asian Seamen's Institute
  Board of Commissioners of Currency §
  Central Supplies Office Tenders Opening Committee
  Committee on Tariff Matters
  Education Advisory Council
  Free Trade Zone Coordination Committee
  Junior Tenders Committee
  Ministry of Interior and Defence Tenders Committee
  Public Accounts Committee (M.P.'s)
  Radio and TV Policy Committee
  Singapore Works Brigade Tenders Committee
  TV Grading Committee
Budget Branch

Accountant-General's Office
Central Supplies Office
Income Tax Review Board
Inland Revenue Department
Liquors Licensing Board *
Organization and Methods Branch
Property Tax Advisory Committee
Valuation Review Board

Economic Development Division
Board of Public Trustees Investment Fund
Board of Trustees of Silver Jubilee Fund
Economic Development Board **
Economic Planning Unit
Junior Tenders Board (Development Estimates)
Malayan Pineapple Industry Board
Malayan Rubber Export Registration Board

Trade Division
Department of Statistics
Electronic Data Processing Unit
Exchange Control Industry Board
Timber Export Industry Board

Minister of Interior and Defence
General Staff Division
Home Affairs Division
Intelligence Division
Logistics Division
Manpower Division

Army Board
Board of Governors, National Youth Leadership Training Institute *
Central Manpower Base
Criminal Investigation Department
Detainees' Aftercare Committee §
Headquarters, People's Defence Force
Headquarters, Singapore Infantry Brigade
Immigration Department
People's Association, Board of Management *
Registrar of Societies
Singapore Armed Forces Training Institute
Singapore Naval Volunteer
Singapore Police Force
Vigilante Corps
Work Brigade

Ministry of Law and National Development
Law Division
Attorney General's Chambers
Corrupt Practices Investigation Bureau †
Land Appeals Board (Land Acquisition)
Land Office: Commissioner of Lands
Pawnbrokers Licensing Board *

Port of Singapore Authority **
Registry of Business Names
Registry of Land Titles and Deeds
Registry of Trade Marks and Patents
Survey Department
Tourist Promotion Board *

High Court
Criminal District and Magistrate's Courts
Maintenance and Juvenile Court
Traffic Courts
Civil District Court
State Coroner's Court
Industrial Arbitration Courts
Justices of the Peace
Board of Visiting Justices
Panel of Advisors to the Juvenile Court Magistrate
Audit Department †
Public Service Commission †
Legal Service Commission †

National Development Division
Boards of Management, Malay Settlements §
Car Parks Division
Chief Building Surveyor's Department
Development Control Committee *
District Offices
Housing and Development Board **
    Building Department †
    Estates and Lands Office †
    Resettlement Department
    Secretariat
    Urban Renewal Section
Master Plan Committee †
Planning Department
Primary Production Department
    Agricultural Development Division
    Fisheries Development
    Rural Development Division
    Veterinary Division
Public Utilities Board **
Public Works Department †
Registry of Co-operative Societies and Co-operative Development Division
Urban and Rural Administration Section
Urban and Rural Services Committee †
Urban and Rural Services Maintenance Committee

Ministry of Education

Accounts Division
Administrative Branch
  Education Societies **
  Lembaga Gerakan Pelajaran Dewasa (Adult Education Board) *
  Nanyang University **
  Ngee Ann College **
  Planning Committee
  School Management Committees **
  Singapore Polytechnic
    Singapore Polytechnic Board of Governors *
  University of Singapore **
  Working Party on School Buildings
Establishment Branch
  English, Tamil, Chinese, and Malay School Sections
  Teachers Training College
Examinations Branch
Inspectorate
Professional Division
Singapore Vocational Institute
  Singapore Vocational Institute Advisory Board †
Textbook and Syllabuses Branch

Ministry of Culture and Social Affairs

  Culture Division
Board of Film Censors §
Cinematographic Films Appeal Committee *
Department of Broadcasting
Dewan Bahasa dan Kebedayaan Kebangsaan
Government Printing Office
National Library
National Library Board *
National Museum
National Theatre Trust §
Publications
Publicity Division
Registry of Publications
Singapore Conference Hall and Trade Union House
Victoria Theatre and Memorial Hall

  Social Affairs Division
Botanic Gardens
Central Complaints Bureau
Fire Brigade
Hindu Advisory Board §

Hotels Licensing Board *
Legal Aid Bureau
Muslim Advisory Board §
Muslim and Hindu Endowments Board
Nature Reserves Board *
Parks and Recreation
Peoples Association Board of Management Committee
Prisons Department (including several boards)
Registry of Marriages
Registry of Muslim Marriages and Shariah Court
Sikh Advisory Board §
Silver Jubilee Fund Board of Management
Social Welfare
Van Kleef Aquarium

Ministry of Health
Chemistry Division
Headquarters Division
Hospitals Division
Public Health Division
Singapore Family Planning and Population Board *
Various professional boards

Ministry of Labour
Central Provident Fund Board *
Citizenship Advisory Committee §
Factory Inspectorate Section
Industrial Relations Section
Labour Court
National Registration Office
Registry of Births and Deaths
Registry of Citizenship
Registry of Trade Unions Section
Seamen's Industrial Relations Section
Training Section

Ministry of Foreign Affairs
Embassies
High Commissions

Groups Providing Liaison among Official Bodies and with the Public

Those bodies marked with an asterisk (*) in Appendix II are listed below, together with an indication of membership. All of these bodies share the characteristic of containing representatives from the general public, along with representatives from two or more government agencies.

Central Provident Fund Board: Ministry of Labour
Members: Lawyer, businessmen, private citizens, Permanent Secretary (Labour) Ministry of Labour, Permanent Secretary (Finance) Ministry of Finance.

Development Control Committee: National Development Division, Ministry of Law and National Development
Members: Chief Building Surveyor, Chief Planner, Director of Public Works, Assistant Director of Medical Services (Health), private architect and engineer.

Hotels Licensing Board: Ministry of Social Affairs
Members: Supreme Court Deputy Registrar, Ministry of Social Affairs representative, union representative, private citizens.

Lembaga Gerakan Pelajaran Dewasa (Adult Education Board): Ministry of Education
Members: Ministry of Education officials, National Trades Union Congress official, Ministry of Finance official, Broadcasting Division official, academics, businessman.

Light Dues Board: Deputy Prime Minister's Office, Marine Department
Members: Marine Department Director, Director of Public Works, Assistant Secretary (Treasury) of Ministry of Finance, Port Master—Port of Singapore Authority, shippers.

Liquors Licensing Board: Ministry of Finance
Members: a judge, private individuals.

National Library Board: Ministry of Culture
Members: Ministry of Culture representative, Ministry of Education representative, Library Association of Singapore representative, university representatives, educator, National Library representative.

National Youth Leadership Training Institute, Board of Governors: Ministry of Interior and Defence

Members: Ministry of Defence official, Ministry of Education representative, Ministry of Finance representative, Permanent Secretary of National Development, People's Association representative, Director Singapore Work Brigade, academics, trade union representative, National Youth Leadership Training Institute representative.

Nature Reserves Board: Ministry of Social Affairs

Members: Chief Planner, Chairman of Botanic Gardens Trustees, private individuals.

Pawnbrokers Licensing Board: Law Division, Ministry of Law and National Development

Members: Public Utilities Board official, Law Division official, lawyer, private individuals.

People's Association, Board of Management: Ministry of Interior and Defence

Members: Prime Minister, Ministry of Defence representative, Ministry of Social Affairs representative, Minister of State (Culture), trade union representative, Ministry of Education Inspectorate representative, private citizens.

Rent Conciliation Board: Ministry of Social Affairs

Members: Ministry of Social Affairs representative, judges, private citizens.

Seafarers' Welfare Board: Deputy Prime Minister's Office, Marine Department

Members: Director of Social Welfare, Marine Department Director, representative of Ministry of Finance, Seamen's Welfare Office representative, bankers, clergyman, shippers, private citizens, social workers.

Seamen's Lodging Houses Licensing Authority: Deputy Prime Minister's Office, Marine Department

Members: Marine Department Director, Permanent Secretary (Health) to Director of Medical Services, Seamen's Welfare Office officer, private citizens, lawyers.

Seamen's Registry Board: Deputy Prime Minister's Office, Marine Department

Members: Ministry of Foreign Affairs official, Deputy Director of Marine Department, Principal Assistant Secretary of Ministry of Labour, Assistant Director of Social Welfare, shipper, private citizens.

Singapore Asian Seamen's Club: Deputy Prime Minister's Office, Marine Department

Members: Social Welfare Department official, Marine Department Director, representative of Permanent Secretary of Ministry of Finance, Port of Singapore Authority official, Singapore Asian Seamen's Club representative, shippers.

Singapore Family Planning and Population Board: Ministry of Health
Members: Ministry of Health officials, hospital and medical representatives, deputy chief statistician, Assistant Director of Social Welfare, Singapore Family Planning Association representative, Ministry of Education representative, Family Planning Institution representatives.

Singapore Polytechnic Board of Governors: Ministry of Education
Members: Deputy Prime Minister, Ministry of Education official, Ministry of Finance official, industrial resettlement official, academics, businessmen.

Singapore Sailors' Institute Committee: Deputy Prime Minister's Office, Marine Department
Members: Marine Department Director, Ministry of Finance representative, Superintendent of Connell House, shippers, clergyman, banker.

Tourist Promotion Board: Law Division, Ministry of Law and National Development
Members: Ministry of Finance official, banker, private individuals involved in tourism.

Groups Providing Liaison among Official Bodies

The following bodies, marked with a dagger (†) in Appendix II, are composed entirely of civil servants or ministry representatives. Their liaison roles, or their membership, are indicated below.

Audit Department: Law Division, Ministry of Law and National Development

Audits all government expenditures.

Building Department, Housing and Development Board: National Development Division, Ministry of Law and National Development

Does some earthmoving for the Economic Development Board.

Corrupt Practices Investigation Bureau: Law Division, Ministry of Law and National Development

Investigates corrupt practices in all segments of government and bureaucracy.

Development Planning Subcommittee

Members: a Treasury officer, Director of Public Works, Permanent Secretary of National Development, Chief Planner.

Economic Development Board: Ministry of Finance

Designs Rural Resettlement Areas for Housing and Development Board.

Estates and Lands Office, Housing and Development Board: National Development Division, Ministry of Law and National Development.

Does resettlement for some other government agencies.

Legal Service Commission: Law Division, Ministry of Law and National Development.

Includes members both from judiciary and Public Service Commission.

Master Plan Committee: National Development Division, Ministry of Law and National Development

Members: Chief Planner, Commissioner of Lands, Director of Public Works, Head of Urban Renewal Section of the Housing and Development Board.

Nautical Advisory Committee, Polytechnic: Deputy Prime Minister's Office, Marine Department

Members: Marine Department, Deputy Prime Minister's Office representatives; Polytechnic academics.

Omnibus Services Licensing Authority: Deputy Prime Minister's Office
Members: Permanent Secretary (Law) Ministry of Law and National Development; Deputy Secretary (National Development) Ministry of Law and National Development; Permanent Secretary of Deputy Prime Minister's Office; Registrar of Vehicles.

Public Service Commission: Law Division, Ministry of Law and National Development
Concerned with all government personnel policy.

Public Works Department: National Development Division, Ministry of Law and National Development
Does construction for a wide variety of other government agencies.

Singapore Airport Commercial Committee: Deputy Prime Minister's Office
Members: Permanent Secretary to Deputy Prime Minister, Director of Civil Aviation, Commissioner of Lands, Permanent Secretary of Ministry of Finance, Director of Tourist Promotion Board, Airport Manager.

Singapore Vocational Institute Advisory Board: Ministry of Education
Members: Ministry of Education members, Ministry of Labour member.

Urban and Rural Services Committee: National Development Division, Ministry of Law and National Development
Members: Parliamentary Secretary (National Development) Ministry of Law and National Development, Parliamentary Secretary to Deputy Prime Minister, Parliamentary Secretary (Social Affairs) to Ministry of Social Affairs, Members of Parliament.

Groups Providing Liaison between an Official Body and the Public

The following bodies, marked with a section mark (§) in 'Appendix II, provide a formal liaison channel between a ministry and some segment of the private citizenry.

Board of Commissioners of Currency: Ministry of Finance
    Consists of Minister of Finance and bankers
Boards of Management, Malay Settlements: National Development Division,
      Ministry of Law and National Development
    Boards of Management consist entirely of members of the settlements.
Citizenship Advisory Committee: Ministry of Labour
    Consists entirely of private citizens.
Detainees' Aftercare Committee: Ministry of Interior and Defence
    Consists of ex-detainees.
Board of Film Censors: Ministry of Culture
    Contains private individuals.
National Theatre Trust: Ministry of Culture
    Contains representatives of Ministry of Culture and of public.
Muslim Advisory Board: Ministry of Social Affairs
    Consists of Muslim members of the public.
Hindu Advisory Board: Ministry of Social Affairs
    Consists of Hindu members of the public.
Sikh Advisory Board: Ministry of Social Affairs
    Consists of Sikh members of the public.

Semi- and Quasi-Official Groups

All educational institutions, with the exceptions of the Singapore Polytechnic and the Adult Education Board (see Appendix III), have private governing bodies without official government members (though there has been a tendency for some government-connected people to be elected to them). Development boards have assets of their own; the membership of their governing bodies (which approve their budgets and make major policy decisions) is indicated below. All educational institutions and development boards are under the jurisdiction of a ministry.

Educational Bodies

Education Societies
Nanyang University
Ngee Ann College   Ministry of Education
School Management Committees
University of Singapore

Development Boards

ECONOMIC DEVELOPMENT BOARD: Economic Development Division, Ministry of Finance

Board consists of Director of Economic Development Board, Permanent Secretary of National Development, trade union representative, businessmen.

HOUSING AND DEVELOPMENT BOARD: National Development Division, Ministry of Law and National Development

Governing board (the Housing Board) consists of private citizens, who are not representatives of any particular groups. Generally, policy initiatives come from administrators in consultation with the Ministry. The Housing Board can veto these initiatives or make revisions. They can also suggest new activities. With regard to the Kallang Basin Reclamation Project, I found them performing none of these functions. They agreed to the policies presented to them for approval, and did not interfere in the policymaking process.

PORT OF SINGAPORE AUTHORITY: Law Division, Ministry of Law and National Development

Members of governing board: Port of Singapore Authority Chairman; official of Law Division, Ministry of Law and National Development; official of Economic Development Division, Ministry of Finance; Marine Department official; bankers; shippers; businessmen.

PUBLIC UTILITIES BOARD: National Development Division, Ministry of Law and National Development

Board consists of private citizens, who are not representative of any particular groups.

SINGAPORE TELEPHONE BOARD: Deputy Prime Minister's Office

Governing board consists entirely of private citizens, who are not representatives of any particular groups.

Bibliography

Singapore

The case study presented in Chapters IV and V benefits from a complete perusal, through January 1, 1968, of all correspondence relating to the Kallang Basin in the following files:

Housing and Development Board, Secretariat
(including the files of the former Singapore Improvement Trust, which are housed there)
Housing and Development Board, Building Department
Housing and Development Board, Urban Renewal
Housing and Development Board, Lands
Planning Department
Public Works Department

Use was also made of correspondence files in the following locations:

Economic Development Board
Housing and Development Board, Resettlement Department

In accordance with a verbal understanding with the Ministry of National Development I have omitted references to these files from the footnotes and bibliography. My notes from these files, complete with file reference numbers, are in my possession.

The University of Singapore Library has extensive holdings on Singapore and Malaya. The libraries of the East-West Center (Honolulu), Cornell University, the University of Michigan, the University of Malaya (Petaling Jaya), and London University are among those with large holdings on Singapore and Malaya.

Books

Allen, R. *Malaysia: Prospect and Retrospect*. London: Oxford University Press, 1968.

Barber, N. *Sinister Twilight: The Fall and Rise Again of Singapore*. London: Collins, 1968.

Brimmell, J. H. *Communism in Southeast Asia: A Political Analysis*. London: Oxford University Press, 1959.

Clutterbuck, K. L. *The Long, Long War: The Emergency in Malaya, 1948–1960*. London: Cassel, 1967.

Gamba, Charles. *The Origins of Trade Unionism in Malaya: A Study in Colonial Labour Unrest*. Singapore: Donald Moore, 1962.

Josey, Alex. *Lee Kuan Yew*. Singapore: Donald Moore, 1968.

Kaye, Barrington. *Upper Nankin Street, Singapore: A Sociological Study of Households Living in a Densely Populated Area*. Singapore: University of Malaya Press, 1960.

Means, Gordon. *Malaysian Politics*. New York: New York University Press, 1970.

Milne, Robert S. *Government and Politics in Malaysia*. Boston: Houghton Mifflin, 1967.

Ness, Gayle. *Bureaucracy and Rural Development in Malaysia*. Berkeley: University of California Press, 1967.

Onreat, René H. *Singapore—A Police Background*. London: D. Crisp, 1947.

Ooi Jin-Bee, and Chiang Hai Ding (eds.). *Modern Singapore*. Singapore: University of Singapore, 1969. Contains extensive bibliography.

Osborne, Milton E. *Singapore and Malaysia*. Ithaca: Department of Far Eastern Studies, Cornell University, 1964.

Purcell, Victor. *The Chinese in Southeast Asia*. 2d ed. London: Oxford University Press, 1965.

——. *Malaysia*. London: Thames and Hudson, 1965.

Puthucheary, J. J. *Ownership and Control in the Malayan Economy*. Singapore: Donald Moore, 1960.

Pye, Lucian W. *Guerilla Communism in Malaya: Its Social and Political Meaning*. Princeton: Princeton University Press, 1956.

Ratnam, K. J., and R. S. Milne. *The Malayan Parliamentary Election of 1964*. Singapore: University of Malaya Press, 1967.

Song, Sir Ong-siang. *One Hundred Years' History of the Chinese in Singapore*. London: J. Murray, 1923. Reprinted Singapore: University of Malaya Press, 1967.

SPUR (ed.). *Singapore Planning and Urban Research Group, 1965–1967*. Singapore: Eurasia Press, circa 1968.

——. *Singapore Planning and Urban Research Group, 1968–1971*. Singapore: Eurasia Press, 1972.

Swift, M. G. *Malay Peasant Society in Jelebu*. New York: Humanities Press, 1965.

Tilman, Robert O. *Bureaucratic Transition in Malaya*. Durham: Duke University Press, 1964.

Van Der Kroef, Justus M. *Communism in Malaysia and Singapore: A Contemporary Survey*. The Hague: Martinus Nijhoff, 1967.

Wang Gung-wu (ed.). *Malaysia: A Survey*. London: Pall Mall Press, 1964.

Wilson, Peter Jay. *A Malay Village and Malaysia: Social Values and Rural Development*. New Haven: Yale University Press, 1967.

Wurtzburg. Charles E. *Raffles of the Eastern Isles*. London: Hodder & Stouphton, 1954.

Articles

Barakbah, Syed Mansor. "The Problem of Illegal Squatters in Urban Areas of Kedah State, Malaysia," *Journal of Administration Overseas*, 10 (July 1971), 201–209.

Bass, Jerome R. "Malaysia and Singapore: Moving Apart?", *Asian Survey*, 9 (February 1969), 122–129.

——. "Malaysia: Continuity or Change?" *Asian Survey*, 10 (February 1970), 152–160.

Beaglehole, John H. "Malay Participation in Commerce and Industry: The Role of RIDA and MARA," *Journal of Commonwealth Political Studies*, 7 (November 1969), 216–245.

Bellows, Thomas J. "The Singapore Party System," *Journal of Southeast Asian History*, 8 (March 1967), 122–138.

Bradley, C. P. "Leftist Fissures in Singapore Politics," *Western Political Quarterly*, 18 (June 1965), 292–308.

Burridge, Kenelm. "Racial Relations in Johore," *Australian Journal of Politics and History*, 2 (1957).

Caldwell, J. C. "Urban Growth in Malaya: Trends and Implications," *Population Review* (Madras), (January 1963).

Catley, R. "Malaysia: The Lost Battle for Merger," *Australian Outlook*, 21 (1967), 44–60.

Chan Heng Chee. "Singapore's Foreign Policy, 1965–1968," *Journal of Southeast Asian History*, 10 (March 1969).

Dodd, Joseph W. "The Colonial Economy, 1966: The Case of Malaysia," *Asian Survey*, 9 (June 1969), 438–446.

Drummond, Stuart, and D. Hawkins. "The Malaysian Elections of 1969: An Analysis of the Campaign and the Results," *Asian Survey*, 10 (April 1970), 320–335.

Ee, Joyce. "Chinese Migration to Singapore, 1869–1941," *Journal of Southeast Asian History*, 2 (March 1961), 33–51.

Gamer, Robert E. "Urgent Singapore, Patient Malaysia," *International Journal* (Toronto), 12 (Winter 1965–1966), 42–56.

Hassan, Ríaz. "Class, Ethnicity and Occupational Structure in Singapore," *Civilisations*, 20 (1970), 496–513.

——. "Population Change and Urbanization in Singapore," *Civilisations*, 19 (1969), 169–185.

Ho, Robert. "Land Ownership and Economic Prospects of Malayan Peasants," *Modern Asian Studies,* 4 (January 1970).

Hooker, M. Barry. "Law, Religion and Bureaucracy in a Malay State: A Study of Conflicting Power Centers," *The American Journal of Comparative Law,* 19 (Spring 1971), 264–287.

Horowitz, Donald L. "Multiracial Politics in the New States: Toward a Theory of Conflict," in Robert J. Jackson and M. B. Stein (eds.), *Issues in Comparative Politics.* New York: St. Martin's, 1971, 164–179.

Jensen, R. "Planning, Urban Renewal, and Housing in Singapore," *Town Planning Review,* 38 (July 1967), 115–131.

Koh Foong-yin and G. W. Betz. "A Business Activity Index for Singapore, 1960–1968," *Malayan Economic Review,* 13 (October 1968), 64–80.

Lau Teik Soon. "Malaysia-Singapore Relations: Crisis of Adjustment, 1965–1968," *Journal of Southeast Asian History,* 10 (March 1969), 155–176.

Leifer, Michael. "Politics in Singapore: The First Term of the People's Action Party, 1959–1963," *Journal of Commonwealth Political Studies,* 2 (May 1964), 102–119.

——. "Singapore in Malaysia: The Politics of Federation," *Journal of Southeast Asian History,* 6 (September 1965), 54–70.

Means, Gordon P. "The Role of Islam in the Political Development of Malaysia," *Comparative Politics,* 1 (January 1969), 264–284.

Milne, Robert S. "Singapore's Exit from Malaysia: The Consequences of Ambiguity," *Asian Survey,* 6 (March 1966), 175–184.

Neville, Warwick. "The Areal Distribution of Population in Singapore," *Journal of Tropical Geography,* 20 (June 1965), 16–25.

Ng Kay-fong and others. "Three Farmers of Singapore: An Example of the Mechanics of Specialized Food Production in an Urban Unit," *Pacific Viewpoint,* 7 (September 1966), 169–197.

Oshima, Harry T. "Growth and Unemployment in Singapore," *Malayan Economic Review,* 12 (October 1967), 32–58.

Pang Cheng Lian. "The People's Action Party, 1954–1963," *Journal of Southeast Asian History,* 10 (March 1969), 142–155.

Png Poh-seng. "The Kuomintang in Malaysia, 1912–1941," *Journal of Southeast Asian History,* 2 (March 1961), 1–32.

Puthucheary, J. J. "Growth and Development of the Trade Union Movement after the Election," *Fajar,* 25 (November 30, 1955).

Pye, Lucian W. "Higher Education and Politics in Singapore," *Minerva,* 3 (Spring 1965), 321–335.

Reid, Anthony. "The Kuala Lumpur Riots and the Malaysian Political System," *Australian Outlook,* 23 (December 1969), 258–279.

Rogers, Marvin. "Malaysia/Singapore: Problems and Challenges of the Seventies," *Asian Survey,* 11 (February 1971), 121–131.

——. "Politicization and Political Development in a Rural Malay Community," *Asian Survey*, 9 (November 1969), 919–934.

Rudner, Martin. "The Malaysian General Election of 1969: A Political Analysis," *Modern Asian Studies*, 4 (January 1970), 1–22.

Saw Swee-Hock and R. Ma. "The Economic Characteristics of the Population of Singapore," *Malayan Economic Review*, 5 (April 1960), 31–51.

Short, Anthony. "Communism, Race and Politics in Malaysia," *Asian Survey*, 10 (December 1970), 1081–1090.

Singh, Vishal. "A Report on Malaysia, Singapore, and Indonesia," *India Quarterly*, 25 (October–December 1969), 321–359.

Snider, Nancy L. "Race, Leitmotiv of the Malayan Election Drama," *Asian Survey*, 10 (December 1970), 1070–1081.

——. "What Happened in Penang?", *Asian Survey*, 8 (1968), 960–975.

Tae Yul Nam. "Singapore's One-Party System: Its Relationship to Democracy and Political Stability," *Pacific Affairs*, 42 (Winter 1969–1970), 465–480.

Wang Gung-wu. "Chinese Politics in Malaya," *The China Quarterly*, 43 (July–September 1970), 1–31.

Yeh Hua-kuo. "The Size and Structure of Households in Singapore, 1957–1966," *Malayan Economic Review*, 12 (October 1967), 97–115.

——. "Housing Conditions in Singapore," *Malayan Economic Review*, 13 (April 1968), 11–38.

Yeo Kim Wah. "A Study of Three Early Political Parties in Singapore, 1945–1955," *Journal of Southeast Asian History*, 10 (March 1969), 115–141.

Yong Ching-fatt. "A Preliminary Study of Chinese Leadership in Singapore, 1900–1941," *Journal of Southeast Asian History*, 9 (September 1968), 258–285.

You Poh-seng. "The Housing Survey of Singapore, 1955," *Malayan Economic Review*, 2 (April 1957), 54–74.

——. "The Population of Singapore, 1966: Demographic Structure, Social and Economic Characteristics," *Malayan Economic Review*, 12 (October 1967), 59–96.

—— and S. H. K. Yeh, "The Sample Household Survey of Singapore, 1966," *Malayan Economic Review*, 12 (April 1967), 47–63.

Government Publications

Abrams, Charles, Susumu Kobe, and Otto Koenigsberger. *Growth and Urban Renewal in Singapore*. New York: United Nations Technical Assistance Department of Economic and Social Affairs, 1963.

Awbery, S., and F. W. Dalley. *Labour and Trade Union Organization in the Federation of Malaya and Singapore*. London: HMSO, 1948.

Boggars, George. *The Tanjong Pagar Dock Company 1864–1905*. Singapore: GPO, 1956.

Goh Keng Swee. *Communism in Non-Communist Asian Countries*. Singapore: Ministry of Culture, 1967.

——. *Urban Incomes and Housing: A Report on the Social Survey of Singapore 1953–1954*. Singapore: GPO, 1956.

Great Britain. Colonial Office. *Malayan Union and Singapore: Statement of Policy on Future Constitution*. London: HMSO, 1946.

Lee Kuan Yew. *The Battle for a Malaysian Malaysia*. Singapore: Ministry of Culture, 1965.

——. *The Battle for Merger*. Singapore: GPO, 1962.

——. *Socialism and Reconstruction in Asia*. Singapore: Ministry of Culture, 1965.

——. *Some Problems in Malaysia*. Singapore: Ministry of Culture, 1964.

Malaysia, Federation of. *Communism in the Nanyang University*. Kuala Lumpur: Jabatan Chetak Kerajaan, 1964.

Murry, J. F. N. *A Report on Control of Land Prices, Valuation and Compulsory Acquisition of Land*. Singapore: GPO, 1957.

Sennet, C. W. A. *Report of the Housing Committee, Singapore, 1947*. Singapore: GPO, 1948.

Singapore, Colony of. *Development Estimates*. 1955–1959. Singapore: GPO.

——. *First Education Triennial Survey, 1955–1957*. Singapore, GPO, 1959.

——. *Master Plan*. Singapore: GPO, 1955.

——. *Master Plan: Report of Survey*. Singapore: GPO, 1955.

——. *Report of the Constitutional Commission*. Singapore: GPO, 1954.

——. *Singapore Annual Report*. 1947–1958. Singapore: GPO.

——. *White Paper on Malayanisation*. Singapore: GPO, 1956.

——, Constitutional Conference, London 1956. *Singapore Constitutional Conference*. London: HMSO, 1956.

——, Constitutional Conference, London 1957. *Report*. Singapore: GPO, 1957.

——, Department of Education. *Education Policy in the Colony of Singapore: Ten Years' Programme Adopted in Advisory Council on 7th August, 1947*. Singapore: GPO, 1948.

——, Legislative Assembly. *The Communist Threat in Singapore*. Singapore: GPO, 1957.

——, Legislative Assembly. *Legislative Assembly Debates: Official Reports*. April 1955–1959. Singapore: GPO.

——, Legislative Assembly. *Singapore Chinese Middle Schools Students' Union*. Singapore: GPO, 1956.

——, Legislative Assembly. *White Paper on Education Policy*. Singapore: GPO, 1956.

——, Legislative Assembly, All-Party Committee on Chinese Education. *Report on Chinese Education.* Singapore: GPO, 1956.

——, Legislative Assembly, Select Committee on the Local Government Bill. *Report.* Singapore: GPO, 1957.

——, Legislative Council. *Memorandum on Bilingual Education and Increased Aid to Chinese Schools.* Singapore: GPO, 1953.

——, Malayanisation Commission. *Interim Report.* Singapore: GPO, 1956.

——, Singapore Improvement Trust. *SIT Annual Report.* 1927–1959. Singapore: GPO.

——, Singapore Riots Inquiry Commission. *Report of the Singapore Riots Inquiry Commission, 1951.* Singapore: GPO, 1951.

——, Statistics Department. *Population Estimates of Singapore by Racial Group and Sex and Administrative Area.* December 31, 1957–1959. Singapore: GPO.

Singapore, Republic of. *Development Estimates.* 1965–present. Singapore: GPO.

——. *Report on the Census of Industrial Production.* 1965–present. Singapore: GPO.

——. *Singapore Year Book.* 1964–present. Singapore: GPO.

——, Ministry of Culture. *The Mirror* (weekly). 1965–present.

——, Ministry of Culture. *Public Housing in Singapore: A Handbook of Facts and Figures.* Singapore: GPO, 1967.

——, Ministry of National Development and Economic Research Centre. *Singapore Sample Household Survey 1966: Report No. 1, Tables Referring to Population and Housing.* Singapore: GPO, 1967.

——, Parliament. *Parliament Debates: Official Reports.* 1965–present. Singapore: GPO.

——, State and City Planning (ed.). *Notes for Consultant Briefing at Node One in the Plan of Operations.* Singapore: GPO, 1967.

——, Statistics Department. *Monthly Demographic Bulletin.* 1965–present. Singapore: GPO.

——, Statistics Department. *Monthly Digest of Statistics.* 1965–present. Singapore: GPO.

——, Statistics Department. *Population Estimates of Singapore by Racial Group and Sex and Administrative Area.* 1965–present. Singapore: GPO.

——, Statistics Department. *Yearbook of Statistics.* 1967–present. Singapore: GPO.

Singapore, State of. *Development Estimates.* 1960–1964. Singapore: GPO.

——. *Singapore Annual Report.* 1959–1963. Singapore: GPO.

——, Economic Planning Unit. *First Development Plan, 1961–1964; Review of Progress for the Three Years Ending 31st December 1963.* Singapore: GPO, 1964.

——, Housing and Development Board. *50,000 Up: Homes for the People.* Singapore, 1965.

——, Legislative Assembly. *Legislative Assembly Debates: Official Reports.* 1959–1965. Singapore: GPO.

——, Legislative Assembly. *Memorandum Setting out Heads of Agreement for a Merger between the Federation of Malaya and Singapore.* Singapore: GPO, 1961.

——, Ministry of Education. *Progress in Education, Singapore 1959–1965.* Singapore: GPO, 1966.

——, Ministry of Finance. *State of Singapore Development Plan 1961–1964.* Singapore: GPO, 1961.

——, Nanyang University Commission. *Report.* Singapore: GPO, 1959.

——, Planning Department. *Revised Master Plan: Written Statement.* Singapore: GPO, 1965.

——, Statistics Department. *Monthly Demographic Bulletin.* 1959–1965. Singapore: GPO.

——, Statistics Department. *Monthly Digest of Statistics.* 1962–1965. Singapore: GPO.

——, Statistics Department. *Population Estimates of Singapore by Racial Group and Sex and Administrative Area.* 1960–1965. Singapore: GPO.

——, Statistics Department. *Report on the Census of Industrial Production.* 1959–1964. Singapore: GPO.

——, Statistics Department. *Report on the Census of Population, 1957.* Singapore: GPO, 1964.

United Nations. Department of Economic and Social Affairs. *Future Population Estimates. Report III, The Population of Southeast Asia 1950– 1980.* Geneva, 1958.

Other Material

Barisan Sosialis. *Plebeian* (also *Plebeian Express*). 1962–. Singapore: Barisan Sosialis.

Bellows, Thomas. "The Singapore Party System: The First Two Decades." Ph.D. dissertation, Yale University, New Haven, 1968.

Buchanan, Ian. "Squatter Resettlement in Singapore." Mimeo. Singapore: Department of Geography, University of Singapore, 1967.

Chan Heng Chee. "Singapore out of Malaysia: The Politics of Survival." Masters thesis, Cornell University, Ithaca, 1967.

Choe, Alan F. C. "Slum Clearance and Urban Renewal in Singapore," in Afro-Asian Housing Congress, 2d., Singapore, 1967. *Papers.* Cairo: Afro-Asian Housing Organization, 1967.

Damu, Asokam. "Problems of Resettlement in Singapore, as Illustrated by the Tanjong Rhu Resettlement scheme." Honours thesis, Department of Geography, University of Singapore, 1962 / 1963.

Eastern Sun (daily newspaper). 1967–1968. Singapore.

Far Eastern Economic Review (weekly). 1946–present. Hong Kong.

Far Eastern Economic Review. *Annual Yearbook*. 1960–present. Hong Kong.

Federation of Unions of Government Employees. "Memorandum to the Malayanisation Commission." Mimeo. Singapore, 1955.

Gamer, Robert E. "Political Socialization in Three Working Class Neighborhoods in Singapore." Mimeo. Singapore, July 1965.

Lee Ting-hui. "Policies and Politics in Chinese Schools in the Straits Settlements and the Federated Malay States, 1786–1941." Masters thesis, University of Malaya, Singapore, 1957.

Lee Yong Hock. "A History of the Straits Chinese British Association, 1900–1959." B.A. Honours thesis, Department of History, University of Malaya, Singapore, 1960.

MacDougall, J. A. "Shared Burdens: A Study of Communal Discrimination by the Political Parties of Malaysia and Singapore." Ph.D. dissertation, Harvard University, 1968.

Malay Action Committee. "Report of Inquiries and Grievances Committee of Malay Action Committee." Mimeo. Singapore, October 7, 1964, and November 25, 1964.

Nanyang University. Curriculum Review Committee. *Report*. Singapore: Nanyang University, 1965.

Neville, Warwick. "Patterns of Change in a Plural Society: A Social Geography of the City State of Singapore." Ph.D. dissertation, London School of Economics, London, 1964.

Penu, Mohan Singh. "Promotion of Private Home Ownership for the Lower Income Group," in Afro-Asian Housing Congress, 2d. Singapore, 1967. *Papers*. Cairo: Afro-Asian Housing Organization, 1967.

People's Action Party. *Petir: Organ of the People's Action Party*. 1956–present. Singapore.

––––. *The Tasks Ahead: PAP's Five-Year Plan, 1959–1964*. Singapore, 1959.

Peritz, R. "The Evolving Politics of Singapore: A Study of Trends and Issues." Ph.D. dissertation, University of Pennsylvania, Philadelphia, 1964.

––––. "A Selected Bibliography of Recent Works in English on Political Processes in Malaysia and Singapore" (1963–1968). Rhode Island: University of Rhode Island, 1969.

Siddiqi, Z. M. S. "The Registration and Deregistration of Trade Unions in Singapore." Masters thesis, University of Singapore, 1967.

Singapore Alliance. *The People*. 1959–1963. Singapore.

Singapore Herald (daily newspaper). 1970–1971. Singapore.

Singapore Labour Front. *The Star: Official Organ of the Singapore Labour Front.* 1955–1956. Singapore.

Singapore UMNO. "Appointments of Malays to the Statutory Boards." Mimeo. Circa 1964.

Stevens, J. T. "The Development of Toa Payoh New Town—Singapore." Unpublished manuscript. Singapore, circa 1966.

Straits Times (daily newspaper). 1845–present. Singapore.

Tan Jake-hooi. "Metropolitan Planning and Development in Singapore," in Afro-Asian Housing Congress, 2d. Singapore, 1967. *Papers.* Cairo: Afro-Asian Housing Organization, 1967.

Tan Tiong-Beng. "The Experiment with the Industrialization Method of Construction of Multi-story Flats in Singapore," in Afro-Asian Housing Congress, 2d. Singapore, 1967. *Papers.* Cairo: Afro-Asian Housing Organization, 1967.

Teh Cheang-wan. "Design and Planning of Public Housing in Singapore," in Afro-Asian Housing Congress, 2d. Singapore, 1967. *Papers.* Cairo: Afro-Asian Housing Organization, 1967.

University Socialist Club. *Fajar.* 1952–1964. Singapore.

Wong Wai-ying. "Modernization of the Local Building Industry for the Construction of Public Housing," in Afro-Asian Housing Congress, 2d. Singapore, 1967. *Papers* Cairo: Afro-Asian Housing Organization, 1967.

Yeh Hua-hui. "Urbanization and Public Housing in Singapore," in International Union for the Scientific Study of Population Conference, Sydney, August 21–25, 1967. *Contributed Papers.* Sydney, 1967.

Yeo Kim Wah. "Political Development in Singapore, 1945–1955." Masters thesis, Department of History, University of Singapore, 1967.

Developing Nations: Introductory Reading

Finkle, Jason L., and R. W. Gable (eds.). *Political Development and Social Change.* 2nd ed. New York: Wiley, 1971.

Gamer, Robert E. "Southeast Asia's Political Systems: An Overview," *Journal of Southeast Asian History,* 8 (March 1967), 139–185.

Gerassi, John. *The Great Fear: The Reconquest of Latin America by Latin Americans.* New York: Macmillan, 1963.

Halpern, Manfred. "The Revolution of Modernization in National and International Society," in Carl J. Friedrich (ed.), *Revolution—Nomos VIII.* New York: Atherton, 1966.

Horowitz, Irving Louis. *Three Worlds of Development.* New York: Oxford University Press, 1966.

———, J. de Castro, and J. Gerassi (eds.). *Latin American Radicalism.* New York: Vintage, 1969.

Houghton, Neal D. *Struggle against History*. New York: Washington Square Press, 1968.

Huntington, Samuel P. *Political Order in Changing Societies*. New Haven: Yale University Press, 1968.

Jackson, Robert J., and M. B. Stein (eds.). *Issues in Comparative Politics*. New York: St. Martin's, 1971.

McCord, William. *The Springtime of Freedom: The Evolution of Developing Societies*. New York: Oxford University Press, 1965.

Pincus, John A. (ed.). *Reshaping the World Economy: Rich Countries and Poor*. Englewood Cliffs: Prentice-Hall, 1968.

Schaffer, Harry G., and Jan S. Prybla (eds.). *From Underdevelopment to Affluence: Western, Soviet, and Chinese Views*. New York: Appleton-Century-Crofts, 1968.

Veliz, Claudio (ed.). *Politics of Conformity in Latin America*. London: Oxford University Press, 1970.

Weisbord, Albert. *Latin American Actualities*. New York: Citadel Press, 1964.

Welch, Claude E. (ed.). *Political Modernization: A Reader in Comparative Political Change*. Belmont, Calif.: Wadsworth, 1967.

Wolf, Eric R. *Peasant Wars in the Twentieth Century*. New York: Harper, 1969.

Urbanization

Abrams, Charles. *Language of Cities*. New York: Viking, 1971.

Balan, Jorge. "Migrant-Native Socioeconomic Differences in Latin American Cities: A Structural Analysis," *Latin American Research Review*, 4 (Spring 1969).

Barakbah, Syed Mansor. "The Problem of Illegal Squatters in Urban Areas of Kedah State, Malaysia," *Journal of Administration Overseas*, 10 (July 1971), 201–209.

Beyer, Glenn H. *The Urban Explosion in Latin America*. Ithaca: Cornell University Press, 1967.

Cornelius, Wayne A., Jr. "Urbanization as an Agent in Latin American Political Instability: The Case of Mexico," *American Political Science Review*, 63 (September 1969), 833–857.

Cousins, Albert N., and H. Nagtau (eds.). *Urban Man and Society*. New York: Random House, 1970.

Delgado, Carlos. "Three Proposals Regarding Accelerated Urbanization Problems in Metropolitan Areas: The Lima Case," *American Behavioral Scientist*, 12 (May–June 1969).

Dwyer, D. J. "The Problem in In-Migration and Squatter Settlement in

Asian Cities: Two Case Studies, Manila and Victoria-Kowloon," *Asian Studies,* 2 (1964), 145–169.

Fava, Sylvia Fleis (ed.). *Urbanism in World Perspective: A Reader.* New York: Crowell, 1968.

Flinn, William L., and David G. Cartano. "A Comparison of the Migration Process to an Urban Barrio and to a Rural Community: Two Case Studies," *Inter-American Economic Affairs,* 24 (Autumn 1970), 37–49.

Gans, Herbert. *People and Plans: Essays on Urban Problems and Solutions.* New York: Basic Books, 1968.

Hauser, Philip M. (ed.). *Urbanization in Latin America.* New York: International Documents Service, 1961.

Jakobson, Leo, and V. Prakash (eds.). *The Urbanization Process in Southeast Asia.* Vol. 1. Beverly Hills: Sage, 1970.

Johnson, Sheila K. "Hong Kong's Resettled Squatters: A Statistical Analysis," *Asian Survey,* 6 (1966), 643–656.

Juppenlatz, Morris. *Cities in Transformation: The Urban Squatter Problem in the Developing World.* St. Lucia: University of Queensland, 1970.

Lewis, John W. (ed.). *The City in Communist China.* Stanford: Stanford University Press, 1971.

Mangin, William. "Latin American Squatter Settlements: A Problem and a Solution," *Latin American Research Review,* 2 (Summer 1967).

——. "Squatter Settlements," *Scientific American,* 217 (October 1967), 21–29.

Meadows, Paul, and E. H. Mizruch (eds.). *Urbanism, Urbanization, and Change: Perspectives.* Reading, Mass.: Addison Wesley, 1969.

Morse, Richard. "Recent Research on Latin American Urbanization," *Latin American Research Review,* 1 (Fall 1964), 35–74.

Turner, Roy (ed.). *India's Urban Future.* Berkeley: University of California Press, 1967.

Urban Planning and Development Administration

Apter, David. *Choice and the Politics of Allocation: A Developmental Theory.* New Haven: Yale University Press, 1971.

Badgley, John. *Asian Development: Problems and Prognosis.* New York: Free Press, 1970.

Banfield, Edward, and J. Q. Wilson. *City Politics.* Cambridge: Harvard University Press, 1963.

Bellush, Jewel, and M. Hausknecht (eds.). *Urban Renewal: People, Politics, and Planning.* Garden City: Doubleday, 1967.

Bernard, Philippe J. *Planning in the Soviet Union.* New York: Macmillan, 1965.

Beyer, John C. "High Growth, Unemployment, and Planning in Venezuela:

Some Observations," *Economic Development and Cultural Change,* 18 (January 1970), 267–277. Includes a reply by M. Hassan.

Beyle, Thad T., and G. T. Lathrop (eds.). *Planning and Politics: Uneasy Partnership.* New York: Odyssey, 1971.

Braibanti, Ralph. *The Civil Service in Pakistan: A Theoretical Analysis.* Durham: Duke University Press, 1959.

Calcutta Metropolitan Planning Organization. *Basic Development Plan for the Calcutta Metropolitan District 1966–1986.* Calcutta, 1966.

Chamberlain, Neil W. *Private and Public Planning.* New York: McGraw-Hill, 1965.

Chenery, Hollis B., and P. Eckstein. "Development Alternatives for Latin America," *Journal of Political Economy,* 78 (July–August 1970), 966–1007.

Daland, Robert T. *Brazilian Planning: Development Politics and Administration.* Chapel Hill: University of North Carolina Press, 1967.

——. "Urbanization Policy and Political Development in Latin America," *American Behavioral Scientist,* 12 (May–June 1969).

—— (ed.). *Comparative Urban Research.* Beverly Hills: Sage, 1969.

Doxiadis, Constantinos A. *Ekistics: An Introduction to the Science of Human Settlements.* London: Oxford University Press, 1968.

Drewnowski, Jan. *Social and Economic Factors in Development: Introductory Considerations on their Meaning, Measurement, and Interdependence.* Geneva: United Nations Research Institute for Social Development, 1966.

Dudley, D. (ed.). *Development in a Divided World.* Baltimore: Penguin, 1971.

Ehrensaft, Philip. "Authentic Planning or Afro-Asian Appalachia?", *American Behavioral Scientist,* 12 (September–October 1968).

Erber, Ernest (ed.). *Urban Planning in Transition.* New York: Grossman, 1970.

Esman, Milton J. "The Politics of Development Administration," in John D. Montgomery and W. Siffin (eds.). *Approaches to Development: Politics, Administration, and Change.* New York: McGraw-Hill, 1966. Pp. 65–71.

Falcon, W. P., and G. F. Papanek. *Development Policy Two: The Pakistan Experience.* Cambridge: Harvard University Press, 1971.

Friedman, John. *Urban and Regional Development in Chile.* Santiago: Ford Foundation, 1969.

Furtado, Celso. *Obstacles to Development in Latin America.* Garden City: Doubleday, 1970.

Galbraith, John K. *Economic Development in Perspective.* Cambridge: Harvard University Press, 1962.

Goodman, William I, and E. C. Freund (eds.). *Principles and Practice of Urban Planning*. Washington, D.C.: International City Managers' Association, 1968.

Grunwald, Joseph. "Some Reflections on Latin American Industrialization Policy," *Journal of Political Economy*, 78 (July–August 1970), 826–857.

Hawley, Amos. "Community Power and Urban Renewal Success," *American Journal of Sociology*, 67 (January 1963), 422–431.

Jakobson, Leo, and V. Prakash (eds.). *Urbanization and National Development*. Beverly Hills: Sage, 1971.

Kammerer, Gladys (ed.). *The Urban Political Community*. Boston: Houghton Mifflin, 1963.

Kaplan, Harold. *Urban Political Systems: A Functional Analysis of Metro-Toronto*. New York: Columbia University Press, 1967.

Keilany, Zind. "A Reappraisal of Development Planning," *Il Politico*, 35 (September 1970), 457–472.

Laquian, A. A. "The Asian City and the Political Process," *The Philippine Journal of Public Administration*, 14 (January 1970), 8–21.

Lewis, W. Arthur. *Development Planning*. London: Allen and Unwin, 1966.

——. *Some Aspects of Economic Development*. London: Panther House, 1970.

Meech, J. V. "Is There an Ideal Relationship between Politicians and Administrators?", *New Zealand Journal of Political Science*, 27 (September 1964).

Meillassaux, Claude. "A Class Analysis of the Bureaucratic Process in Mali," *The Journal of Development Studies*, 6 (January 1970).

Milne, Robert S. "Administrators, Experts, and Training in the Public Service," *The Philippine Journal of Public Administration*, 6 (October 1962).

Mountjoy, A. (ed.). *Developing the Underdeveloped Countries*. New York: Wiley, 1971.

Moynihan, Daniel P. *Maximum Feasible Misunderstanding: Community Action in the War on Poverty*. New York: Free Press, 1969.

Ness, Gayle. *Bureaucracy and Rural Development in Malaysia*. Berkeley: University of California Press, 1967.

Olorunsola, Victor A. "Patterns of Interaction between Bureaucratic and Political Leaders: A Case Study," *The Journal of Developing Areas*, 3 (October 1968).

Ortiz, Sutti. " 'The Human Factor' in Social Planning in Latin America," *The Journal of Development Studies*, 6 (July 1970).

Osborn, Robert J. "How the Russians Plan Their Cities," in Sylvia Fleis Fava (ed.). *Urbanism in World Perspective: A Reader*. New York: Crowell, 1968.

Oshima, Harry T. "Labor-Force 'Explosion' and the Labor-intensive Sector in Asian Growth," *Economic Development and Cultural Change,* 19 (January 1971), 161–183.

Pratt, R. Cranford. "The Administration of Economic Planning in a Newly Independent State: The Tanzania Experience 1963–1966," *Journal of Commonwealth Political Studies,* 5 (March 1967), 38–59.

Prosser, A. R. G. "Community Development and Its Relation to Development Planning," *Journal of Administration Overseas,* 8 (July 1969).

Rabinovitz, Francine F. *City Politics and Planning.* New York: Atherton, 1969.

Reps, John W. *Town Planning in Frontier America.* Princeton: Princeton University Press, 1969.

Riggs, Fred W. (ed.). *Frontiers of Development Administration.* Durham: Duke University Press, 1971.

——. "Relearning an Old Lesson: The Political Context of Development Administration," *Public Administration Review,* 20 (March 1965), 70–79.

Robinson, R. (ed.). *Developing the Third World: The Experience of the Nineteen Sixties.* Cambridge: Cambridge University Press, 1971.

Rodwin, Lloyd. *Nations and Cities: A Comparison of Strategies for Urban Growth.* Boston: Houghton Mifflin, 1970.

——. (ed.). *Planning Urban Growth and Regional Development: The Experience of the Guyana Program of Venezuela.* Cambridge: M.I.T. Press, 1969.

Rosser, Colin. "Action Planning in Calcutta: The Problem of Community Participation," *The Journal of Development Studies,* 6 (July 1970), 121–140.

Scherer, F. *Development of Smallholder Vegetable Production in Kigezi, Uganda.* New York: Humanities Press, 1971.

Sharma, Prabhu Datta. "Urban Government and Community Development: The Turkish Experience," *The Philippine Journal of Public Administration,* 12 (October 1968).

Shils, Edward. "The Intellectuals in the Political Development of the New States," *World Politics,* 12 (April 1960), 329–368.

Smallwood, Frank. *Greater London: The Politics of Metropolitan Reform.* Indianapolis: Bobbs-Merrill, 1965.

Sorokin, G. *Planning in the USSR.* Moscow: Progress Publishers, 1967.

Spitz, Alan A., and E. A. Weidner (eds.). *Development Administration: An Annotated Bibliography.* Honolulu: East-West Center, 1963.

United Nations Department of Economic and Social Affairs. *Urbanization: Development Policies and Planning.* New York: United Nations, 1968.

Van Huyck, Alfred P., and J. D. Herbert. *Urban Planning in Developing Countries.* New York: Praeger, 1968.

Veliz, Claudio (ed.). *Obstacles to Change in Latin America*. London: Oxford University Press, 1965.

Violich, Francis, and J. B. Astica. *Community Development and the Urban Planning Process in Latin America*. Los Angeles: University of California Press, 1967.

Walinsky, Louis J. *The Planning and Execution of Economic Development*. New York: McGraw-Hill, 1963.

Waterston, Albert. *Development Planning: Lessons of Experience*. Baltimore: Johns Hopkins, 1965.

Housing and Urban Renewal

Abrams, Charles. *Man's Struggle for Shelter in an Urbanizing World*. Cambridge: M.I.T. Press, 1964.

——. *Forbidden Neighbors*. Port Washington, N.Y.: Kennikat, 1971.

——. "The Uses of Land in Cities," *Scientific American,* 213 (September 1965).

Adde, Leo. *Nine Cities: the Anatomy of Downtown Renewal*. Washington, D.C.: Urban Land Institute, 1969.

Anderson, Martin. *The Federal Bulldozer: A Critical Analysis of Urban Renewal 1949–1962*. Cambridge: M.I.T. Press, 1964.

Beyer, Glenn H. *Housing and Society*. New York: Macmillan, 1965.

Blumenfeld, Hans. "The Modern Metropolis," *Scientific American,* 213 (September 1965).

Brolin, Brent C., and John Zeisel. "Mass Housing: Social Research and Design," *Architectural Forum,* 68 (July / August 1968), 66–71.

Burns, Leland S., R. G. Healy, D. M. McAllister, and B. K. Tjioi. *Housing: Symbol and Shelter*. Los Angeles: University of California Press, 1970.

Clinard, Marshall B. *Slums and Community Development: Experiments in Self-Help*. New York: Free Press, 1966.

Dietz, A. G. H., M. N. Koth, and J. G. Silva. *Housing in Latin America*. Cambridge: M.I.T. Press, 1965.

Dwyer, D. J. "Urban Squatters: The Relevance of the Hong Kong Experience," *Asian Survey,* 10 (July 1970), 607–614.

Eckbo, Garret. *Urban Landscape Design*. New York: McGraw-Hill, 1964.

Frieden, Bernard J. (ed.). *Urban Planning and Social Policy*. New York: Basic Books, 1968.

Gottlieb, Lois D. *Environment and Design in Housing*. New York: Macmillan, 1965.

Grebler, Leo. *Urban Renewal in European Countries: Its Emergence and Potentials*. Philadelphia: University of Pennsylvania Press, 1964.

Greer, Scott. *Urban Renewal and American Cities: The Dilemma of Democratic Intervention*. Indianapolis: Bobbs-Merrill, 1965.

Grigsby, William G. *Housing Markets and Public Policy.* Philadelphia: University of Pennsylvania Press, 1963.

——. "Housing and Slum Clearance: Elusive Goals," *Annals of the American Academy of Political and Social Science,* 352 (March 1964), 101–118.

Hong Kong Government. *Review of Policies for Squatter Control, Resettlement, and Government Low Cost Housing.* Hong Kong, 1964.

Hong Kong Housing Board. *Report of the Housing Board, 1967–1968.* Hong Kong, 1968.

Hopkins, K. "Public Housing Policy in Hong Kong," *Supplement to the Gazette,* 16. Hong Kong: University of Hong Kong, 1969.

Lansing, John B. *New Homes and Poor People: A Study of Chains of Moves.* Ann Arbor: Survey Research Center, 1969.

Logan, J. A. (ed.). *Environmental Engineering and Metropolitan Planning.* Evanston: Northwestern University Press, 1962.

Meyerson, Martin, B. Terret, and L. C. Wheaton. *Housing, People, and Cities.* New York: McGraw-Hill, 1962.

Milone, Paula. "The Disaster Cities," *Far Eastern Economic Review,* 43 (October 23, 1971), 57–63.

Nakamura, Koji. "Poor Little Rich People," *Far Eastern Economic Review,* (October 23, 1971), 63–66.

Page, Alfred, and W. R. Seyfried (eds.). *Urban Analysis: Readings in Housing and Urban Development.* Glenview: Scott, Foresman, 1970.

Pepper, Simon. *Housing Improvement: Goals and Strategies.* New York: Wittenborn, 1971.

Pucak, Stjepan. "Brick Revolution," *Far Eastern Economic Review,* 43 (October 23, 1971), 66–68.

Sazanomi, Hidehiko. *Housing in Metropolitan Areas.* Toronto: Bureau of Municipal Research, 1967.

Solon, Anatole A. *Housing Conditions of Urban Low Income Families in Relation to Levels of Social and Economic Development in Latin America.* Pittsburgh: University of Pittsburgh Graduate School of Public and International Affairs, 1966.

Staples, John H. "Urban Renewal: A Comparative Study of Twenty-two Cities, 1950–1960," *The Western Political Quarterly,* 23 (1970), 294–304.

Stegman, M. (ed.). *Housing and Economics: The American Dilemma.* Cambridge: M.I.T. Press, 1971.

Taeuber, Karl E., and Alma F. Taeuber. *Negroes in Cities: Residential Segregation and Neighborhood Change.* Chicago: Aldine, 1965.

United Nations. *Major Long-Term Problems of Government Housing and Related Policies.* New York, 1966.

——. *Reports of the United Nations Committee on Housing, Building, and Planning.* 1963–present. New York.

—— *United Nations Report of the Latin America Seminar on Housing Statistics and Programmes.* Copenhagen, 1962.

——, Economic Commission for Asia and the Far East. *Review of Housing Situation in ECAFE Countries.* Bangkok, 1965.

——, Economic Commission for Europe. *European Housing Progress and Policies in 1953.* Geneva, 1954.

——, Economic Commission for Europe. *Report of the Urban Renewal Symposium.* Geneva, 1962.

United States Department of Housing and Urban Development. *Housing and Urban Planning References.* 1965–present. Washington, D.C.

Walker, M. L. *Urban Blight and Slums: Economic and Legal Factors in Their Origin, Reclamation and Prevention.* New York: Russell and Russell, 1971.

Wendt, Paul F. *Housing Policy—the Search for Solutions: A Comparison of the United Kingdom, Sweden, West Germany, and the United States since World War II.* Berkeley: University of California Press, 1962.

Wheaton, William (ed.). *Urban Housing.* New York: Free Press, 1966.

Wilson, James Q., (ed.). *Urban Renewal: The Record and the Controversy.* Cambridge: M.I.T. Press, 1966.

Case Studies: Citizen Participation in Urban Redevelopment

Abrahamson, Julia. *A Neighborhood Finds Itself.* New York: Harper, 1959.

Altshuler, Alan A. *The City Planning Process: A Political Analysis.* Ithaca: Cornell University Press, 1965.

Banfield, Edward C. *Political Influence.* New York: Free Press, 1961.

Dahl, Robert. *Who Governs?* New Haven: Yale University Press, 1961.

Davies, J. Clarence, III. *Neighborhood Groups and Urban Renewal.* New York: Columbia University Press, 1966.

Donella, Frank, and Anne Sarka. *Metro-North-INRA-CRRA: A Report on a Unique Collaboration.* New York: International Research Associates, 1966.

Ecco Project. *Neighborhood Foundations Memoranda.* Washington, D.C.: Institute for Policy Studies, circa 1966.

Frieden, Bernard J. *The Future of Old Neighborhoods: Rebuilding for a Changing Population.* Cambridge: M.I.T. Press, 1964.

Gans, Herbert L. *The Urban Villagers.* New York: Free Press, 1962.

Heller, Robert M., and M. A. Jacoby. "Citizen Participation in Urban Renewal," *Columbia Law Review,* 66 (March 1966).

Kaplan, Harold. *Urban Renewal Politics: Slum Clearance in Newark.* New York: Columbia University Press, 1963.

Keyes, Langley Carleton, Jr. *The Rehabilitation Planning Game: A Study in the Diversity of Neighborhood*. Cambridge: M.I.T. Press, 1969.

Lowi, Theodore J. *The End of Liberalism: Ideology, Policy, and the Crisis of Public Authority*. New York: Norton, 1969.

Meyerson, Martin, and E. C. Banfield. *Politics, Planning, and the Public Interest: The Case of Public Housing in Chicago*. Glencoe: Free Press, 1955.

Millspaugh, Martin, and G. Breckenfield. *The Human Side of Urban Renewal: A Study of Attitude Changes Produced by Neighborhood Rehabilitation*. New York: Ives Washburn, 1958.

Perman, Dagmar H. *The Girard Street Project*. Washington, D.C.: All Souls Unitarian Church, 1964.

Rossi, Peter H., and R. A. Dentler. *The Politics of Urban Renewal: The Chicago Findings*. New York: Free Press, 1961.

Boston

Fried, Marc. "Grieving for a Former Home," in Leonard J. Duhl (ed.), *The Urban Condition*. New York: Basic Books, 1963. Pp. 151–171.

Gans, Herbert. *People and Plans: Essays on Urban Problems and Solutions*. New York: Basic Books, 1968. Pp. 208–230, 260–265.

——. *The Urban Villagers*. New York: Free Press, 1962.

Hartman, Chester. "The Housing of Relocated Families," *Journal of the American Institute of Planners,* 30 (November 1964).

Jacobs, Jane. *The Life and Death of Great American Cities*. New York: Random House, 1961. Pp. 8–12.

Keyes, Langley Carleton, Jr. *The Boston Rehabilitation Program: An Independent Analysis*. Cambridge: Harvard University Press, 1970.

——. *The Rehabilitation Planning Game: A Study in the Diversity of Neighborhood*. Cambridge: M.I.T. Press, 1969.

Thernstrom, Stephan. *Poverty, Planning, and Politics in the New Boston: The Origins of the ABCD*. New York: Basic Books, 1969.

Cuba

Baum, P. *Cuba: Continuing Crisis*. New York: Putnam, 1971.

Bernardo, Robert M. *The Theory of Moral Incentives in Cuba*. Alabama: University of Alabama Press, 1971.

Boorstein, Edward. *The Economic Transformation of Cuba*. New York: Monthly Review Press, 1968.

Dumont, R. *Cuba: Socialism and Development*. New York: Grove Press, 1970.

Fagen, Richard R. *The Transformation of Political Culture in Cuba*. Stanford: Stanford University Press, 1969.

———, R. A. Brody, and T. J. O'Leary. *Cubans in Exile: Disaffection and the Revolution.* Stanford: Stanford University Press, 1968.

Goldenberg, Boris. *The Cuban Revolution and Latin America.* New York: Praeger, 1965.

Lockwood, Lee. *Castro's Cuba, Cuba's Fidel.* New York: Macmillan, 1967.

Mesa-Lago, Carmelo (ed.). *Revolutionary Change in Cuba.* Pittsburgh: University of Pittsburgh Press, 1971.

Ruiz, Ramon E. *Cuba: The Making of a Revolution.* Amherst: University of Massachusetts Press, 1968.

Valdes, Nelson P., and Edwin Lieuwen (comps.). *The Cuban Revolution: A Research-Study Guide, 1959–1969.* New Mexico: The University of New Mexico Press, 1971.

Viator. "Cuba Revisited after Ten Years of Castro," *Foreign Affairs,* 48 (January 1970).

Yglesias, Jose. *In the Fist of the Revolution: Life in a Cuban Country Town.* New York: Vintage, 1969.

Zeitlin, Maurice. "Cuba—Revolution without a Blueprint," *Transaction,* 6 (April 1969).

———. *Revolutionary Politics and the Cuban Working Class.* Princeton: Princeton University Press, 1967.

Changing Social Environment

Anderson, Nels. "The Urban Way of Life," *International Journal of Comparative Sociology,* 3 (December 1962).

Aron, Raymond. *Eighteen Lectures on Industrial Society.* London: Weidenfeld and Nicolson, 1967.

Bacon, E. E. *Central Asians under Russian Rule: A Study in Cultural Change.* Ithaca: Cornell University Press, 1966.

Bailey, F. G. *Politics and Social Change, Orissa in 1959.* London: Oxford University Press, 1963.

Bloomberg, Warren, and H. Schmandt (eds.). *Power, Poverty, and Urban Policy.* Beverly Hills: Sage, 1968.

Blumer, Herbert. "Industrialization and the Traditional Order," *Sociology and Social Research,* 48 (January 1964), 129–138.

Boeke, Julius H. *Economics and Economic Policy of Dual Societies, as Exemplified by Indonesia.* New York: Institute of Pacific Relations, 1953.

Braibanti, Ralph, and J. J. Spengler. *Tradition, Values, and Socioeconomic Development.* Durham: Duke University Press, 1961.

Cohen, Ronald, and John Middleton (eds.). *Comparative Political Systems: Studies in the Politics of Pre-Industrial Societies.* Garden City: Natural History Press, 1967.

Doob, Leonard. *Becoming More Civilized: A Psychological Exploration.* New Haven: Yale University Press, 1960.

Dube, S. C. *India's Changing Villages.* Ithaca: Cornell University Press, 1958.

Durkheim, Emile. "Social Change in an Indian Village," *Economic Development and Social Change,* 1 (1952–1953), 153.

Edwards, Adrian C. *The Ovimbundu under Two Sovereignties.* London: Oxford University Press, 1962.

Eggan, Frederick R. *The Social Organization of the Western Pueblos.* Chicago: University of Chicago Press, 1960.

Eisenstadt, S. N. *The Political Systems of Empires.* New York: Free Press, 1963.

Firth, Raymond. *Malay Fishermen: Their Peasant Economy.* London: Kegan Paul, 1946.

Fischer, W. "Social Tensions at the Early Stages of Industrialization," *Comparative Studies in Society and History,* 9 (October 1966), 64–83.

Foster, George M. *Traditional Cultures and the Impact of Technological Change.* New York: Harper, 1962.

Fox, Richard D. *Kin, Clan, Raja, and Rule: State-Hinterland Relations in Preindustrial India.* California: University of California Press, 1971.

Fromm, Erich, and M. Maccoby. *Social Character in a Mexican Village: A Psychoanalytic Study.* Englewood Cliffs: Prentice-Hall, 1970.

Geertz, Clifford. *Agricultural Involution: The Processes of Ecological Change in Indonesia.* Berkeley: University of California Press, 1968.

——. *Islam Observed: Religious Development in Morocco and Indonesia.* New Haven: Yale University Press, 1968.

——. *Peddlers and Princes: Social Development and Economic Change in Two Indonesian Towns.* Chicago: University of Chicago Press, 1968.

——. *Religion in Java.* Glencoe: Free Press, 1960.

——. *The Social History of an Indonesian Town.* Cambridge: M.I.T. Press, 1965.

Hagen, E. E. *On the Theory of Social Change: How Economic Growth Begins.* Homewood, Ill.: Dorsey, 1962.

Hahn, Hariah. *Urban-Rural Conflict: The Politics of Change.* Beverly Hills: Sage, 1970.

Halpern, Joel. *The Changing Village Community.* Englewood Cliffs: Prentice-Hall, 1967.

Hammond, J. L., and B. Hammond. *The Village Labourer.* London: Longmans, 1911, 1966.

——. *The Town Labourer.* London: Longmans, 1917, 1966.

Hanson, Robert C., and O. G. Simmons, "Differential Experience Paths of

Rural Migrants to the City," *American Behavioral Scientist,* 13 (September–October 1969).

Hauser, Philip M. "On the Impact of Urbanism on Social Organization, Human Nature and the Political Order," *Confluence,* 7 (Spring 1958).

Hetzler, Stanley A. *Technological Growth and Social Change.* New York: Praeger, 1969.

Hooker, M. Barry. "Law, Religion and Bureaucracy in a Malay State: A Study in Conflicting Power Centers," *The American Journal of Comparative Law,* 19 (Spring 1971), 264–287.

Hunter, Guy. *The New Societies of Tropical Africa.* New York: Oxford University Press, 1963.

Johnson, John J. *Political Change in Latin America: The Emergence of the Middle Sectors.* Stanford: Stanford University Press, 1958.

Kasperson, Roger E. *The Dodecanese: Diversity and Unity in Island Politics.* Chicago: University of Chicago, Department of Geography, 1966.

Lerner, Daniel. *The Passing of Traditional Society.* Glencoe: Free Press, 1958.

Lewis, Oscar. *The Children of Sanchez.* New York: Random House, 1961.

———. *La Vida: A Puerto Rican Family in the Culture of Poverty.* New York: Random House, 1966.

———. *Life in a Mexican Village: Tepoztlan Restudied.* Urbana: University of Illinois Press, 1951.

———. "Urbanization without Breakdown: A Case Study," in Dwight B. Heath and R. N. Adams (eds.), *Contemporary Culture and Societies in Latin America.* New York: Random House, 1965.

McClelland, Charles. *The Achieving Society.* Princeton: Van Nostrand, 1961.

Mair, Lucy. *Primitive Government.* Baltimore: Penguin, 1962.

Mead, Margaret (ed.). *Cultural Patterns and Technological Change.* Paris: UNESCO, 1953.

Morris, Donald R. *The Washing of the Spears: The Rise and Fall of the Zulu Nation.* New York: Simon and Schuster, 1965.

Morse, David A. "Unemployment in Developing Countries," *Political Science Quarterly,* 85 (March 1970), 1–16.

Myrdal, Jan. *Report from a Chinese Village.* New York: Pantheon Books, 1965.

Omer-Cooper, J. D. *The Zulu Aftermath: A Nineteenth Century Revolution in Bantu Africa.* Evanston: Northwestern University Press, 1966.

Paredes, A., and E. J. Stekert. *Urban Experience and Folk Tradition.* Austin: University of Texas Press, 1971.

Payne, Raymond. "Leadership and Perception of Change in a Village Confronted with Urbanism," *Social Forces,* 41 (March 1963).

Peattie, Lisa Redfield. *The View from the Barrio.* Ann Arbor: University of Michigan Press, 1968.

Pratt, Raymond B. "Community Political Organizations and Lower Class Politicization in Two Latin American Cities," *The Journal of Developing Areas,* 5 (July 1971), 523–543.

Ray, Dalton F. *The Politics of the Barrios in Venezuela.* Berkeley: University of California Press, 1969.

Reader, D. H. *Zulu Tribe in Transition.* Manchester: Manchester University Press, 1966.

Redfield, Robert. *The Primitive World and Its Transformation.* Ithaca: Cornell University Press, 1962.

——. *The Village That Chose Progress: Chan Kam Revisited.* Chicago: University of Chicago Press, 1950.

Rogers, Everett M. *Modernization Among Peasants.* New York: Holt, 1969.

Rogers, Marvin L. "Politicization and Political Development in a Rural Malay Community," *Asian Survey,* 9 (November 1969), 919–934.

Rohrer, Wayne C., and L. H. Douglas. *The Agrarian Transition in America: Dualism and Change.* Indianapolis: Bobbs-Merrill, 1969.

Salmen, Lawrence F. "A Perspective on the Resettlement of Squatters in Brazil," *America Latina,* 12 (January–March 1969), 73–95.

Schapera, I. *Government and Politics in Tribal Societies.* London: C. A. Watts, 1956.

Shanin, Teodor (ed.). *Peasants and Peasant Societies.* Baltimore: Penguin, 1971.

Simush, P. I. "The Impact of the Scientific and Technological Revolution on the Socialist Village," *International Social Science Journal,* 21 (1969), 256–264.

Sjoberg, Gideon. *The PreIndustrial City, Past and Present.* New York: Free Press, 1960.

Smelser, N. J. *Social Change in the Industrial Revolution.* Chicago: University of Chicago Press, 1965.

Smith, T. Lynn. *The Process of Rural Development in Latin America.* Gainesville: University of Florida, 1967.

Sorenson, John L. "The Social Bases of Instability in Rural Southeast Asia," *Asian Survey,* 9 (July 1969).

Spicer, E. *Human Problems in Technological Change.* New York: Russell Sage Foundation, 1952.

Steward, Julian H. (ed.). *Contemporary Change in Traditional Societies.* Urbana: University of Illinois Press, 1967.

Swartz, Marc J., V. W. Turner, and A. Tuden. *Political Anthropology.* Chicago: Aldine, 1966.

Szyliowicz, Joseph S. *Political Change in Rural Turkey*. The Hague: Mouton, 1966.

Tawney, R. H. *The Agrarian Problem in the Sixteenth Century*. New York: Harper, 1967.

Wagley, Charles. *Amazon Town: A Study of Man in the Tropics*. New York: Macmillan, 1953.

Wertheim, William F. *Indonesian Society in Transition: A Study of Social Change*. New York: Institute of Pacific Relations, 1956.

Whiteford, Andrew H. *Two Cities of Latin America: A Comparative Description of Social Classes*. New York: Doubleday, 1964.

Wilson, Peter J. *A Malay Village and Malaysia: Social Values and Rural Development*. New Haven: Yale University Press, 1967.

Wolf, Eric R. *Peasant Wars of the Twentieth Century*. New York: Harper, 1969. Contains excellent bibliography.

Community Building

Bamberger, Michael. "A Problem of Political Integration in Latin America: The Barrios of Venezuela," *International Affairs,* 44 (October 1968).

Casaco, Juan A. "The Social Function of the Slum in Latin America: Some Positive Aspects," *America Latina,* 12 (July–September 1969), 87–112.

Cloward, R. A., and L. E. Ohlin. *Delinquency and Opportunity: A Theory of Delinquent Gangs*. New York: Free Press, 1960, 1966.

Fava, Sylvia Fleis. "Contrasts in Neighboring: New York and a Suburban County," in Ronald L. Warren (ed.), *Perspectives on the American Community*. Chicago: Rand McNally, 1966. Includes a lengthy bibliography.

French, Robert Mills (ed.). *The Community: A Comparative Perspective*. Itasca: Peacock, 1969.

Fromm, Erich. *The Revolution of Hope: Toward a Humanized Technology*. New York: Harper, 1968.

Gans, Herbert L. *The Levittowners: Ways of Life and Politics in a New Suburban Community*. New York: Pantheon, 1967.

——. *People and Plans: Essays on Urban Problems and Solutions*. New York: Basic Books, 1968.

Goldrich, Daniel, R. B. Pratt, and C. R. Schuller. "The Political Integration of Lower-Class Urban Settlements in Chile and Peru," in Irving L. Horowitz (ed.), *Masses in Latin America*. New York: Oxford University Press, 1970.

Goodman, Paul. *Communitas, Ways of Livelihood and Means of Life*. New York: Random House, 1960.

——. *The New Reformation: Notes of a Neolithic Conservative*. New York: Random House, 1970.

Gorz, André. *Strategy for Labor: A Radical Proposal.* Boston: Beacon Press, 1967.

Harrington, Michael. *Toward a Democratic Left: A Radical Program for a New Majority.* Baltimore: Penguin, 1969.

Jacobs, Jane. *The Life and Death of Great American Cities.* New York: Random House, 1961.

Keller, Suzanne. *The Urban Neighborhood: A Sociological Perspective.* New York: Random House, 1968.

Kramer, Ralph N. *Participation of the Poor: Comparative Case Studies of the War on Poverty.* Englewood Cliffs: Prentice-Hall, 1969.

Lowi, Theodore J. *The End of Liberalism: Ideology, Policy, and the Crisis of Public Authority.* New York: Norton, 1969.

——. *The Politics of Disorder.* New York: Basic Books, 1971.

Mangin, William. "Poverty and Politics in Cities of Latin America," in Warren Bloomberg, Jr., and H. Schmandt, *Power, Poverty, and Urban Policy.* Beverly Hills: Sage, 1968. Pp. 397–432.

Mannheim, Karl. *Man and Society in an Age of Reconstruction.* New York: Harcourt Brace, 1940.

Mar, José Matos. "The Barriadas of Lima: An Example of Integration into Urban Life," in Philip Hauser (ed.), *Urbanization in Latin America.* New York: International Documents Service, 1961.

Marris, Peter M., and M. Rein. *Dilemmas of Social Reform: Poverty and Community Action in the United States.* New York: Atherton, 1967.

Merton, Robert K. *Social Theory and Social Structure.* Glencoe: Free Press, 1957.

Minar, David W., and S. Greer. *The Concept of Community: Readings with Interpretations.* Chicago: Aldine, 1969.

Pahl, R. E. (ed.). *Readings in Urban Sociology.* Oxford: Pergamon Press, 1968.

Silberstein, Paul. "Favela Living: Personal Solution to Larger Problems," *America Latina,* 12 (July–September 1969), 183–221.

Smith, T. Lynn. *The Process of Rural Development in Latin America.* Gainesville: University of Florida Press, 1967.

Spiegel, Hans (ed.). *Citizen Participation in Urban Development.* Vol. 1. Washington, D.C.: Center for Community Affairs, 1968.

Talton, Ray F. *The Politics of the Barrios of Venezuela.* Berkeley: University of California Press, 1969.

Tönnies, Ferdinand. *Community and Society (Gemeinschaft and Gesellschaft).* New York: Harper Torchbooks, 1963.

Tucker, Robert C. *Philosophy and Myth in Karl Marx.* Cambridge: Cambridge University Press, 1961.

Turner, John. "Dwelling Resources in South America," *Architectural Design*, 8 (August 1963).

Violich, Francis, and J. Astica. *Community Development and the Urban Planning Process in Latin America*. Los Angeles: University of California Press, 1967.

Warren, Roland L. *The Community in America*. Chicago: Rand McNally, 1963.

Index

THE POLITICS OF URBAN
DEVELOPMENT IN SINGAPORE

Designed by R. E. Rosenbaum.
Composed by Vail-Ballou Press, Inc.,
in 10 point Linofilm Times Roman, 3 points leaded,
with display lines in Helvetica
Printed offset by Vail-Ballou Press.
Bound by Vail-Ballou Press
in Interlaken book cloth
and stamped in All Purpose foil.

Library of Congress Cataloging in Publication Data
(For library cataloging purposes only)

Gamer, Robert E   , date.
    The politics of urban development in Singapore.

    Bibliography: p.
    1. Cities and towns—Planning—Singapore.
2. Urban renewal—Singapore. I. Title.
HT169.S55G34   309.2'62'095952   78-37778
ISBN 0-8014-0708-7